Eagles, Ravens, and Other Birds of Prey

A History of USAF Suppression of Enemy Air Defense Doctrine, 1973–1991

James L. Young Jr.

Eagles, Ravens, and other Birds of Prey

© 2022, James Young

Typesetting: Anita C. Young
Cover Design: Anita C. Young
ISBN-13: 9798423221218
Printed in USA

Acknowledgements

If I tried to thank everyone who had a hand in this, there'd be over a thousand pages. From my former boss who gently asked, "Haven't enough people written about [the Allied Bombing Campaign in World War II]?" to the hotel staff during numerous research trips, I was blessed to have many assistants. Therefore, rather than engage in what would be an ultimately futile exercise to remember every teacher, mentor, or individual who aided me in ways great and small, I'd simply like to say "Thank you." It has been a long haul, and I am grateful you were there to help.

Contents

Dedication

For Doctor Albert Hamscher. Scholar, Eagles fan, and one of the best mentors any writer could ever have.

CENTURIES AND LINEBACKERS

On the evening of January 3rd, 1973, B–52D #55–0056, call sign "Ruby 2" was struck by an SA–2 *Guideline* missile near Vinh, North Vietnam. With the *Stratofortress* heavily damaged, aircraft commander Lieutenant Colonel Gerald Wickline immediately turned the aircraft towards the South China Sea and likely safety. After crossing the North Vietnamese coastline and conducting a damage assessment, Lt. Colonel Wickline believed that he and his crew could reach a friendly airfield in Da Nang, South Vietnam. Unfortunately for Wickline and his crew, the damage to the B-52 was far more extensive than they believed. When their primary hydraulic system failed a little over 25 miles away from Da Nang, the six men aboard Ruby 2 were forced to eject into the darkness and leave the *Stratofortress* to crash into the South China Sea.[1]

The shootdown of Ruby 2 was significant for three reasons in addition to the loss of a multi-million dollar aircraft. First, the B-52D was the final United States Air Force (USAF) aircraft shot down by North Vietnam's Integrated Air Defense System (NV-IADS). Second, the *Stratofortress*'s demise marked the nadir of the USAF's Suppression of Enemy Air Defense (SEAD) doctrine and execution thereof.[2] Despite heavy electronic warfare (EW) and defense suppression support, Ruby 2 had been destroyed by an obsolescent weapons system that was a full two generations behind the surface-to-air missiles (SAMs) USAF and its NATO allies could expect to face in Western Europe. As the 2,257th aircraft the NV-IADS had destroyed, Ruby 2 seemed to indicate not only the death of the manned strategic bomber, but also the ascendancy of ground-based defenses over all jet aircraft.[3] This, in turn, led to the final reason why Ruby 2's loss was particularly fateful for the United States' strategic doctrine: If the USAF could not deliver ordnance against defended targets, NATO's conventional deterrence against

Warsaw Pact forces was significantly reduced, if not nonexistent. Much like the late bomber's crew, the USAF found itself listless and adrift in a dark sea of troubles as the Vietnam War slowly ground to a close.

MiG Alley Assumptions

The events preceding Ruby 2's shootdown could not have been more unlikely to the USAF's leaders when the service was created. The USAF was born via the National Defense Act of 1947, having purchased its independence with operations over Nazi Germany and Imperial Japan. Ostensibly organized to fight conflicts across the full spectrum of warfare, the Air Force's mission became synonymous with the delivery of atomic weapons against the growing threat of the Soviet Union. For President Harry Truman, this reliance on the United States' atomic monopoly seemed an easy way to stabilize the newly formed Department of Defense's (DoD's) budget.[4] The United States Army (USA) and USAF leaders concurred with Truman's chosen approach, with only the United States Navy (USN) breaking ranks to argue that the DoD still needed the ability to conduct large-scale conventional warfare.[5]

The folly of the United States' reliance on its atomic monopoly was demonstrated when North Korea, a Soviet client state, crossed the 38th parallel in force on June 25th, 1950. As with the rest of the United States military, the USAF was unpleasantly surprised by the Korean War. At inception, the Air Force had was divided into two commands, the Strategic Air Command (SAC) and Tactical Air Command (TAC). SAC was solely responsible for the delivery of nuclear weapons and thus considered the USAF's premier command. Tactical Air Command was responsible for air defense, establishment of air superiority over the tactical battlefield, and close air support (CAS) to United States Marine Corps (USMC), USN, and USA forces.[6] In reality, Air Force officers such as General Carl Spaatz, General Hoyt S. Vandenberg, and Lieutenant General Curtis LeMay had concentrated the majority of their service's budget on enhancing SAC's ability to deliver the United States' limited atomic arsenal in a single, debilitating strike against the Soviet Union.[7] Thus, TAC found itself woefully unprepared to fight a limited conventional conflict half a world away from the United States.

The USAF's conduct in the Korean War has been well recorded elsewhere, and space precludes a definitive recounting here.[8] For the purpose of developing SEAD doctrine, the Korean War was a particularly poor crucible. First and foremost, air defense technology had not markedly changed since the conclusion of World War II. From 1950 to 1953, North Korean anti-aircraft artillery (AAA) of various calibers remained the most prevalent ground-based system to complement aerial interceptors. In contrast, jet propulsion and improved aerodynamics had improved the speed of the typical United Nations' single-seat fighter by over one hundred miles per hour.[9] Thus even with radar-controlled guns, North Korean forces had difficulty in engaging enemy fighters. As for manually aimed weapons, the USAF's decision to change its tactics and jet aircraft's increased speed made hitting attacking fighter bombers more a matter of luck rather than skill.[10]

Regarding North Korean interceptors, USAF leaders looked at their operations and made several reasonable assumptions about the relative effectiveness of MiG-15 interceptors versus USAF aircraft in general and B-29 *Super-fortresses* in particular. First and foremost, USAF leaders assumed that the relatively high kill ratio achieved by F-86s versus Communist MiG-15s proved the superiority of American pilot training methods and technology. Following from this, the Air Staff thus believed the relatively short loiter time of American F-86 *Sabres* had contributed significantly to the MiGs' success against both attack and bomber aircraft. Given the *Sabres'* short range, there were ample opportunities for MiGs to bounce the USAF's bombers / attack aircraft after the F-86s departed. Finally, unlike what could reasonably be expected in a general nuclear war, rules of engagement precluded USAF and other United Nations' forces from conducting airfield attacks against the MiG-15 bases in China.[11]

Despite the rhetorical pillorying that subsequent

USAF officers, historians, and civilian leaders would deliver upon Vandenberg, LeMay, and other senior Air Force leaders, these assumptions were not merely superficial justifications for later acquisitions.[12] Instead, they were very much based in the present of 1953. For example, the B-29 was a weapon system that had been developed at the conclusion of World War II. By contrast, the B-36 *Peacemaker* and B-47 *Stratojet* flew faster (411 miles per hour for the *Peacemaker* and 607 mph *Stratojet* versus 329 miles per hour for the B-29) and higher (43,600 feet for the *Peacemaker* and 39,300 for the *Stratojet* versus 33,600 for the B-29) than the *Superfortress*. The Air Force's collective leadership assumed that this combination of high altitude and speed would make the MiG-15s' job far more difficult. Similarly, even if the leaders had been able to foresee the revolutions in electronics and computer miniaturization that would take place over the next decade, the vast majority of anti-aircraft artillery was ineffective over 35,000 feet. American senior leaders failed to understand that the strong leavening of World War II veterans had more to do with the F-86s' success than any issues inherent to Communist bloc pilot training programs.[13] Far more important than these tactical and operational factors, however, would be something the Air Force had no control over: the Eisenhower administration.

The Seven Centuries of the Apocalypse

Upon assuming office in January 1953, President Dwight D. Eisenhower began seeking ways to reorient and streamline the United States' national defense policy. Having run strenuously against President Truman's economic policies, spending, and the Korean War, President Eisenhower believed that the United States was far more likely to implode economically than face direct destruction at the hands of the Soviet Union and its allies. Therefore, one of Eisenhower's first acts was to direct the National Security Council to conduct a strenuous series of exercises dubbed Operational Solarium. From this, his administration derived what President Eisenhower called the "New Look" but what his opponents (and some supporters) referred to as "Massive Retaliation." Stemming from Operation Solarium's recommendations, Eisenhower's New Look relied upon the United States' ability to deliver its new thermonuclear weapons with great speed and in large quantities to complement the economic and political stabilization of Europe. Rather than being merely brandished should a conflict arose, the United States' nuclear sword of Damocles was to be swung rapidly and violently until such time as the Communist Bloc lay in ruins. Furthermore, the Department of Defense would execute this course of action regardless of the relative scale of hostile action against an American ally. In this manner, the potential cost of aggression, no matter how slight, would be too great to justify future Communist aggression such as that which precipitated the Korean War. In addition, by being able to purchase relatively cheap thermonuclear weapons, the United States' economy would be saved from the ravages of maintaining a large standing Army in Central Europe, Korea, or anywhere else where Moscow may been tempted to strike.[14] Regardless of its merits, the Eisenhower Administration's decision to pursue its New Look national strategy had a deleterious effect on the Air Force's development of SEAD doctrine, its acquisition of the necessary weapons systems to attack both ground-based and airborne defenses, and the training of personnel to ensure they could operate effectively against an IADS.

The Role of Doctrine[15]

Doctrine is a word that has numerous definitions, but for purposes of this dissertation two are most pertinent. According to *The Dictionary of Modern War*, doctrine consists of "[o]fficially enunciated principles meant to guide the employment of military forces under specified conditions."[16] The current Department of Defense dictionary, Joint Publication (JP) 1-02, considers doctrine to be, "[f]undamental principles by which military forces or elements thereof guide their actions *in support of national objectives* [emphasis added]."[17] Merging these two explanations, it becomes readily apparent that doctrine is basically a military organization's methodology and thought process for the conduct of war in support of a national strategy. Once it has decided on a doctrine, a military service must ensure that this doctrine is widely propagated among its leaders so that, should war break out, the entire organization is on the same page. Otherwise, a wide range of unfortunate military and strategic outcomes may occur.

It was this kind of disjunction between Air Force doctrine and procurement that General Twining and General LeMay sought to avoid in the early 1950s. To both men, Pearl Harbor was both a cautionary tale and a traumatic event.[18] They, and their political leaders, fervently believed that everything possible had to be done to ensure such a disaster never befell the United States again.[19] Both men realized that nuclear warfare, more than any other type in history, rewarded the side that struck first and hardest. Therefore, they wanted to ensure that the United States had sufficient nuclear firepower to annihilate the Communist Bloc's nuclear delivery systems and command apparatus in one massive strike. Alternatively, should the Soviet Union and its allies surprise the United States with a "bolt from the blue," a large nuclear force distributed through both TAC and SAC would ensure that enough delivery systems would survive to destroy most of the U.S.S.R. in turn. Given the Eisenhower administration's strict limitations on military budgets, the delivery systems available at the time, and the perceived relative sizes of the

U.S.S.R. and United States' nuclear arsenals, such an approach made sense.[20]

This mindset became codified in 1953 when the USAF published Air Force Manual (AFM) 1-3 *Theater Operations*, its "bible" for conducting combat operations. With guidance from former bomber leaders Nathan F. Twining, Thomas D. White, and LeMay, USAF doctrine authors wrote AFM 1-3 with a heavy focus on nuclear delivery.[21] Indeed, a layman reading *Theater Operations* could have easily believed that the Korean War had not occurred. Rather than discussing how to establish and maintain air superiority in a prolonged conflict, AFM 1-3 emphasized tactical nuclear delivery as a means of supporting the United States' strategic operations. By its conclusion, the reader is left with the clear impression that the USAF expected to operate as a homogenous force whose operations would cause the swift, decisive immolation of the Soviet Union and its allies within a matter of days, if not hours. TAC's fighters, rather than acting as escorts to clear the way for SAC's bombers, would shatter enemy squadrons and the infrastructure needed to support them with "tactical" nuclear weapons.[22] SAC's strategic bombers would, in turn, sail majestically at high altitude to deliver their far larger strategic nuclear payload against Soviet cities, command centers, and industrial locations.[23]

U.S. Tactical Fighter Acquisition, 1953–1965

As noted above, doctrine often drives a military organization's materiel acquisition, personnel development, and training processes. The pre-Vietnam USAF, tasked with ushering in the Apocalypse, took this mindset to a new, terrifying level. From lumbering strategic bombers to sleek, supersonic fighters, almost every Air Force airframe purchased from 1954 through 1965 was viewed through the simple prism of whether it helped deliver nuclear weapons against the Communist Bloc or could prevent the Soviet Union's bombers from striking the United States. Furthermore, the USAF engaged in a public relations program to convince the American people that this was the best course for securing the United States' present and future security. Despite congressional, secretarial (both Defense and Air Force), and even presidential directives to the contrary, the Air Force paid less and less consideration to the accomplishment of tactical tasks such as close air support, air superiority, or battlefield area interdiction (BAI) when acquiring TAC systems.[24]

This refusal to diversify fighter capabilities manifested itself in the seven tactical fighters the USAF acquired from 1953–1965. Colloquially dubbed the "Century Fighters" due to their triple digit nomenclature, these aircraft began with the F-100 *Super Sabre* (first flight 1953 / service acceptance 1954) that was intended to rapidly impart the lessons of Korea in a supersonic platform. By the end of the decade, the F-100 was joined by the F-101 *Voodoo* (1954 / 1957), F-102 *Delta Dart* (1953/1956), F-104 *Starfighter* (1956/1958), F-105 *Thunderchief* (1955 / 1958), and the F-106 *Delta Dagger* (1956-1959), with the F-110 / F-4 *Phantom* being forced upon a recalcitrant Air Force in 1962. Although each airframe had its unique features, in general they shared three major characteristics that reflected the effects of Air Force doctrine: speed, technological complexity and, most importantly, the ability to deliver nuclear weapons.

Although not inherently detrimental, the focus on speed required aerodynamic tradeoffs. The need for high-speed penetration flights or, for interceptors, the ability to gain altitude quickly and then close with incoming Soviet bombers restricted designers to employing "area rule" designs on all Air Force fuselages from the F-100 through the F-106. With the U.S. Navy-designed F-4, the limitation on fuselage design was only overcome by employing two powerful engines to make the *Phantom* the fastest aircraft of its era. This resort to brute force, in addition to making the *Phantom* more expensive than its predecessors, gave the McDonnell Douglas product a large visual and infrared signature. In order to carry what was considered a useful nuclear payload at near top speed or catch hostile aircraft in a reasonable amount of time, the *Phantom*'s design teams made sacrifices with regard to maneuverability, airframe strength, and/or armor. The Air Force's leaders, both civilian and military, believed that none of these negative attributes would be of any importance should the seven fighters be called upon to carry out their wartime mission. Nuclear delivery and bomber interception was considered to be a relatively straightforward mission, and it was unlikely that any aircraft would have to fly more than one or two sorties if Massive Retaliation was carried out.[25]

In addition to pressing the boundaries of aerody-namics, the Century Fighters epitomized an era of "technological exuberance," i.e., the belief that a myriad number of issues could be solved by the application of science and engineering.[26] In every conflict from World War I to Korea, air combat had been a chaotic, dynamic experience whose outcome seemed to hinge on luck, weather conditions, and pilot skill almost as much as equipment. Between Korea and Vietnam, USAF (and to a slightly lesser extent, USN) leaders believed, future air combat would likely be a contest determined by precision engineering, sophisticated electronics, and advanced weapon systems. As demonstrated in test after test by both the Air Force and Navy, missiles were so reliable that the aircraft which could acquire, track, and fire its onboard ordnance first would almost always prevail. Based on these experi-mental engagements and on limited operational use by the Republic of China's F-86 and F-100 fighters, Air Force leaders considered missiles so lethal that they denied requests to equip the service's two most advanced aircraft, the F-106 *Delta Dart* and F-4 *Phantom*, with either external or retrofitted cannons.[27]

While seemingly imprudent in retrospect, at the time and given the war foreseen in Air Force doctrine, these decisions made perfect sense. In the case of the *Delta Dart*, almost the entire interception was controlled by a series of ground-based control stations that made up Air Defense Command's Semi-Automatic Ground Environment (SAGE) system. Equipped with a nuclear rocket (the *Genie*) that had a lethal blast radius of over a thousand meters and *Falcon* missiles with a three-mile range, the F-106 was never expected to get close enough to its prey to require a short-ranged cannon.[28] Similarly, the *Phantom*'s battery of eight missiles included the beyond visual range (BVR) *Sparrow* and either *Falcon* or *Sidewinder* heat-seeking weapons.[29] Even without the F-106's ground-based support, the F-4 was expected to create the same comparable effects as SAGE via its powerful internal radar and second crewman. Thus, as Eisenhower's administration gave way to John F. Kennedy's, the Air Force's concept of a "fighter" became almost completely indistinct from what had previously been known as "interceptors."[30]

As the Kennedy administration began to shrink the Air Force's portion of the Department of Defense's budget, the F-4's ability to serve as a multi-role strike aircraft became almost as important as its air-to-air potential. As noted above, the delivery of nuclear weapons had become central to the development of all Air Force fighters. Although retrofitted F-100 *Super Sabres* (e.g., the F-100C) and F-105s were seemingly adequate against visual range only Eastern bloc interceptors, Air Force officers began to see the potential in the F-4 for a "self-escorting" fighter bomber that would destroy MiGs before being detected itself. Furthermore, by virtue of requiring only slight modifications to its on-board fire control equipment, having space to add an additional bombing computer, and having still more room for possible later modifications, the *Phantom* seemed perfect for the tactical strike role required AFM 1-3.[31]

Air Force Fighter Pilot Training, 1953-1965

As the Air Force's airframes evolved to meet the roles envisioned if AFM 1-3, there was a similar change in what constituted a fighter pilot. In 1953, the Air Force exited the Korean War with a mixture of fighter pilots who were World War II veterans, recalled reservists who had also fought in that conflict, and neophytes that the service trained using almost the same methods as their older comrades. In all cases, combat pilots had received roughly 100 hours of training that included air combat maneuvering (ACM), air-to-ground conventional ordnance delivery, and instruction on how to evade enemy ground defenses (albeit almost solely AAA).[32] By

1965, as the Air Force prepared to launch the first airstrikes to initiate Operation Rolling Thunder, its pilot cadre was almost wholly college-educated regular officers with some form of science or engineering degree. More importantly, except for the dwindling number of Korean War and World War II veterans, these officers almost wholly ignorant of how to conduct conventional warfare.[33]

There were many reasons for this decay in conventional capability. First and foremost was the nuclear mission that had spawned the Century Fighters. As the USAF transitioned to a system that saw pilots receive limited training time on their particular airframe, increasingly fighter wing/group commanders were expected to ensure their pilots proficiency in nuclear delivery. Furthermore, under General Twining and then General LeMay, TAC began to conduct regular inspections such as those the latter had begun with SAC. Chief among the numerous pass/fail criteria for these events were the number of training hours spent conducting practice nuclear deliveries, the accuracy of bombing during nuclear delivery practice missions, and inspections of individual units' "go to war" maps, flight plans, and aircrew knowledge of both of these. As wing/group leaders began to be relieved for failing these inspections, regardless of their previous performance in either Korea or World War II, it became readily apparent where Air Force's leaders expected its commanders to concentrate their efforts.[34]

Providing further encouragement to avoid training active Air Force wings in ACM or conventional munitions delivery was the inherent danger of flying such missions. As had become apparent to the Air Force after 1945, flying jets was inherently more dangerous due to their increased operating speeds. Beginning with the F-100, the Century Fighters' accident rates increased to an almost unsustainable level. The *Super Sabre*'s operators quickly found that its supersonic level speed had been purchased with a truly unforgiving flight envelope whenever a pilot slowed to near stall speed.[35] The F-102 and F-106's pilots discovered that their aircraft quickly lost speed and controllability if they placed the big delta-winged fighters into any type of high-g turn. The F-104, in addition to taking literal miles to turn at high speed, required far too delicate handling when coming in to land due to its own stall problems.[36] The F-105 combined both poor turning radius with initially unreliable engines and an airframe that was known to disintegrate if pressed too far.[37] Lastly, the F-4's tendency to depart controlled flight at a high angle of attack became so notorious that one *Phantom* wing did not fly any ACM missions for over three years by order of its commander.[38] Even in the cases where all these dangers were overcome and commanders were willing to assume risk, ACM was conducted against similar aircraft, i.e., *Phantom* vs. *Phantom* or *Thunderchief* vs. *Thunderchief* as opposed to dissimilar engagements. Combined, these factors meant that the Air Force's flying officers were quite capable of flying missions that involved annihilating entire cities but were all but helpless when it came to destroying singular enemy aircraft.

Even worse than their unawareness of the tactics, techniques and procedures necessary to attain victory in aerial combat was TAC aircrew's ignorance of advances in ground-based air defenses from 1953 through 1965. As noted above, the ubiquitous anti-aircraft gun, ranging from light machine guns through large-caliber, high-angle cannon, was difficult to employ against high speed fighter aircraft due to the likelihood of tracking errors.[39] In reviewing the Korean War and other international conflicts, TAC's leadership assumed optically-aimed anti-aircraft artillery would be a lethal nuisance but hardly a major threat.[40] Unfortunately, advances in radar miniaturization and ruggedness meant that AAA was often laid onto target with the assistance of ballistic computers, while design tradeoffs made in the quest for supersonic capability meant even rifle-caliber weapons could destroy a multi-million dollar aircraft.[41] TAC pilots remained unaware of these vulnerabilities, and thus prepared to avoid AAA systems by flying at high speed and low level along sparsely populated paths to their Eastern bloc targets.

Even though the Air Force had an understanding, albeit outdated, of the AAA threat to TAC's fighters, the service's senior officers had paid almost no attention to SAMs as a potential tactical threat. Originally fielded by the Soviet Union in 1957, the U.S.S.R.'s military conceived SAMs as a counter to SAC's high-flying bombers. Most famous for shooting down Francis Gary Powers' U-2 in 1960 and for destroying another U-2 during the Cuban Missile Crisis, the primary Soviet SAM was the SA-2 *Guideline*. A two-stage weapon that was fired either singly or as part of a salvo from a fixed site, the *Guideline* and its accompanying *Fan Song* radar van formed a system capable of engaging an aircraft up to 25 miles away. With a maximum effective altitude in excess of 80,000 feet, a speed over three times the speed of sound, and a 420-lb. warhead, the *Guideline* could not be outclimbed or outrun, nor could a direct hit by one be survived by USAF tactical fighters.[42]

Due to the United States' own air defense doctrine and Soviet deployments before 1965, USAF commanders and national intelligence services considered it unlikely that TAC would encounter *Guideline* missiles in a conventional conflict. Therefore, unlike SAC bombers, which were equipped with extensive electronic countermeasures (ECM) equipment and radar homing and warning (RHAW) detection gear, TAC fighters were built lacking the bulky, heavy equipment. Using terrain analysis and intelligence information, TAC fighter wings/groups merely marked the fixed sites in the Eastern Bloc and then planned their attack routes either to avoid these or to use terrain masking to get within the SA-2's five-mile minimum range.[43]

This was considered sufficient, since even if Congress had allocated the necessary funds to purchase ECM or RHAW for fighters, early models of these systems were known to interfere with the onboard radar and navigational equipment. As these were critical to accurate nuclear delivery, TAC understandably decided not to invest time in further ECM or RHAW development. Exacerbating this problem was the lack of training facilities on which electronic warfare courses could be taught. Given that using available facilities would have detracted from their availability for SAC electronic warfare officers (EWO), the Air Force's predilection to not research pods or sensors seemed to be a prudent one.[44]

The end result of this lack of training, combined with the materiel decisions made with regard to the Century Fighters, was a TAC that looked extremely capable for all levels of warfare but was only suited for nuclear conflict. There was no discussion of even rudimentary SEAD tactics at the wing and squadron level. Indeed, the majority of fighter pilots believed that speed and terrain masking would allow them to penetrate any defensive system in the world.[45] Unlike their Navy counterparts, the majority of whom had at least been exposed to air defense radars due to task force training operations, USAF pilots lacked even a rudimentary understanding of SAM or radar-directed gunfire's capabilities. As noted in an Air Force monograph, as the Air Force prepared to attack North Vietnam in February 1965, "over 50 percent of fighter pilots had more than 2,000 total flying hours" in jet aircraft yet had not conducted a practical application of firepower in a modern air defense environment.[46]

Operation Rolling Thunder

General Curtis LeMay is said to have stated, in response to concerns that the Air Force would not be able to conduct small-scale wars, "If we can lick a cat, we can lick a kitten."[47] It can be said without equivocation that LeMay's confidence was proven to be spectacularly misplaced. How the United States' long, painful intervention in Southeast Asia began has been well documented elsewhere and will not be recounted here. By February 1965, President Lyndon B. Johnson believed that it would serve America's strategic interests to intensify operations in Vietnam. Deciding that the application of airpower would intimidate the North Vietnamese into no longer providing support for the South's Viet Cong guerillas, President Johnson directed the Navy and Air Force to begin sustained aerial operations against the Democratic Republic of Vietnam (DRV). Whereas previous air raids had been specifically targeted reprisals, the President intended for these raids (dubbed Operational Rolling Thunder) to gradually increase pain across all of North Vietnamese society until Communist leader Ho Chi Minh accepted the division of Vietnam into northern and southern halves as had been done with Korea.[48] When the United States called a bombing halt in November 1968, not only had this not been accomplished but the USN and USAF combined had lost over 900 aircraft.[49] Far from demonstrating the USAF's prowess, Operation Rolling Thunder had seemingly demonstrated just how far the service's conventional capability had atrophied since the end of the Korean War.

"Handcuffing" the Incapable

It is necessary, before discussing Air Force doctrine's detrimental effect on Rolling Thunder's outcome, to address the persistent historical legend that civilian interference was the primary cause for American losses. It is undeniable that the Johnson administration failed to achieve optimal employment of American airpower against North Vietnam from March 1965 through November 1968. First, President Johnson and, to a lesser extent, Secretary of Defense Robert McNamara did not provide a unified strategic focus. Indeed, at any particular moment during Operation Rolling Thunder there were as many as four broad, often competing, objectives. Leading this was Johnson's desire to avoid conducting an air campaign so intense that the People's Republic of China (PRC) or the Soviet Union would feel compelled to enter the conflict. Competing with it was how airpower, at this time a blunt instrument, could both prevent PRC or Soviet entry yet inflict enough pain to break the DRV's will. Moreover, there were few attempts to determine what would break the North Vietnamese people's will, how long it would have to remain broken, and whether doing so in the first place would be in the United States' long-term strategic interests.[50]

Further complicating the matter of applying sufficient force against the DRV was the Johnson administration's simultaneous directive to interdict supplies flowing from North Vietnam to the Viet Cong. With a limited number of airframes throughout the Pacific Air Force's (PACAF's) area of responsibility, there was a physical limit to how many aircraft could be assigned to Vietnam. Inexplicably, neither McNamara nor his staff, despite their background in science and systems engineering, ever rigorously applied either of these disciplines to determining just how much bombing ability would be necessary to conduct interdiction, simultaneously provide close air support to South Vietnam, and still maintain a credible deterrence force in other regions such as Korea. If they had done so, then subtracted these airframes from PACAF's contemporary order of battle, they would have realized that Seventh Air Force (as the entity responsible for bombing North Vietnam was designated) simply lacked the capability to mount a sustained bombing campaign. Instead, in an effort to continue to demonstrate American resolve (the final Johnson administration objective), President Johnson and Secretary McNamara expected aircrews that had just prepared to bomb Hanoi on one day to simply and adroitly switch to flying interdiction raids against amorphous, ill-defined targets in Laos or northwestern South Vietnam the next.[51]

Combined, this strategic ambivalence has led to much of the intervening years' historiography blaming these two men for the many losses that followed. This began with relatively benign comments in CHECO reports (e.g., "JCS [Joint Chiefs of Staff] targeting practices added a distinct, and as it turned out, significant variable to tactical planning").[52] After Rolling Thunder, however, the Air Force was openly critical of its former civilian masters, culminating with the CHECO report on Operation Linebacker stating that "Rolling Thunder was conducted under severe, often crippling, restraints."[53] In 1976, General William W. Momyer, 7th Air Force commander, bluntly stated he "deeply resented the proscription of attacks on North Vietnamese airfields, SAM and AAA sites, and other targets."[54] This was relatively sedate compared to junior officers such as Colonel Jack Broughton, who called the strategic ambiguity and resultant restraints "sick" in his bestseller *Thud Ridge*.[55] Broughton then went on to elaborate:

> It's sick because we handcuff ourselves on tactical details. First we oversupervise and seem to feel that four-star generals have to be flight leaders and dictate the details of handling a type of machinery they have never known. Second, we have lost all sense of flexibility, and we ignore

tactical surprise by insisting on repeated attacks without imagination. Third, our intelligence, and the interpretation and communication of that intelligence, is back in the Stone Age. Fourth, our conventional munitions are little improved over 1941 and those who insist on dictating the ultimate detail of their selection, fuzing and delivery do not understand or appreciate their own dictates. (This, of course, assumes that they have adequate quantities and varieties on hand to be selective.) Fifth, we have not advanced far enough in the field of meteorology to tell what we will have over the homedrome an hour from now. Our degree of accuracy on vital details like bombing winds over the target is abominable. Sixth, many of our high-level people refuse to listen to constructive criticism from people doing the job.[56]

The majority of memoirs, documents, and secondary sources written about the Vietnam War follow the thrust of the above paragraph. Indeed, if simply taken at face value, the preponderance of books, articles, and memoirs would indicate that President Johnson and McNamara, in addition to providing poor strategic direction, completely handcuffed the military. In turn, this handcuffing is what led to the destruction of almost 1,000 American aircraft over North Vietnam from 1965 through 1968, prevented the Air Force and Navy from bringing the North Vietnamese to the peace table, and set in motion the long path that culminated in Saigon's defeat in 1975.

No matter how colorful or how prevalent the presentation, putting the blame for Operation Rolling Thunder's failure on civilian control of the military ignores the United States' martial tradition. As Lieutenant Colonel Ed Cobleigh put it in his own memoir *War For the Hell of It*, "[c] ivilian control of the U.S. military is a cornerstone of our democracy and must not be compromised, no matter how dire the situation."[57] Put another way, President Johnson and Secretary McNamara were acting well within their constitutional authority and duty in sharply limiting the military's actions during Operation Rolling Thunder. It was not McNamara and Johnson's first responsibility to win the war in Vietnam but to preserve the United States. Put in the language of a different scenario, no one in the Johnson administration was ready to trade Chicago for Saigon.

In this light, it becomes much easier to understand that Johnson and McNamara did not intend to conduct their actions in a capricious manner. Instead, both men were erring well on the side of safety in ensuring the accomplishment of their first strategic goal. Both men had observed the damage done to the nation when President Truman failed to keep General MacArthur in check during the halcyon days after the Inchon landings. Whereas in 1950 this had led to Chinese intervention and near destruction of U.N. forces on the Korean peninsula, there was a real possibility that Russian and Chinese intervention in Vietnam could quickly lead to a broadened (and nuclear) conflict.[58] When General LeMay said that this event would be positive by allowing a first strike on the PRC's nascent nuclear program, he probably did little to lessen either President Johnson's or Secretary McNamara's fears. If one considers the civil-military climate, especially given the various crises of 1961 through 1964, it is easy to understand why the Air Force was given very clear directives and limitations.[59]

By constantly focusing on these directives, those who attempt to demonize President Johnson and Secretary McNamara almost completely ignore the process that led to the friction between those two men and their military commanders. They also ignore General White's and General LeMay's refusal to modify their service's doctrine in accordance with three successive presidents' directives. In 1958, President Eisenhower had made it quite clear that massive retaliation was no longer the United States' overarching military policy. In 1960, John F. Kennedy had run on the principle that a chief executive ought to have more options than defeat or mass murder and selected Secretary McNamara to make this happen. Rather than going along with either President's reforms, the Air Force had fought them via means both explicit and implicit.[60] This had greatly slowed both President Kennedy's and Johnson's attempted military reforms and contributed a great deal to the Air Force's unpreparedness for conventional warfare.

Therefore, when President Johnson turned to air power to salvage the U.S. effort in Vietnam, his restrictions should not have been a surprise nor can failure be wholly blamed on them. As Momyer himself stated, "self-imposed restraint has been a fact in all U.S. conflict since World War II, and obviously our hope in the age of nuclear and thermonuclear weapons is that some restraint will be exercised by all superpowers in all future conflicts."[61] Instead, it was the decision of the Air Force's leaders, consciously or not, to not acknowledge the effects that strategic parity (perceived or real) had on the conduct of American foreign policy which contributed the most to the service's heavy losses during Rolling Thunder. Rather than "scream[ing] for changes to the operational conduct of the air war," as one Air Force officer put it, the service's leaders rightfully sought ways to minimize losses in the conventional environment for which they had not prepared.[62] To their sorrow, they found that their service was incapable of penetrating a wholly unexpected foe in the NV-IADS.

North Vietnamese Weapons

The NV-IADS began humbly with optically-aimed guns, the overwhelming majority of which were heavy machine guns or automatic cannons, supplemented by large-caliber cannons controlled by obsolescent radars.[63] However, this situation rapidly changed once China and the Soviet Union chose to supply North Vietnam with weapons, equipment, and training as part of their larger Cold War strategy. In addition to giving the appearance of aiding a fellow Communist state, the Chinese and Soviets were also given an opportunity to test their weapons and techniques in a realistic environment versus their likely opponents. Combined, these factors meant that, by November 1968, the NV-IADS grew from its humble beginnings to the deadliest air defense network in the world outside of the Soviet Union itself.[64]

It was not merely the weapons themselves that made this network deadly but also how the North Vietnamese employed them. Unsurprisingly, the North Vietnamese did not strictly adhere to either Chinese or Soviet air defense doctrine. Lacking the operational depth of either of their larger patrons or the means to strike back at the USN's carriers or USAF bases in Thailand, the North Vietnamese could not conduct a traditional air superiority campaign. Instead, realizing that the United States intended to fight a limited war and that there was no single North Vietnamese target that was irreplaceable, the North Vietnamese military opted to conduct a strategy that was roughly analogous to that of their ground forces. Whenever possible, North Vietnamese defenses would concentrate their most sophisticated ground- and air-based systems where they could be employed from a position of strength. Just as they intended to exhaust the United States Army in the South, the North's leaders expected to bleed the United States Air Force white as long as it attempted to strike the DRV.[65]

Command and Control

Orchestrating this campaign was the responsibility of the NV-IADS command and control (C^2) nodes. The most important component of the NV-IADS, these four North Vietnamese Air Defense Command (NVADC) sub-headquarters were located within Hanoi and Haiphong. Tasked with coordinating the movements of the other three components (AAA, MiGs, and SAMs) in order to avoid fratricide and cause the most damage to American air strikes, each center was commanded by a North Vietnamese Army flag officer. These command nodes, in turn, was fed information by multiple subordinate commands. First, there was an extensive network of early warning radars whose medium- and high-altitude coverage extended across neighboring Laos to the west and well out into the Gulf of Tonkin to the east. By detecting American strike aircraft well in advance, these systems allowed the North Vietnamese to quickly determine the speed and direction of an approaching American strike. Second, there were numerous electronic intelligence (ELINT) and radar intercept stations that would attempt to discern what the 7th Air

Force had targeted for the day. Finally, there were the reports given by defense assets in action, all of whose secondary job was to keep higher headquarters abreast of the Americans' progress so North Vietnamese commanders could direct additional forces against a strike if conditions were especially favorable.[66]

AAA Systems

The simplest of these three assets were the aforementioned guns. By 1968 almost the entire North Vietnamese populace was engaged in anti-aircraft defense. The regular anti-aircraft forces of the North Vietnamese Army (NVA) used a suite of cannons that were almost wholly controlled by *Fire Can* radars and associated fire control computers. Capable of tracking multiple, high-speed targets from low altitude (around 1,000 feet) through roughly 60,000 feet, the *Fire Can* drastically increased AAA weapons' accuracy.[67] Although the *Fire Can* could be jammed, 7th Air Force strikes ignored the system to their peril, as they controlled heavy and automatic cannon capable of reaching jets flying up to 39,000 feet.[68]

Complementing the radar-controlled weapons were the countless small arms wielded by the North Vietnamese populace. As one USAF report noted:

> Added to all [the heavy weapons] was what one THUD pilot called the "Hanoi

Habit": even waitresses would run outside and start firing when the sirens sounded, using weapons from 7.62 rifles to the WW II Browning M–2 .50 calibre (*sic*) machine gun.[69]

Although the mental image of a cocktail waitress leaving her patrons in order to go outside and fire a few rounds up into the air may be amusing in the abstract, in reality those rounds costing a few cents were only slightly less likely to contribute to the destruction of a multi-million dollar jet aircraft than their larger cousins. Flying over North Vietnam at less than 10,000 feet was an exercise in calculated risk. Thanks in no small part to the waitresses, farmers, and other militia members flying at 5,000 feet altitude near a target would almost assuredly end in casualties. Like citizens playing a macabre lottery, every North Vietnamese saw an American air strike as an opportunity to strike a jackpot.[70]

The Air Force's leaders had not taken these defenses into account when determining their attack tactics. As they had planned to do in Europe, F–105s began air operations against North Vietnam by ingressing at low altitude, pulling up to 10,000 feet to dive-bomb their targets, then egressing using the *Thunderchief*'s superior speed. The North Vietnamese, after determining the most common USAF ingress and egress routes, then began siting the guns accordingly. By Rolling Thunder's conclusion, Air Force fighter were forced to ingress and egress at high altitudes.[71]

SAMs

This solution to the ferocity of North Vietnam's AAA defenses brought USAF's fighters squarely into contact with the SA-2. The Air Force's passing familiarity with the *Guideline* became a lethal, regular relationship on July 24th, 1965 with the destruction of Leopard 2, an F-4 *Phantom*.[72] With this single stroke, the North Vietnamese and their Soviet advisors greatly complicated the American bombing offensive. Unable to simply avoid the SA-2 sites as they had planned to do in Europe, and often unable to spot the sites before they fired, USAF fighter pilots were forced to devise methods to try and outmaneuver the "flying telephone poles." While these were somewhat successful, they either necessitated the jettisoning of weapons or, alternatively, depleted the targeted aircraft's energy.[73] When the *Guideline* was fired as part of a salvo (a common tactic), American aircrews often found themselves blundering squarely into the path of a second *Guideline* or, even worse, the NV-IADS AAA envelope.[74]

It was at this point that the Air Force's dearth of SEAD doctrine began to have terrible consequences for the 7th Air Force's squadrons. Attempting to attack SAM sites with conventional fighters was quickly shown to be almost suicidal due to the concentration of anti-aircraft weapons around each site. Hurriedly fitting the two F-105 wings based in Thailand with RHAW sensors, 7th Air Force then directed that tracked fighter bombers only begin anti-SAM maneuvers if they received a warning that their fighter was being tracked.[75] Even though this was better than nothing, it was far from optimal given the similarity between the *Fan Song's* and *Fire Can's* signals, with lethal consequences for an incorrect guess. To a pilot transitioning through the densest North Vietnamese defenses (e.g., Route Packages 5 and 6), reacting to the RHAW transformed a mission into a virtual roller coaster ride into and out of the heart of the AAA envelope.[76]

As losses continued to mount, the Air Force developed two final solutions for dealing with the SAM sites: Wild Weasel aircraft and ECM pods.[77] The Air Force had first explored employing ECM pods in 1957, but initial efforts were less than optimal and required up-to-date intelligence on what hostile systems would be present at the target.[78] Unimpressed with the outcome and believing that tactical fighters would not need jammers in order to penetrate defenses at low level, the Air Force had decided that continued development was not a budgetary priority.[79] With the North Vietnamese providing deadly impetus for rethinking how their doctrine viewed air defense, the Air Force initiated a crash program to develop a more effective jamming pod.

The resultant second-generation ECM pod,

dubbed the QRC-160, was first fielded to protect the F-105 strike force and then, as numbers increased and the pods improved, their F-4 escorts. Although carrying the jamming pod meant that an aircraft could carry less ordnance, pilots and Air Force leaders considered the protection gained from turning a *Fan Song* or *Fire Can*'s screen into an unreadable mass of lines worth the cost. As long as the equipped aircraft flew straight and level at around 18,000 feet, the various pods greatly reduced the effectiveness of radar defenses. This protection grew almost exponentially if the aircraft was part of a tight, precise flight dubbed the "pod formation." Although the *Fan Song* could burn through the jamming at around six miles, the SA-2's minimum range of 4-5 miles meant that effective engagements would have required an extremely proficient crew. Losses to the SA-2 initially dropped after the pods' introduction, but there were periods of increased vulnerability due to North Vietnamese *Fan Song* operators changing their radars' frequency in November 1967.[80] Even though American ELINT quickly ascertained these new frequencies, with Air Force systems command making the necessary modifications to maintain effectiveness, it was clear that the pods as well as the formations were not the optimal solution to stop the *Dvina*.[81]

Guerillas of the Sky: MiGs

Part of the reason for dislike of the pods had to do with the final component of the NV-IADS: MiGs. Named for the Mikoyan-Gurevich Design Bureau, their usual manufacturer, these interceptors attempted to destroy USAF strike aircraft by using air-to-air missiles or mounted cannon. Ground control intercept (GCI) stations guided these North Vietnamese Air Force (NVAF) fighters to their prey by radio.[82] The pod formation, as the Air Force quickly found out, made this process much easier. Striking most often from behind and above, MiGs usually made a single pass on an American formation in an attempt to destroy, damage, or force the targeted aircraft to jettison its ordnance.[83] In this manner, they usually frustrated USAF attempts to force them into extended dogfights.

Fighting the IADS: USAF SEAD Doctrine During Rolling Thunder

The strength and skill with which the North Vietnamese defended their nation came as an unpleasant shock to the USAF's senior leaders. Although rules of engagement did limit the 7th Air Force's options, the simple fact of the matter was that Air Force tactical fighters lacked the capability to impose their will on the NV-IADS due to the prior overemphasis on nuclear doctrine.[84] Almost all of these shortcomings, including the inability to react to restrictive rules of engagement, could be blamed on one culprit: the USAF's lack of attention to SEAD doctrine in AFM 1-3. Indeed, AFM 1-3 devoted less than a page to enemy defenses, discussing them in this manner:

(8) Countermeasures:

(a) The nerve center of any modern air defense system consists essentially of electronic devices and equipment. It is primarily by these means that invading air forces are detected and located. After they are located, electronic devices assist in their interception and destruction. Antiaircraft artillery fire also is, to a large extent, controlled electronically.

(b) Certain types of offensive airforce operations are facilitated and their success enhanced by the complementary actions of electronic countermeasures operations. Such complementary operations tend to disrupt and confuse the enemy, and thus permit greater success to the main operation. Airborne countermeasure devices are complex and require highly trained personnel for effective operation.

(c) Due to the far-reaching implications of countermeasure operations their planning and employment transcend the responsibility of any single theater. The

overall agency charged with the direction
of the war determines the role each
theater will perform in accomplishing
certain countermeasures. The theater
countermeasures' program is controlled
at theater level, and is harmonized with
the global plan on a continuing basis.
In this manner, a concerted action
is achieved which provides all forces
irrespective of assigned tasks optimum
benefit from such measure to deceive and
confuse the enemy.[85]

It can be seen from above that the Air Force
considered destruction of enemy defenses to be
a *theater* (i.e., operational level) task. Despite
this, there was no doctrine to state just how
such a destruction should be conducted. Without
an overarching operational-level doctrine,
USAF wing commanders were forced to attack
the NV-IADS with a hodgepodge of techniques
that reflected each wing commander's personal
preferences. This, in turn, made coordination of
matters such as tanker support, fighter escort,
and jamming even more difficult for non-at-
tacking wings.[86] Finally, the Air Force's rotation
policies and senior leader attrition further
exacerbated this approach as new officers rotated
into wing command and senior staff positions.

This initial lack of an operational SEAD doctrine
followed by a failure to embark on an emergency
program to remedy it served to exacerbate the
materiel and tactical shortcomings exposed

in Operation Rolling Thunder's early days. The former manifested against all three facets of the NV-IADS in spectacular fashion. USAF fighters lacked ordnance that allowed them to target specifically *Fan Songs* and *Fire Cans* that made AAA and SA-2s so dangerous. Thus initial efforts to engage SAM sites using high explosive bombs and napalm resulted in heavy casualties both for the suppression flights and the strike packages they were attempting to protect.[87] Even after the development of *Shrike* radar-homing missiles and *Wild Weasel* aircraft, the lack of an operational SEAD plan made every foray into North Vietnam analogous to a parent betting on a pet mongoose's ability to kill a cobra before it struck their children. In many cases, the "Iron Hand" and "Wild Weasel" hunter-killer packages were able to suppress the North Vietnamese defenders into lesser effectiveness. However, all too often either a change in NVAF doctrine, a lack of available *Wild Weasel* airframes, or the inevitable friction of trying to coordinate between hundreds of airframes led to American strikes suffering increased losses from guns, SAMs, and MiGs.

It was North Vietnamese fighters' continued effectiveness that was most surprising and frustrating to USAF's leaders. Due as much to a lack of suitable ordnance as to restrictive rules of engagement, 7th Air Force was unable to destroy the North Vietnamese Air Force (NVAF) fighters on the ground. Even though MiGs fought in a style reminiscent of aerial guerillas, given the relative technological levels and investment in pilot development, fighting MiGs in the air should have been relatively simple. Indeed, in Korea, USAF fighter pilots had established a kill ratio of eight to ten MiGs for every United Nations aircraft lost to enemy fighters. During Rolling Thunder, this plunged precipitously to slightly over 2:1 against the obsolescent MiG-17 and only slightly more modern MiG-21. Although this could be understood due to the F-100, F-102, F-104's shorter range and the F-105's design parameters, it was perplexing to USAF leaders when F-4 *Phantoms* often found themselves outmaneuvered and then destroyed by North Vietnamese MiGs.[88]

It was only after hurried analysis that the Air Force realized the truly detrimental effect that their prewar doctrine had on their readiness for air-to-air combat. The *Phantom*'s lack of an internal gun, touted as proof of its modernity, quickly proved to be a liability as NVAF MiGs swiftly closed within the *Falcon*, *Sparrow* and *Sidewinder*'s minimum range. The missiles themselves, so reliable in tests, quickly began to malfunction due to both Southeast Asia's humidity and poor maintenance practices employed by draftee airmen facing pressure for rapid sortie rates.[89] Within the cockpit, systems designed to ensure that there was careful, thoughtful release of nuclear weapons proved ergonomically unsuitable to use during the chaotic, high-G dance of aerial combat. Perhaps most importantly, pilots taught for years to fly precise, rigid flight formations that placed a premium on flight integrity proved wholly unsuited to fighting against dissimilar aircraft manned by increasingly experienced NVAF operators.[90] All of these problems were exacerbated by questionable USAF personnel policies dictating that 7th Air Force personnel would be rotated after 100 missions, with no officer required to return against his will until virtually all TAC officers had been sent to Southeast Asia at least once.[91]

The State of the Air Force, November 1968

This problem with manning was only one of the numerous issues facing the Air Force as Rolling Thunder ended in November 1968. First and foremost, it was clear that USAF leaders had wildly exaggerated the likelihood of nuclear war when writing the service's doctrine. This had led to several poor decisions with regard to acquisition, training, and ordnance development. Second, the severe cost of Rolling Thunder had indicated that the Air Force's views about hostile air defense systems were fatally flawed. The NV–IADS had not only taken its measure of 7th Air Force but it had also shot down so many *Thunderchiefs* that the Air Force was forced to withdraw the F-105D from active service.[92] Third, conventional training and pilot proficiency had been clearly lacking at the beginning of the bombing campaign and only faced haphazard improvement over the previous three years. Unfortunately, the psychological effect of these devastating losses, frustration with what the pilots perceived as indifference of Air Force leaders, and wide availability of jobs in the civilian sector resulted in many combat-experienced pilots opting for civilian life.[93] This exodus occurred concurrently with the accelerated exit of the World War II and Korean War pilots who had led Rolling Thunder's squadrons and wings. With most of the experienced officers leaving, the Air Force was in great danger of losing most of the lessons it had learned from Operation Rolling Thunder.[94]

OF LULLS AND DOCTRINE

Generall McConnell and the Air Staff took several steps in order to try and preserve the knowledge gained at great cost over North Vietnam. Although senior leaders did not take the drastic step of outright preventing officers from leaving the Air Force, the LOYAL LOOK (later dubbed CORONA HARVEST) oral history program was initiated to interview as many of the departing individuals as possible.[95] The Air Staff also gave increased priority to updating its doctrine, a process that it had begun just prior to the initiation of Operation Rolling Thunder.[96]

Unfortunately for the USAF, ongoing operations in Southeast Asia, as well as continued responsibilities throughout the rest of the world, constantly distracted the individuals tasked with updating AFM 1-3. The end result of this upheaval was almost no change in actual SEAD doctrine from November 1968 through March 1972. Lacking the pervasive guidance of doctrine, the Air Force made few advances toward fixing the vulnerabilities exposed by the NV-IADS during Rolling Thunder. There is little evidence that USAF leaders at any level attempted to determine how Air Force units were to identify or destroy an IADS's command and control elements. With regard to AAA, from 1968 to 1972 the Air Force continued to preach the gospel of terrain avoidance and low-level ingress and egress in training and European commands. This directly contradicted the medium-altitude ingress followed by dive-bombing delivery that 7th Air Force had almost universally adopted by October 1968 after completing a hasty study of North Vietnamese air defenses and F-105 losses.[97]

Anti-radar efforts faced a similar organizational malaise throughout TAC in particular and the USAF in general. In addition to its own experience in Rolling Thunder, the Air Force was able to observe the Israeli Air Force's (IAF's) issues in facing Egyptian defenses from late 1967 through 1972 in the "War of Attrition."[98] Despite this, minimal emphasis was placed upon making advances in anti-radar capability through either advanced ECM pods, internal jammers, or physical attack. The EB-66, despite its creeping obsolescence and inability to accompany strike packages, continued to be the Air Force's primary jamming aircraft. As for Wild Weasels, the USAF once again attempted to use an obsolescent airframe (the F-4C) rather than attempting to develop a wholly new system or diverting new *Phantom* production for modification. In addition to not being able to carry *Standard* anti-radiation missiles (*StARMs*), the F-4C had serious issues with its avionics suite and physical maneuverability in comparison to the new production F-4Es.[99] These proved difficult to resolve and, as the Air Force's leaders failed to make development a priority, meant that the F-105Fs/Gs would be the primary defense suppression aircraft when combat resumed in 1972.[100]

The sum effect of these changes was that Air Force aircraft went to war in 1972 with less electronic warfare capability than they had when Operation Rolling Thunder ended. On the positive side, the ability to carry more *StARMs* on the F-105G, better jammers, minor improvements in avionics, and an increase in the total available airframes meant that Wild Weasels were somewhat more capable. This increase in capability, however, was more than counterbalanced by the increased proficiency of the North

Vietnamese, the F-105F/G's age, the *Thunder-chiefs*' lower speed at medium altitude, and the need for Wild Weasels to be provided with an additional flight of escorts. Whether or not one believes that the Air Force's anti-radar capability actually regressed, there is overwhelming evidence that markedly improving Wild Weasel capability had not been a priority of the intervening four years.[101]

The Air Force appeared similarly disinterested in making major improvements in its ability to destroy airborne MiGs. Despite the heavy losses suffered from NVAF interceptors, especially in the final months of Rolling Thunder, the Air Force did not increase its focus on ACM. Instead, the number of aerial combat training flights flown by new pilots actually decreased.[102] Even worse, those missions which were left in the syllabus were the same rigidly controlled exercises that had passed for training prior to Rolling Thunder.[103] Rather than learning how to use their *Phantoms*' strengths against an enemy's weaknesses, new pilots were often sent to war with only a rudimentary understanding of their fighters' capabilities.[104]

This lack of training made the improvements the Air Force completed to the *Phantom* itself superfluous. Equipping the "E" model of the *Phantom* with a gun did little good if no one taught the pilots how to bring their cannon to bear. Improved avionics and ergonomically modified cockpits had little effect if the Air Force did not ensure that pilots received the number of training sorties to make their use second nature When TAC did not develop a training regimen that instructed pilots how to fly an F-4 throughout its flight regime, expecting these same pilots to take advantage of maneuvering slats that were designed to improve the *Phantom*'s performance in air-to-air combat was somewhat wishful thinking. Finally, the continued problems with the *Sparrow* and *Sidewinder* meant that the F-4s' primary armament remained ineffective.[105] SEAD doctrine was not a panacea for all of these issues. However, it is clear that, in its absence, the Air Force continued most of the same policies that had caused the heavy losses during Operation Rolling Thunder. From the lack of movement on SEAD doctrine, equipment, or training from 1968 through 1972, it appeared that Air Force leaders focused on the wrong issues after rolling Thunder. As noted by Air Force historian Michael Worden, "TAC worked closely with Systems Command to develop cluster-bomb munitions (CBU), precision-guided munitions (PGM), radar warning systems...F-4E gatling guns...electronic warfare aircraft, and long-range aid to navigation (LORAN) systems." But the majority of these efforts were conducted without thought to their integration with each other.[106] For almost four years the Air Force, in focusing on individual aircraft components and ordnance effects on targets, did not give enough effort to training their aircrews how to penetrate an integrated air defense system.

Thoughts on Air Defense

Noting the Air Force's lack of SEAD doctrine is not intended to imply that the 1971 edition of AFM 1-1 *United States Air Force Basic Doctrine* completely ignored the enemy air defenses. Indeed, if the Air Force had not just spent three years being mauled over North Vietnam, its treatment of a possible enemy IADS would have appeared to be sufficient given the dearth of other information for analysis. At the tactical level, the Air Force's revised doctrinal manual provided a doctrine of what the "counterair mission" consisted of [bold in original copy]:

> **3-4.   Conventional   Mission Characteristics.** In a conflict involving only conventional weapons, the following mission characteristics will generally apply:
>
> **a.   The   Counterair   Mission.** Conventional operations require the use of aircraft of such a scale as to be impracticable without air superiority. The counterair mission can best be accomplished by multiple attacks against the enemy's airbases, air order of battle, and his command and control facilities, but must also include the interception and destruction of enemy aircraft in flight. If sanctuary is permitted near the battle zone, air superiority will depend on air-to-air combat.[107]

This tactical definition complemented the counterair operational task [bold in original copy]:

> a. **Counterair.** Counterair operations are conducted to gain and maintain air superiority by destruction or neutralization of an enemy's offensive and defensive air capability. The counterair mission involves both offensive and defensive air action.
>
> (1) Offensive counterair operations are normally conducted throughout enemy territory to seek out and destroy aircraft in the air or on the ground, missile and anti-aircraft artillery sites, air bases, air control systems, fuel stores and other elements which constitute or support the enemy air order of battle.
>
> (2) Defensive counterair operations are generally reactive to enemy initiative. Air defense operations involve destroying enemy air vehicles attempting to penetrate friendly airspace. While air defense is vital to the overall counterair program and to the security of friendly forces and installations, the most rapid and conclusive results are obtained through offensive action.
>
> (3) Centralized allocation and direction of air forces is essential to achieve

maximum effectiveness of the counterair effort and to insure coordination of the overall air campaign.[108]

In order to accomplish these tasks, according to AFM 1–1, aerospace forces would have to be "capable of":

(1) Sustained operations under austere conditions.

(2) Continuous mission performance under all conditions of light and weather.

(3) Continued and effective operations in a sophisticated enemy electromagnetic environment.

(4) Survivability under enemy fire.

(5) Obtaining complete and timely intelligence on enemy activities.

b. Underlying the foregoing capabilities is the requirement for a secure, responsive, flexible control system to direct the forces, integrate their efforts, and coordinate operations with those of other friendly forces.

c. Standardized equipment, ordnance, and operational procedures are desirable, however, efforts to standardize should not compromise mission flexibility nor create stereotyped operational patterns.

d. Combat aircraft are designed to accomplish specific operational tasks. At the same time to achieve flexibility, combat aircraft are capable of performing multiple missions.[109]

Finally, the ordnance which these aircraft would carry would meet the following description [bold in original text]:

3-3. **Conventional** **Weapons Capabilities.** Conventional weapon capabilities should not be considered as fixed or static. Since military capability is sensitive to new types of weapons and improved delivery systems, efforts to upgrade conventional systems must proceed alongside comparable efforts in the field of nuclear warfare. Smoke, incendiary agents and riot control agents are included within the concept of conventional air operations.

These descriptions and analyses would have been understandable if written in 1965. However, the Air Force went through great effort (e.g., CORONA HARVEST) to record lessons learned during Operation Rolling Thunder with the intent that these historical records would influence later doctrine and training. In addition, the Nixon administration had made its plans to use airpower as a national instrument very clear. Despite this, there appears to be a clear incongruity between the Air Force's intellectual efforts, stated national policy, and the doctrine stated above. The USAF was tasked with myriad worldwide missions. Of these, senior Air Force leaders repeatedly emphasized that a potential war in Central Europe was their paradigm for measuring units' effectiveness and the basis for the service's most important contingency plans.110 AFM 1-1's authors wrote the above paragraphs as if many of these contingencies would not entail fighting the very same systems that had just savaged 7th Air Force over the DRV. Indeed, looking at AFM 1-1, an outside observer would have believed that an individual AAA site was as worthwhile a target as fuel stores for a major airbase. If one accepts the purpose of doctrine as providing clear guidelines, AFM 1-1 did not meet this standard with regard to SEAD.

This shortcoming did not end with target prioritization. Based on the document's own definitions, it was impossible for a theater commander to organize an effective SEAD aerospace force from systems available in 1971. With only limited capability to operate at night, marginally better suitability to operations in an electronic environment, and no innate reconnaissance capabilities, the F-4 airframe did not even meet most of the criteria for aerospace power in the document. Thus, commanders who were expected to carry out SEAD would not be able to employ the proposed Wild Weasel IV aircraft against ground-based threats even as the document was being written, much less in the near future. This dissonance becomes even more pronounced when one considers that the F-105 F/G, not the F-4C, was still the Air Force's primary suppression aircraft in September 1971.

The conflict between doctrinally stated require- ments and existing Air Force capabilities in 1971 continues with regard to conventional weapons. Although AFM 1-1 alludes to conventional weapons, there is no mention of what these weapons are expected to do to targets. SEAD weapons are not even described at all. Previously the Air Force had used doctrine as a tool to drive procurement of the Century Fighters for a theoretical conflict. Having learned through painful experience over North Vietnam that not all conventional weapons were created equal, it is curious that its foundational doctrine omitted any mention of SEAD. As the intent of AFM 1-1 was to serve as a doctrinal foundation, having the central doctrinal text list every weapon by type would likely have been unwieldy. However, given the impact of the NV-IADS, the Air Force's doctrine writers could likely have delivered a general description of SEAD weapons and how they affected to ability to employ aerospace power in a short number of pages. The Air Force's doctrinal writers did not do this and, in addition to leading to later weapons procurement mischief, this omission increased the likelihood that the bomber, fighter, and electronic warfare communities would suffer confusion when communicating with one another.

Finally, AFM 1-1 continued to tie Air Force

conventional and nuclear capabilities together as part of a warfighting whole rather in a manner that did not make much sense. By 1971 the Soviet Union had achieved near parity in nuclear weapons, and thus it was highly unlikely a general nuclear exchange would occur. Simultaneously, this paradigm increased the probability of a conventional conflict. By stating that Air Force efforts, in everything from research and development (R&D) through procurement, should be "comparable," USAF leaders indicated their belief that thermonuclear exchange continued to be a viable national strategy Further evidence of this mindset can be seen in the fact that conventional weapons operations were covered in one chapter yet AFM 1-1 dedicated two chapters to nuclear warfare. This is especially confusing given the concurrent use of conventional weapons in Vietnam, their previous use in Korea, and likely future use should deterrence fail in Central Europe. Put more starkly, although it was possible that there could be a high-intensity nuclear conflict in 1971, the Air Force had yet to see one. In contrast, almost forty percent of its time as a separate service had been spent in conventional combat[111]

It is even harder to understand is why the Air Force included these two chapters yet did not include one on SEAD. Using obsolescent systems, North Vietnam's air defenses had accounted for the downing of almost 1,000 aircraft. The Air Force was well aware that the Soviet Union possessed systems that were far more capable than the SA-2. A Central European scenario where most of these weapons could be expected was central to most of the Department of Defense's planning. Furthermore, after Operation Rolling Thunder and concurrent wars in the Middle East, Air Force leaders and pilots were also cognizant of the Soviet Union's willingness to provide advanced systems to client states.[112]

Despite this knowledge, AFM 1-1's writers saw fit to provide only three paragraphs on this threat. Thus, in effect, the doctrine published in September 1971 was fundamentally unchanged from that published in 1953. There was no guidance in how a theater commander would reduce an IADS. Future procurement officers could not foresee what changes needed to be made in future systems to meet a doctrinal intent. Finally, there was no discussion as to how the Air Force could conduct joint or combined operations in support of national objectives. Subsequently, in both the near and mid-term, the Air Force would be doctrinally adrift.

Explaining the Excluded

There is no single event or cause that explains why Air Force SEAD doctrine did not evolve from 1968 to 1972. The Air Force remained a large organization and, like all similar entities, had many complexities, personnel movements, and daily unit activities that served to hinder change through bureaucratic inertia. However, historical evidence indicates that three major incidents influenced the development of AFM 1-1 in general and the exclusion of SEAD doctrine in particular. First, the election of Richard Nixon and the appointment of his cabinet not only changed the Air Force's civilian leadership in 1968 but revamped the USAF's strategic focus to conventional warfare. The 1969 appointment of General John D. Ryan to succeed General McConnell as Air Force Chief of Staff meant that this reorientation occurred in a period when military leadership was also transitioning. Finally, in yet another shift, General McConnell appointed General William Momyer, formerly the 7th Air Force commander, to become head of Tactical Air Command. Having all three of these positions change hands simultaneously had interesting effects on Air Force doctrine.

President Nixon, in addition to wanting to end the Vietnam War, also sought to reduce American military responsibilities worldwide. The first step towards doing this was the enunciation of the Nixon Doctrine, in which President Nixon outlined the United States' responsibilities towards its allies. No longer could allied nations expect the open-ended commitment of American ground forces in order to combat communist incursions against their territory. Nor would the United States, given the Soviet Union's increasingly modern strategic arsenal, provide a blanket nuclear guarantee to counteract gross disparities in conventional forces between allied nations and their Communist neighbors. Instead, the United States could be expected to provide two things: military hardware and training to equip allied forces at reasonable prices and, more importantly, conventional airpower. Though this was intended to have major implications for NATO and Western Europe, the first test of this theory would come with "Vietnamization," i.e., the withdrawal of U.S. ground combat forces from 1969 to 1972.[113]

Unfortunately for the U.S. Air Force, President Nixon's clarity in enunciating his new doctrine and the military's role met with immediate resistance within the Pentagon. The primary cause of these difficulties was President Nixon's relationship with Secretary of Defense Melvin R. Laird. Laird had not been Nixon's first choice to head DoD. Since the President did not know Laird well, the new secretary did not enjoy the Chief Executive's full confidence.[114] As would be the case with many of his other appointees, military leaders, and members of Congress, Nixon's paranoia caused him to regard Laird with increasing acrimony. Laird's actions during a crisis that ensued after North Korea shot down an American spy plane followed shortly by Nixon's suspicions that Laird was the source of a leak regarding operations in Cambodia did not help matters.[115] Eventually, the friction between the two men grew to the point that their relationship was barely functional, as Nixon began to believe that Laird was more interested in simply abandoning South Vietnam than achieving any semblance of victory.[116] Although a degree of tension between a President and his Secretary of Defense in time of war may be typical or even healthy, the relationship between Nixon and Laird exceeded this standard. This friction, combined with the damage done to the Department of Defense during the Johnson administration, prevented Laird from acting as Nixon's agent of change within the Pentagon.

Unlike the tense relationship between Laird and Nixon, the tie between Secretary of the Air Force Robert Seamans, Jr. and General Ryan was much too friendly. Air historian Walter J. Boyne describes Seamans as "able" and an "excellent match" for General Ryan when the latter became Air Force Chief of Staff.[117] If one accepts that the Air Force needed change, it stands to reason that this was not a good thing. Seamans not only reestablished the Air Force's Central European focus but gave every indication that the Air Force's leaders did not have to worry about a return to North Vietnam.[118] With this lackadaisical approach to solving the war at hand, Seamans likely contributed, as Earl Tilford puts it, to the "sense within the Air Force that the [Vietnam] war was over" in 1971.[119] There are also no indications that Seamans questioned the Air Force's continued attempts to develop a successor to the B-52 or the Air Staff's prioritization of this project over rushing the successor to the F-4 *Phantom* and F-105 *Thunderchief* into service. Given both the Nixon Doctrine and the attrition suffered by TAC airframes in Southeast Asia, it is puzzling why the Secretary of the Air Force did not take a more active role in overseeing his service's refurbishment efforts.[120] Taken altogether, these actions strongly indicate that Secretary Seamans was not interested in forcing major modifications to any doctrine, much less specific areas such as SEAD, on the Air Force's military leadership.

Air Force Leaders

It is apparent that the impetus for sweeping changes would have to come from an external source after examining the three Air Force officers who were responsible for conventional readiness prior to Operation Linebacker. The first of these, General McConnell, was only briefly on the scene. Having served as Air Force Chief of Staff for the entirety of Rolling Thunder, McConnell blamed most of that campaign's shortcomings on civilian leaders' restrictions.[121] Furthermore, McConnell felt that the Air Force had allowed its strategic strength to decline to dangerous levels.[122] Although he had cut SAC's research and development budget to the bone in order to support tactical fighters in contact, McConnell had also strongly resisted cutting prohibitively expensive bomber programs in order to expedite the production of conventional fighters.[123] It was clear that General McConnell believed the Air Force should reallocate the bulk of its budget from conventional operations to rebuilding SAC as soon as the Vietnam War was over. It is not hard to imagine how the Chief of Staff's views may have influenced doctrine writers in general, and almost certainly by what he found unimportant. McConnell gave no formal guidance to TAC on training, nor did he seem to believe that suppressing enemy air defenses was a pressing task.

General John D. Ryan, McConnell's successor, believed even more strongly in the primacy of strategic forces. General McConnell, desiring Ryan to be his successor, appointed the latter as Commander in Chief, Pacific Air Forces at the beginning of Operation Rolling Thunder. McConnell did this specifically so that Ryan, who had spent his entire career within SAC, could gain some experience overseeing tactical fighters. This appointment did not go well. General Ryan regularly demonstrated ignorance of what his pilots were going through and gave few indications that he wished to learn.[124] He displayed a very poor leadership style which often prevented the flow of information between PACAF and 7th Air Force and also had a negative impact on pilots' morale. Finally, on more than one occasion he seemed to demonstrate a lack of integrity to his subordinates.[125]

Had Ryan not become Air Force Chief of Staff, his personality traits would not have had much bearing on how USAF developed doctrine. However, General Ryan carried these same traits to Washington when he succeeded McConnell. Two incidents will suffice to illustrate this point. First, after tacitly encouraging 7th Air Force commander General John D. Lavelle to interpret liberally his rules of engagement with regard to striking North Vietnamese targets in 1971, Ryan did not defend his subordinate when these incidents drew the ire of President Nixon.[126] Second, after having dispatched then Brigadier General Robin Olds to conduct an evaluation of 7th Air Force's capabilities, General Ryan did not reward the World War II ace and MiG killer for his candor. Instead, General Olds was shuffled off to the Air Force Inspector General's office, effectively ending his career.[127] Justifiably or not, General Ryan began to develop a reputation for not wanting to hear bad news or have subordinates confront him in public.[128] Although the effect this environment had on doctrinal development cannot be quantified, it is unlikely that it was positive.

The last Air Force leader who, by virtue of position and experience, could have had a great influence on Air Force doctrine was General William Momyer, commander of TAC. Of all three military leaders, it is General Momyer's unwillingness to force change that is hardest to explain. The commander of 7th Air Force throughout Rolling Thunder, Momyer had been an approachable leader who often visited his wing commanders.[129] Unlike Ryan at PACAF, Momyer had been well aware of the NV–IADS's effect on his forces. In response to the strength of the

DRV's defenses, General Momyer had regularly scheduled tactics meetings involving all of his subordinate leaders then disseminated the collective input throughout his organization.[130] When General McConnell appointed Momyer as head of TAC, it was with the understanding that the latter would bring these same techniques with him to his new posting. General Ryan reaffirmed this expectation when he succeeded McConnell as Chief of Staff.[131] Therefore, it is hard to understand why General Momyer did not ensure that AFM 1-1 encapsulated more of the lessons, to include the necessity for SEAD, which 7th Air Force had learned.

One possible cause could be combat fatigue, as Momyer had overseen the longest bombing campaign in the Air Force's short history while simultaneously running the air war over South Vietnam. Another is that Momyer may have believed that the Air Force, and himself especially, had executed Rolling Thunder to the best of their ability given the resources at hand and civilian restrictions in place. Momyer espouses this view throughout his book *Airpower In Three Wars* and it is hard to believe that this opinion did not affect his actions as TAC commander. Providing further evidence that this stance may have been a factor is a 1974 memorandum that accompanied the CORONA HARVEST report on operations over North Vietnam and Laos during Rolling Thunder. In it, Momyer states:

> Many of the restrictions on the attack

EAGLES, RAVENS, AND OTHER BIRDS OF PREY | 75

of SAMs and AAA came from the location of these weapons. The North Vietnamese deliberately sited many of these weapons in civilian areas knowing full well there would be a reluctance to strike these sites because of the civilian casualties that would ensue. The question of expected collateral damage became a major consideration in the selection of targets at the highest level. The SAMs and AAA that were located in the ten and thirty mile circle were usually surrounded by civilian structures. Collateral damage could be significant when striking these targets which invariably had a political effect on the international scene.[132]

Momyer proceded to give a similar treatment to air-to-air combat during Rolling Thunder:

> With the **projected weapon systems now being developed and procured,** [emphasis added] we should have a vastly improved potential for air to air combat. Although the air to air engagements were dramatic in the Vietnam War, they were of **limited significance** [emphasis added] in terms of operations against the warmaking structure of the North Vietnamese. The MiG force was relatively small and the size of the engagements was limited to four to five aircraft at any given time. Even under the intensive effort by the North Vietnamese, the number of MiGs

up for battle never exceeded fifteen to twenty aircraft. We should, therefore, be cautious about the lessons derived from these limited combats. Most certainly, relative performance of aircraft could be judged and restricted conclusions on air to air tactics could be deduced, but one should not try to extrapolate these limited experiences in generalizing about the character of an air war in Europe where thousands of fighters would be involved.

Recommendation. **Current actions are considered adequate** [emphasis added]. Care should be exercised in the application of the Vietnam experience to our tactical operations manuals. TAC should be directed to review such publications for applicability to a large scale war.[133]

Considering that General Momyer wrote this in 1974, i.e., two years after the Linebacker Operations, it is safe to assume that Momyer had these same opinions from 1968 to 1972. This means that, in Momyer's view, it was not the Air Force's current doctrine or its lack of guidance that explained 7th Air Force's inability to combat the NV-IADS. Nor was it the USAF's inability to reliably detect active *Fan Song* and *Fire Can* radars, lack of a suitable anti-radiation missile or conventional munitions to destroy SAM sites, or dearth of pilot training in the delivery of these weapons that explained the resiliency of North Vietnam's defenses.

Instead, in Momyer's view it was the DRV's cunning use of civilian structures coupled with President Johnson and Secretary McNamara's unwillingness to suffer a loss of international prestige that explained 7th Air Force's issues with ground defenses. Likewise, the missiles that had failed to work reliably in Rolling Thunder had done so, in part, due to a lack of a target-rich environment or high-altitude clash between droves of MiGs and squadrons of *Phantoms*. Finally, as long as the Air Force could wait until new systems were produced, there was no need to change training or ensure that pilots knew how to use their high-technology mounts once they began to arrive in the Air Force.

Combined, these factors meant that TAC, like the remainder of the Air Force, marked time and focused on attempting to repair the damage Operation Rolling Thunder had caused. Although Momyer did make several changes, the majority of these did not require strenuous action or risk-taking on his part. By emphasizing TAC's focus on the development of guided bombs, all-weather capability, and sensor systems, General Momyer attempted to ensure that the USAF's next generation of warriors would go to war with the ability to threaten an ever growing list of targets.[134] Unfortunately for the generation he commanded, however, the North Vietnamese did not wait until these projects came to full fruition.

The Linebacker Operations

On March 30th, 1972, the DRV launched a surprise conventional assault against South Vietnam. Dubbed the "Easter Offensive" by the United States, the attack demonstrated that the NVA had finally evolved from an organization that employed traditional guerilla and light-infantry tactics into a modern, mechanized army capable of employing armored vehicles in multi-divisional attacks. The purpose of the Easter Offensive was threefold. First, the NVA would discredit the regime of President Thieu, South Vietnam's leader, by occupying several of Republic of Vietnam's (RVN's) regional capitals. Second, by virtue of targeting population centers, the NVA would force the Army of the Republic of Vietnam (ARVN) into pitched battles for which its American advisors considered its small unit leaders poorly prepared. Finally, even if the first two goals were not fully realized, the NVA expected that they would gain lodgments within South Vietnam from which they could launch future offensives.[135]

Given the North Vietnamese decision to pursue their objectives with the South in the midst of Vietnamization, the Easter Offensive seemed to be a perfect opportunity to test the Nixon Doctrine. To both stabilize the wavering South Vietnamese government and to punish the DRV's leadership, President Richard Nixon ordered the United States Air Force and Navy to resume bombing North Vietnam, with initial operations beginning on March 30th, 1972. Unlike his predecessor, President Nixon committed these forces with reasonably clear strategic goals and the latitude to accomplish them. The North Vietnamese, in response to this onslaught, defended their country with the same systems they had used from 1965 to 1968. Beginning with Operation Freedom Train, transitioning seamlessly to Linebacker I, and then, after a two-month pause (October–November 1972), ending with Linebacker II, the USN and USAF once again put America's air power theories to the test.

The Air Staff derived four major objectives from President Nixon's guidance. First, USAF aircraft, with USN support, would seek to interdict the NVA's supply lines sufficiently to preclude continued conventional operations in South Vietnam. Second, the White House had explicitly stated that the Air Force was to inflict sufficient punishment on North Vietnam so that the DRV Politburo would be deterred from authorizing further aggression against South Vietnam. Third, as implied by the Nixon Doctrine, the USAF was to establish convincingly its ability to conduct conventional operations in support of an allied nation during a major conflict.[136] Finally, with the introduction of B-52 bombers in December 1972, the Air Force was to maintain the credibility of manned strategic aircraft as part of American nuclear deterrence policy.

Measuring Effectiveness

There are many opinions about the outcome of this test. Many of these judgments depend on how one views the ultimate objectives. As one Air Force historian has noted, a football linebacker disrupts the offense through speed, strength, and the application of controlled violence.[137] Although urban legend has it that Linebacker I was so dubbed "because of [President Nixon's] fondness for football," the moniker was an apt analogy given American intentions to disrupt North Vietnam's strategic war aims from March 30th to October 23rd, 1972.[138] However, as "disruption" is a vague term, clearly enumerating President Nixon's objectives will better serve further discussion. Generally speaking, the Air Force and USN were dispatched to accomplish the following objectives:

(1) Interdict the NVA's supply lines in order to prevent the success of the Easter Offensive;

(2) Sufficiently punish North Vietnam, both by destroying its military capability and civilian infrastructure, so that its leadership was compelled to accept American peace terms and would deterred from future aggression;[139]

(3) Validate the USAF and USN's ability to conduct conventional operations in a high-threat air defense environment;

and

(4) If USAF introduced strategic bombers, all elements were to ensure that the deterrent value of the manned strategic bomber was preserved.

Goal #1: Battlefield Interdiction

The first two tasks were clearly and repeatedly stated by President Nixon. By deploying the North Vietnamese Army in a modern combined-arms mechanized assault, the Politburo had made their forces vulnerable to a traditional aerial interdiction campaign. If DRV's leaders had been correct in their analysis of Nixon, this vulnerability would have been of no consequence — South Vietnam did not have an Air Force capable of many operations beyond close air support. However, when his military leaders made clear to Nixon the extent and type of the North's attack, the President made several clear comparisons between the North Vietnamese offensive and the *Wehrmacht*'s Ardennes Offensive of December 1944. Equally direct were his indications that he expected the North Vietnamese offensive to suffer a fate similar to that of the German one: strangulation and destruction under the weight of American air power.[140]

Whether air power caused the NVA's offensive to fail is arguable even if the importance of American airstrikes to South Vietnamese morale is not. On one hand, the Linebacker strikes wrought great destruction on the North Vietnamese logistical network through the destruction of bridges, railways, and supply caches throughout that country.[141] On the other, the NVA had foreseen just this possibility and stockpiled sufficient supplies to conduct the initial phase of their offensive.[142] This simple preparation meant that any interdiction campaign, no matter how rapid, would have taken several weeks to show any effect.

The massive amounts of air power directed against the NVA's offensive forces, however, ensured that the exposed North Vietnamese divisions suffered losses far exceeding what their leaders had prepared for. With myriad aircraft including everything from U.S. Army AH-1 *Cobra* helicopter gunships through South Vietnamese A-1 *Skyraiders* up to B-52 Arc Light missions dropping 60,000–180,000 pounds of high explosive every thirty minutes, the NVA's armored spearheads faced firepower unlike any seen to that point in warfare. As Nixon desired, this resulted in the defeat of the North Vietnamese offensive in conjunction with the interdiction campaign. Regardless of which phase caused more damage, the NVA's general offensive did not achieve the physical conquest of the South nor did it cause the Thieu government to abruptly topple. Therefore, it can be argued that the USAF and USN airstrikes met President Nixon's first stated goal.[143]

EAGLES, RAVENS, AND OTHER BIRDS OF PREY | 83

Goal #2: Punishment

The military could not so easily meet the second objective -- to punish North Vietnam. From Nixon's perspective, the DRV's Politburo had rewarded three years of good-faith negotiating with an overt, aggressive betrayal. Moreover, North Vietnam's actions threatened to undermine Nixon and National Security Advisor Henry Kissinger's Cold War détente policies with the People's Republic of China and Soviet Union. Also, Nixon had watched his predecessor's attempt at a gradual campaign become a spectacular failure. Finally, and most importantly, Nixon wanted to make certain that the North Vietnamese were keenly aware of the penalties involved should the DRV force the United States to intervene again in Southeast Asia. All four of these aspects compelled Nixon to ensure that the military understood his intent for the Linebacker operations to be an act of violence so extreme as to deter any future large-scale North Vietnamese offensives against South Vietnam for at least the remainder of his first term. Contrary to what the DRV's Politburo had expected, Nixon had the will to aid South Vietnam. Even worse, as they were about to be made aware, the American President had the necessary vindictiveness to ruin North Vietnam's civil and industrial capability if this would result in the DRV's leadership being cowed into giving South Vietnam breathing room.[144]

A potent force of will aside, it is unknowable whether what Nixon asked of the U.S. military was even achievable. Like President Johnson's goal of demonstrating "resolve," Nixon's desire to "punish" the North Vietnamese cannot be quantified. The DRV's Politburo was highly motivated to expedite the United States' exit, as they felt this was the only way to ensure the fall of South Vietnam. After the death of Ho Chi Minh in 1969, some observers noticed that North Vietnamese Politburo members had become increasingly concerned they would die before Vietnam was unified. Ho Chi Minh's passing also increased the North Vietnamese people's motivation to reunite their country.[145] Combined, these two factors meant that it was unlikely that the United States could achieve a sufficient level of violence to persuade these men to accept a divided Vietnam or, for that matter, any dictated American objectives. That Nixon's goals kept changing also hindered this process by making it unclear how much and what type of pain the USAF's aircrews and their USN counterparts needed to inflict.[146]

Regardless of these facts, one possible guideline did exist: Operation Rolling Thunder. The North Vietnamese people and their leaders had weathered the USAF and USN's efforts from 1965 to 1968. Considering North Vietnam's continued intransigence from 1968 to 1972, infiltration of NVA regular units into South Vietnam, and the launch of the Easter Offensive, Operation Rolling Thunder had not greatly affected the DRV's society nor deterred its leaders. Therefore, in order to have achieved Nixon's "punishment," the Linebacker operations would have had to at least equal if not surpass that earlier effort.

Before attempting to see if the level of effort in the Linebacker operations surpassed that of Operation Rolling Thunder, it is necessary to examine some technical factors. In 1972, the USAF did not deploy as many aircraft to Southeast Asia as it had in 1968. During Linebacker Operations, the 7th Air Force had roughly 100 fewer aircraft capable of striking Vietnam than its Rolling Thunder predecessor.[147] The material quality of this force, however, was far greater. During operations from April to October, the 7th Air Force's primary strike aircraft was the F-4 *Phantom*, each of which was capable of carrying slightly more tonnage than the F-105. More importantly, the Air Force had developed the *Paveway* (laser) and *GBU / HOBO* (optical or electro-optical) families of guided weapons. In clear conditions, both of these systems allowed the F-4 to engage targets that had been previously unassailable due to their proximity to urban centers or sensitive buildings. In addition, they allowed the rapid destruction of bridges, bunkers, and other hardened North Vietnamese structures. The General Dynamics F-111, the outcome of Secretary McNamara's TFX program, provided an all-weather, night-attack capability from September 1972 forward.[148]

Taken altogether, these new capabilities meant that General John W. Vogt, 7th Air Force's commander, possessed a far deadlier force than General Momyer had. When one added SAC's B-52s, first used in April 1972 and fully committed in December 1972, Vogt and his superiors in SAC and the White House believed the USAF had more than enough firepower to break the will of the North Vietnamese people and their leaders.[149] Contrary to the claims of some authors, this did not happen, and thus the Air Force did not achieve its second objective of inflicting "punishment" in the manner that President Nixon intended. A major reason for this shortcoming was the continued strength of the NV-IADS. This, in turn, stemmed primarily from the Air Force's inattention to SEAD doctrine between Operation Rolling Thunder and the start of Linebacker operations.

The impact of insufficient development of SEAD doctrine and inadequate training can be seen from how the NV-IADS affected the employment of 7th Air Force's increased capabilities. For instance, a typical laser-guided bomb (LGB) strike began with an F-4 flight arriving in the vicinity of the targeted structure armed with three aircraft carrying *Paveway* bombs and one aircraft (usually the flight leader) equipped with a *Pave Knife* laser pod.[150] This pod was an improvement on an earlier system that had required the designating aircraft to remain in a gentle, predictable orbit while other aircraft dropped bombs. When in the target area, the flight leader would designate the strike's objective and, on his signal, the entire flight would drop the allocated number of *Paveway*s on the target. The control units on these bombs then detected the light reflected from the *Pave Knife*'s laser and guided the ordnance to impact.[151]

EOGB operations were somewhat similar to those of LGBs. Once again, a flight of F-4s approached a target area at medium altitude. Upon sighting the objective, the F-4's backseater would acquire the desired target visually. The *Phantom*'s pilot would then bring the aircraft into the correct attitude, altitude, and air speed to release the glide bomb as the backseater attempted to lock the EOGB's self-contained television camera onto the target's contrast with its surroundings. In optimal conditions, this process could take 5-10 seconds. Over North Vietnam it could take up to 30 seconds depending on the ground haze, target contrast, and position of the sun. Once lock-on was achieved, the bomb was released and, provided there was no further interference, impacted its target.[152]

Unfortunately, there were severe limitations on both LGBs and EOGBs. First, the weather had to be fairly clear and with low winds over the proposed target area. Second, there had to be no more than a minimal amount of smoke or dust in the vicinity of the structure to be destroyed. In the case of LGBs, obscurants scattered the guidance laser and caused the weapon to "go stupid" and follow a ballistic path. EOGBs, on the other hand, had a tendency to lose their contrast unless light conditions remained ideal. Finally, and most importantly, the NV-IADS was more than capable of providing "further interference" before, during, and after weapons launch. The release parameters for both EOGBs and LGBs were in the heart of the SA-2's envelope, and it was difficult for the F-4s carrying the large bombs to carry out the SAM evasion maneuver. These problems grew even worse once the *Phantoms* entered the target area. While the EOGBs could be launched as "fire and forget" weapons, the more accurate *Paveways* required target illumination throughout.[153] This illumination would be problematic if the designating aircraft was performing the SAM evasion maneuver. This was also true if the *Pave Knife* F-4 had to evade a determined MiG attack while designating its target. In order to avoid a MiG's cannon or *Atoll* missiles, the *Phantom* would have to perform a high-g maneuver. As the *Pave Knife*'s gimbal-mounted laser had specific g-limits, this meant saving the aircraft would lead to the pod's laser being slewed off the target.[154]

Collectively, all of these factors greatly constrained how 7th Air Force could use its most effective weapons. Exacerbating these problems was the fact that there were only six *Pave Knife* pods in the 7th Air Force's inventory at the start of the Linebacker operations.[155] The only crews certified to use the *Pave Knife* pods were concentrated in a single unit (the 8th Tactical Fighter Wing [TFW]). Likewise, the 8th TFW was also the only unit whose backseaters were extensively trained in the use of the EOGB. Seventh Air Force's guided weapon capability, in other words, resided in a half-dozen pods, a little more than twenty F-4s, and the fifty or so men who manned them. The fragility of this force was not lost on General Vogt and his staff, and they immediately set about determining methods to create the necessary permissive air defense environment. It was at this point that AFM 1-1's lack of SEAD doctrine reared its head. Rather than being able to refer to a common doctrine that established how to engage an IADS, 7th Air Force was left to find their own way to prevent destruction of 8th TFW aircraft.

The method General Vogt and his staff chose had three major components. First was the use of "chaff bombers," i.e., a fleet of F-4s equipped with droppable chaff dispensers. When these containers opened, they spread radar reflective metal strips that had been specifically manufactured to jam the *Fan Song* radar. This "chaff corridor" then descended slowly and prevented North Vietnamese SA-2 sites from locking onto the following strike force. Complementing this technique were direct attacks on North Vietnamese radars by Wild Weasel aircraft as long as the F-105s could stay on station. In order to counter the NVAF's interceptors, several flights of F-4s served as MiG Combat Air Patrol (MiGCAP).[156]

In one way, this approach was successful—the Air Force lost only one *Pave Knife* to enemy action throughout the Linebacker operations, with the overall loss rate being far lower than that of

Rolling Thunder.[157] Yet the inefficiency of 7th Air Force's SEAD technique more than balanced the positives of lower casualties and preservation of capability. From March 30th through October 23rd, 1972 the 7th Air Force had to dispatch 4-8 sorties of support aircraft (Wild Weasels, jammers, chaff bombers, and escorts) for every F-4 actually delivering bombs to a target.[158] In numerical terms, this meant that the NV-IADS forced the 7th Air Force to forswear 4-8 *Phantoms'* worth of ordnance (typically 16,000-32,000 lbs. maximum) for every two to four LGBs (2,000-6,000 pounds maximum) delivered by an 8th TFW F-4. Operationally, such effort meant the USAF had enough aircraft to conduct interdiction missions or strikes against North Vietnamese infrastructure, but seldom both.

Strategically, this meant that the 7th Air Force could not deliver enough consistent firepower against North Vietnam to shake its resolve. It is true that targets which had resisted every effort to attack them in 1968 (e.g., the Paul Doumer and Than Hoa bridges) were destroyed to great psychological and materiel effect.[159] Similarly, the precision weapons placed targets such as NV-IADS command posts at risk for the first time in the war.[160] However, the effort required to accomplish these feats meant that the 7th Air Force was unable to strike a great many others. Without doctrinal guidance on dismantling the NV-IADS, the 7th Air Force had chosen a method that had denied air power its greatest strength: flexibility. In turn, because the NV-IADS forced

USAF to employ so much of its force in protecting the 8th TFW's F-4s, 7th Air Force's lower loss rate and ability to place all targets at risk was not fully realized. By not being able to replicate the fury of Rolling Thunder, much less exceed it, the USAF provided no incentive for the DRV's leaders and populace to change their course of action.[161]

Goal #3: Conventional Deterrence

In addition to preventing the delivery of sufficient punishment, the amount of effort required for the USAF to penetrate North Vietnamese air space called into question its conventional capabilities. This was not a small matter given the primacy of theUSAF in many alliance and individual allies' defense plans. For example, United States Air Force Europe (USAFE) was considered to be the primary interdiction and deep strike organization for the entire NATO alliance. Similarly, the Republic of Korea Air Force (ROKAF) was organized primarily for close air support with the understanding that the USAF would carry the bulk of interdiction and strike missions against North Korean forces should a second conflict erupt on the Korean peninsula.[162] In these and other contingencies, American allies expected that USAF would be able to achieve and exploit air superiority quickly and thus planned their own national strategies accordingly. The Nixon Doctrine only served to formalize this practice.

USAF leaders recognized this reality as evidenced both in AFM 1-1's acknowledgments of conventional operations and the war plans developed with allied nations. However, thoughts and theories were one thing whereas 7th Air Force's difficulties in striking Hanoi were quite another. During Linebacker operations, the NV–IADS was able to force the USAF to adopt measures that were only feasible due to the unique situation in Southeast Asia. Furthermore, with the NVAF possessing only a feeble strike force incapable of reaching American bases in Thailand, the 7th Air Force could largely ignore air defense responsibilities. This would not be the case in the majority of the contingencies for which allied or national interest compelled the Air Force to plan. Similarly, the NV–IADS continued to use the obsolescent SA–2 rather than being equipped with the far more modern systems available to North Korea, the Warsaw Pact, or other potential American enemies. Finally, although NVAF's MiGs operated in a favorable environment due to GCI and the existence of sanctuary, they were not present in the numbers that the USAF could expect to face in a likely Central European, Korean, or Middle Eastern contingency.[163]

Combined, these factors led to a lack of internal confidence in the USAF's conventional capability. By the conclusion of Linebacker operations, Air Force pilots did not have faith in their ability to defeat modern Soviet-bloc air defense systems either singly or when part of an integrated whole.[164] Indeed, the mere possibility that the

North Vietnamese may have possessed the SA-3 *Goa* during 1972 caused many anxious moments both to 7th AF's planners and, once the B-52s were committed, their SAC counterparts.[165] Similarly, Air Force pilots had begun to doubt their ability to combat hostile interceptors in a major conflict.[166] Finally, TAC's and SAC's own leaders came to believe that the 7th Air Force's performance indicated that the USAF's conventional capability was far beneath that needed to achieve deterrence or, should that fail, to execute NATO's wartime missions.[167]

This lack of internal faith clearly indicated a breakdown in the Air Force's conventional deterrence capability. The President and Congress could not expect national policy to be executed by a service that had lost faith in itself. Moreover, the Air Force's performance had left the United States' civilian leaders questioning the service's capability to carry out any of its missions.[168] Both of these outcomes, in light of the facts, were to be expected and stemmed from a lack of SEAD doctrine. Had the Air Force's leaders provided the 7th Air Force with guidance on how to destroy an integrated air defense system, there is a possibility that it could have done so and demonstrated American conventional capability. However, as with the objective of punishment, the USAF's doctrinal vacuum and subsequent *ad hoc* arrangement made this unfeasible. The effort required to attack North Vietnam left the Air Force's own pilots, America's civilian leaders, and, more than likely, allies and enemies alike questioning USAF's ability to project power against a hostile air defense system. This undermined the Nixon Doctrine and was hardly what the President expected from the Air Force's efforts.

Goal #4: Preserving the Manned Strategic Bomber Deterrent

The inability of the 7th Air Force to inflict sufficient punishment on the North Vietnamese forced President Nixon to seek alternate means of persuasion. In addition, Nixon needed to convince South Vietnam's President Thieu to trust American promises of a long-term commitment towards the RVN's survival. With this in mind, President Nixon committed SAC's B-52s against North Vietnam in December 1972.[169] In his memoirs, Nixon indicates that he was well aware of the risks when he made this decision but settled upon it with the expectation that the Air Force would be able to carry out this assault with little difficulty.[170]

Nixon's confidence prior to the start of Linebacker II was quite reasonable. General LeMay, during his time as head of SAC, Vice Chief of Staff of the Air Force, and USAF Chief of Staff had made the *Stratofortress* a symbol of American security. Over two decades, to much of the American public, the big Boeing bomber had become what the Royal Navy's (RN's) warships had been to the British people.[171] To the Soviet

Union, the B-52 was a system so fearful that it had elicited the development of numerous weapons systems and the wholesale modernization of *PVO Strany* after SAC had accepted the bomber into service.[172] In deploying the bomber that the *Dictionary of Modern War* described as "the mainstay of SAC's bomber force," Nixon intended not only to send the North Vietnamese a message but also to demonstrate America's power projection capabilities to the entire world.[173]

Had the Air Force published a unified SEAD doctrine, it is likely that this gambit would have worked. Two raids against the North Vietnamese panhandle in April 1972 had demonstrated the B-52s' ability to penetrate the NV-IADS with appropriate TAC and naval air support. At that time, desiring to cut the NVA's southernmost

Vietnam-era B-52 (Courtesy of Redwood 8 via Dreamstime.com)

supply link, PACAF staff had conceived and directed a comprehensive plan that limited the big bombers' vulnerability to SAMs and NVAF fighters. Even though the North Vietnamese defenders damaged one B-52, the shock effect on the NV-IADS and destruction of materiel made the mission a great success.[174]

Unfortunately for USAF, this planning had not resulted from adherence to doctrine. Instead, it had largely been the result of a theater staff applying their experience and knowledge of North Vietnamese defensive tendencies. Furthermore, the raids in question had been small, sharp affairs involving less than twenty-five bombers. These small attacks, in turn, did not require the length or breadth of defensive suppression that a much larger raid would require. A raid in November 1972 had led to the loss of a B-52. Ominously, the techniques used by the North Vietnamese to down this bomber indicated that the NV-IADS had begun to adapt to both the B-52s' internal ECM as well as tactical SEAD measures.[175]

Regardless of this loss's implications, the Air Force's leaders still believed that USAF could carry out the massive raids President Nixon desired. Due to the size of the B-52 force, SAC refused to delegate any authority for the operation to forces in the Pacific theater. Determined to demonstrate their command's capabilities, SAC's staff did not consult either their PACAF or 7th Air Force counterparts during the planning phase. Instead, SAC's commander, General

John C. Meyer, with the full consent of General Ryan, used his command's staff to compose the operations orders for the initial strikes.[176] These orders were then, in turn, passed down to a subordinate unit, the 8th Air Force. Based in Omaha, the 8th's primary focus was preparing for nuclear strikes against the Soviet Union, but it had developed plans for striking against North Vietnam in April.[177] SAC staff, ostensibly concerned with collateral damage, ignored this previous work and developed its own set of orders that it dictated to 8th Air Force. SAC headquarters did not give the 8th Air Force the option of modifying the directives, citing the subordinate headquarters' involvement in the coordination of support assets and the sundry details inherent in such a massive undertaking.[178]

Given these facts as well as the internecine warfare that dominated the Air Force during this period, it is debatable just how much influence SEAD doctrine would have had on the development of SAC's plan. However, it is clear that the lack of guidance strongly influenced both the planning and execution of operations conducted in support of the bombing raids. Due to the choices made by the 7th Air Force in the absence of SEAD doctrine, the NV–IADS did not suffered permanent degradation from April through December 1972. On the contrary, emphasis on passive measures had allowed SAM operators and crews to gain in proficiency and develop countermeasures throughout Linebacker operations.[179] Similarly, despite the effect that mining Haiphong coupled with President Nixon's diplomatic efforts had on retarding Soviet and Chinese resupply, 7th Air Force's SEAD techniques had not resulted in a gradual attriting of *Fan Song* or early warning radars.[180] Finally, instead of eliminating NVAF's MiGs, 7th Air Force's *Phantom*s had once more been fought to a virtual draw. Therefore, rather than concentrating on using the tactical fighters to maximum effect, American staffs had to develop an escort plan that placed F-4s on MiGCAP. Combined, these circumstances meant that SAC was, for all practical purposes, engaging the NV-IADS when the latter was both experienced and at peak strength.

The resulting carnage not only came as an unpleasant shock to the USAF but also signaled the shattering of the strategic triad's manned bomber leg. Fifteen B-52s were destroyed and ten more damaged during what the Air Force called Operation Linebacker II but participating SAC crews would dub "The Eleven Days of Christmas." Only the strenuous intervention of fighter bombers, naval gunfire support, changes in tactics, and electronic jamming aircraft prevented losses from being far worse.[181] Contemporary Air Force monographs and papers attempted to sugarcoat the losses by pointing out that the majority of lost B-52s either had their electronic countermeasures improperly configured, flew poorly, or simply blundered into the path of volley-fired SAMs.[182] These statements, given SAC's alleged strategic mission, were sophistry at best. Regardless of the reason, the world had observed a second-tier military force equipped with obsolescent weapons inflict heavy losses on what was allegedly the premier Air Force in the world.

It is not hard to surmise the effects this had on the manned bomber as a strategic deterrent. Linebacker II provided President Nixon with even more evidence that USAF could not perform its anticipated wartime missions despite requesting additional budgetary outlays. In addition to being incensed by the casualties the losses represented, Nixon was concerned at what effect the U.S. loss of bombers had on the North Vietnamese.[183] Given that the North Vietnamese dubbed the B-52 raids the "Dien Ben Phu" of the skies, President Nixon's anxiety was quite justified.[184] Just how unconcerned the North Vietnamese were about return visits from the B-52s can be seen by how quickly the NVA set about violating the 1973 Paris Accords.[185] The fact that the USAF no longer deterred even North Vietnam speaks volumes to how greatly Linebacker II broke the B-52s' mystique.

The United States' primary strategic opponent, the Soviet Union, echoed this disdain for the bombers. The first night's situation (e.g., short warning time, prepared enemy defenses, and limited tactical fighter support) closely replicated those to be expected during a nuclear war. The U.S.S.R., as North Vietnam's main arms supplier, was well aware of three things. First, the equipment of the North Vietnamese was far inferior to that of PVO *Strany*. Although Soviet doctrine dictated that military services retain obsolescent systems in order to maintain a defense in depth, PVO *Strany* had been equipped with faster, larger, and more sophisticated SAMs than the SA-2 for almost five years. Second, the North Vietnamese had been able to inflict heavy losses on USAF without the full use of the NV-IADS due to a lack of pilots trained in night flying. The Red Air Force, on the other hand, maintained at least a limited night capability with all of its interceptor squadrons.[186] With the Soviet Union's strategic depth serving to limit tactical fighter support, the majority of these elements would be able to operate without the interference of Wild Weasels or escorting fighters that proved so critical to limiting SAC's losses after the first three days' of bombing.[187] Even with total losses far beneath those expected by SAC, Linebacker II all but finished the manned bomber as a nuclear deterrent until more modern weapons were introduced.[188]

This erosion of the B-52s' deterrent value was far from necessary, and the Air Force's response to the first three nights' losses demonstrates this fact. Stung by the strength of the NV-IADS, the Air Force quickly began to revise its tactics and operational focus. First, both SAC and the 7th Air Force began to consider the NV-IADS as an entire operational system, complete with supply lines and vulnerable points. Second, after determining these vulnerable points, General Vogt and his staff began to place pressure against them. Using all the weapons within their arsenal, SAC, 7th Air Force, PACAF, and the USN's TF 77 began to strike at MiG airfields, SAM assembly sites and, in a couple of cases, SAM batteries that had displayed an above-average level of proficiency. Finally, after the Christmas break, SAC routed the B-52s in a manner that facilitated 7th Air Force's defense suppression efforts.[189]

Although it is hard to quantify the effects of these efforts or to separate them from the other, non-SEAD countermeasures being conducted, the precipitous drop in SAM launches and number of B-52s destroyed indicates that they had a positive effect. Whether a SEAD doctrine which directed these efforts at the start of Linebacker II would have lessened the losses and maintained the viability of the manned bomber remains an open question. Regardless of one's answer, however, the sharp decrease in losses strongly indicates that the Air Force's initial problems stemmed from the lack of guidance. It is hard to imagine a situation where a manual that laid out a proper SEAD doctrine prior to the start of Linebacker II would have been detrimental given these results.

Nadir

Even with the improvements the USAF had been able to cobble together at the conclusion of Linebacker II, Ruby 2's loss on January 3rd,

1973 constituted the nadir of the USAF's SEAD doctrine. President Nixon had dispatched the Air Force to Southeast Asia with the intent of disrupting North Vietnam's offensive, punishing the DRV's leaders, proving the USAF's conventional capabilities, and maintaining the strategic deterrence value of the manned bomber fleet. The USAF's only success had been the interdiction of North Vietnamese supply lines, with the inability to complete the other three objectives due to the improvised nature of USAF's SEAD efforts. With a well-thought out doctrine that laid out the steps necessary to disrupt or destroy an enemy air defense, the Air Force might have had a chance to achieve its goals. Without it, however, Air Force commanders were left to develop a plan that not only botched the suppression of the NV-IADS but also ensured that the North Vietnamese had little fear of future attacks. In the end, rather than serving as a success, the Linebacker operations were a stunning defeat brought about by the Air Force's military and civilian leaders' decisions concerning SEAD doctrine development after Operation Rolling Thunder. As Ruby 2's crew awaited rescue in the South China Sea, the Air Force's ability to conduct conventional warfare seemed similarly adrift.

REFLECTIONS AND ATONEMENT

With the conclusion of the Paris Acccords on January 27th, 1973, the United States Air Force's involvement against North Vietnam came to an official end. Although there would be a handful of subsequent operational losses in operations over Cambodia and Laos, by June 1973 the Air Force had completed its final combat operations over Southeast Asia. Having lost over

2,000 fixed and rotary-wing aircraft and suffered almost 3,000 aircrew casualties while dropping over triple the ordnance it had employed in World War II, the Air Force had gained a wealth of painful experience over eight years. As its final aircraft departed Southeast Asia, it was now up to its tactical, operational, and senior leaders to apply these lesson to the service's primary focus on a possible war in Central Europe.[190]

The State of TAC, January through October 1973

At the tactical level, TAC and its subordinate organizations made few immediate changes in the aftermath of Vietnam. The four-plane flight remained the primary formation for Air Force fighter operations. Although the Navy's formation explained much of its success against MiGs during Linebacker I and II, the Air Force continued to employ the "fluid four." The former formation's role in the USN's success against MiGs during Linebacker was acknowledged by Momyer and TAC's staff. However, the Air Force had several sound reasons to resist such a transition. First and foremost, the "fluid four" greatly simplified command and control in larger formations. Second, squadron and wing commanders considered the "fluid four" to be superior for the accurate, concentrated employment of air-to-ground ordnance. Third, the Air Force's continued reliance on ECM pods and lack of a dedicated EW aircraft that could keep pace with the F-4 *Phantom* meant flight cohesion was necessary for maximum protection against radars. Finally, the Air Staff, General Momyer, and many of TAC's wing commanders considered the effort necessary to retrain current pilots in "Double Attack" (as the Air Force dubbed the "loose deuce" in 1972) to be cost prohibitive.[191]

This tactical decision was not a minor one. The USN had largely negated North Vietnamese MiGs as a threat to its strike aircraft during Linebacker. This had been due in no small part to the Navy's use of the "loose deuce" formation and, more importantly, training F-4 pilots how to properly employ it against the NVAF. By consciously deciding not to engage in a similar revision, the USAF was all but ensuring that it would either have to continue employing a prohibitive number of *Phantoms* as escorts for potential strike packages. Furthermore, air combat maneuvering training remained too expensive and dangerous since the fluid four retarded the experiential growth of junior flight members. Although changes were discussed via articles written for *The Fighter Weapons Review*, at USAF Fighter Weapons School (FWS) Symposiums, and in the aftermath of Aggressor training missions that pitted T-38 trainers against F-4 *Phantoms*, tactically TAC did not change its formations before the end of 1973.[192]

With the exception of the increased acquisition

of GBU and *Paveway* precision munitions, TAC's conventional air-to-ground tactics also did not change in 1973. Aircraft continued to employ the standardized Mark 80-series series of bombs matched to the F-4 *Phantom*'s bombing computer. With regard to Wild Weasel and Iron Hand tactics, the long-delayed replacement of the F-105 with the F-4C *Wild Weasel IV* did not come with a commensurate update in attack methodology. While the F-4C could maintain pace with the F-4 strike packages favored by TAC, it continued to be plagued by wiring and hardware problems. Despite known advances in Soviet missile technology, F-4C Wild Weasels continued to employ the increasingly obsolescent *Shrike* due to their inability to carry the larger *StARM*. To achieve full destruction of a SAM site or vehicle, the F-4Cs continued to rely on cluster and high-explosive bombs. In rare cases, Wild Weasel aircraft were equipped with the new AGM-65A *Maverick* television-guided missile, but a shortage of this advanced weapon meant it was usually reserved for dedicated strike aircraft. In effect, SEAD pilots of 1973 were expected to use the same tools as their Rolling Thunder predecessors.[193]

Operationally, the Air Force continued to employ the Tactical Fighter Wing as its primary unit for supplying airpower in theater operations. Still consisting for 3 or 4 squadrons of 12 to 16 aircraft apiece, the TFW in 1973 was expected to act as a homogenous unit to accomplish its wartime mission. In the aftermath of Linebacker, it was clear that fighter wings would need external assets to allow the penetration of enemy air defenses. Unfortunately, while the 1971 edition of AFM 1–1 detailed electronic warfare as a "supplemental task," it did not outline how the aircraft that performed this task were to be arrayed with those conducting attack missions.[194] Therefore, rather than a mutually understood process for executing SEAD, Air Force wings usually employed *ad hoc* method of coordinating defense suppression support as they began conducting post–Vietnam training exercises.

That such exercises existed was due to General Momyer's belated realization that TAC, despite its leavening of new combat veterans, lacked a broad knowledge of how to conduct an air campaign. Despite publicly stating that "[t]hrough pilot skill, improvisation, and training, the air battle [*sic*] over the skies of North Vietnam were fought and won," in private Momyer was much more circumspect about inefficiencies he perceived in the 7th Air Force's staffing process, C², and post–strike integration of lessons learned.[195] Momyer felt that these problems also existed at the wing level during Linebacker I and II. Time and time again, it seemed that wing and squadron commanders did not demonstrate the ability to rapidly receive, evaluate, plan, and execute the missions they received from higher headquarters. This, in turn, led to the 7th Air Force having to override the wing staffing process and directly control the composition of the ever larger, tightly choreographed "gorilla packages" used over North Vietnam. It was clear that a far more flexible process was going to have to be developed and, more importantly, trained in a realistic environment that replicated a full IADS.[196]

TAC's first post-Vietnam attempt at just such an exercise was the ninth Operation CORONET ORGAN. The first eight CORONET ORGANs had been conducted between August 1969 and December 1972 at irregular intervals due to TAC's funding and equipment shortages.[197] Directed by General Momyer, the initial CORONET ORGAN began with a reinforced fighter wing acting both as the friendly force and enemy interceptors. In addition to training aircrews in dealing with an IADS, CORONET ORGANs were also intended to test operational mission concepts, flight tactics, tactical fighter wings' ability to deploy over long distances, and crews' conventional bombing capabilities. The exercises slowly grew more complex, with Army air defense batteries and USAF Air Defense Command fighters taking part in attempts to simulate an integrated air defense system. In August 1973, on the ninth iteration, the Air Force added a new asset: Aggressors.[198]

The 64th Fighter Weapons Squadron (later also known as the 64th Tactical Fighter Squadron) grew from CORONA HARVEST and PROJECT RED BARON interviews of returning Vietnam veterans. In response after response, *Phantom* and *Thunderchief* aircrews had stated that their first experience facing a dissimilar aircraft had been on an operational mission over North Vietnam. In contrast, the USN's Top Gun program, as well as unofficial policy, had ensured that most Navy aircrews had several opportunities to conduct an ACM flight against either an A-4 *Skyhawk*, F-8 *Crusader*, or borrowed USAF T-38 trainers before deployment to Yankee Station. The results spoke for themselves, and General Momyer, with assistance from Air Defense Command, placed increased emphasis on assigning aircraft to dissimilar aircraft training in late-1972. This did not, however, yield the best results, as F-106s had not been able to replicate the same performance as Soviet MiG-17s, -19s, or -21s. Therefore, General Momyer turned to the Air Force's Training Command and its T-38 *Talon*, with the expectation the TAC would eventually purchase Northrop's F-5E *Freedom Fighter*. [199]

Thus, the 64th FWS employment in CORONET ORGAN was a harbinger of TAC's growing commitment to ACM training. In effect, by purchasing the F-5E and creating a squadron that was trained solely in Soviet-style tactics, General Momyer was choosing to expend some TAC resources on a weapons system and personnel he would not be able to use in time of war. However, as CORONET ORGAN demonstrated, *Phantom* crews gained valuable experience from having to acquire, track, and maneuver against a smaller, more nimble opponent. Although still far behind the Navy's Top Gun program, CORONET ORGAN was at least the beginning of developing techniques to operate within an IADS. Moreover,

CORONET ORGAN spurred the Fighter Weapons School to begin recommending changes to the Air Force's tactical "bible," TAC Manual 3-1 (TACM 3-1). Although this was not as authoritative or officially binding as AFM 1-1, TACM 3-1 guided all TFWs in their conduct of training operations and expected activities in warfare. It was, at long last, a start to developing a comprehensive SEAD doctrine.[200]

General Momyer's Thoughts on Task Organization and TAC Equipment

General Momyer's willingness to invest TAC's resources into attempting new techniques reflected a willingness to avoid the same mistakes made from 1968 through 1972. As his tenure as TAC commander came towards an end in September 1973, Momyer prepared a memorandum for Air Force Vice Chief of Staff Richard Ellis. A continuation of a similar memorandum he had written in 1969, Momyer attempted to frankly capture his observations and recommendations based on his time commanding Operation Rolling Thunder and TAC. In addition to providing a window to Momyer's thoughts, the Ellis memorandum also provides a benchmark into how the service's most experienced operational commander viewed its current capabilities.[201]

The Fighter Wing

Momyer was a strong proponent of the tactical fighter wing as an organizational entity and believed it should be retained. Although he praised the F-4 as the premier fighter of its time, he strongly believed that the Air Force should make every effort to expedite transition to the F-15 and future Light Weight Fighter (LWF) rather than maintain the current rate of procurement.[202] Momyer strongly believed that it would be a mistake to consolidate Wild Weasel or other potential SEAD aircraft into separate, consolidated wings. Instead, Momyer stated his opinion that Wild Weasel aircraft should be integrated into established TFWs at the flight level. In Momyer's view, with each 12- to 16-aircraft squadron having one flight of Wild Weasels, organizing and controlling strikes would be greatly simplified.[203] Momyer noted that currently this capability was provided by variants of the F-4. Ultimately Momyer proposed that the Air Force modify the F-15's avionics so that every aircraft would have SEAD capability available. Like combat against enemy fighters, defeating SAM sites would be an additional task that USAF pilots would be trained in at the unit level via exercises. To facilitate the execution of this mission, the USAF should expedite the development of an anti-radar standoff missile with greater capability than the current *Shrike*.[204]

Electronic Warfare

Momyer also proposed additional solutions that involved purchasing equipment specifically intended for disrupting an IADS. Stating that "ECM is here to stay for all forces," Momyer noted that as 7th Air Force commander he had been unable to fully employ EB-66 *Destroyers* as he would have desired. Although one of these issues as organizational (EB-66s were a SAC asset), the preponderance of the problem laid with the fact the *Destroyers* could not keep up with even heavily laden F-4s and F-105s. Momyer proposed that the Air Force invest in an electronic warfare variant of the F-111 strike fighter, a so-called "EF-111."[205] Given the expected strength and capabilities of Warsaw Pact air defenses in a proposed European conflict, Momyer was adamant that all future fighters be equipped with both active (i.e., jammers) and passive (i.e., RHAW displays) ECM capabilities. These capabilities should be internal to the aircraft's fuselage, rather than in pods, in order to maximize offensive capability. Lastly, the ECM capabilities should not require predictable, limiting formations that precluded independent maneuver by each individual fighter.[206]

Solutions for MiGs and SAMs

Momyer stated that "air to air engagements were dramatic in the Vietnam War." However, he believed that these were ultimately "of limited significance" since the numbers of NVAF MiGs was small and those present had enjoyed sanctuary for much of the conflict.[207] Regardless, the increased potential inherent in the F-15 and LWF would likely reduce weaknesses exposed in the F-4's capabilities. According to Momyer, providing TAC with an all-weather system that allowed precise engagement of specific enemy C^2 and GCI targets without a long, predictable bomb run would also provide a remedy to the MiG issue. Without capable controllers or radars, both current and projected Soviet tactical interceptors (e.g., the MiG-17, -19, and -21) would be relatively helpless at night or in bad weather.[208]

Momyer stressed that personnel training was just as important as more Wild Weasel aircraft in the fighter wings, new fighters, or all-weather capability. Several CORONET ORGANs had been completed by the time the memo was written, and Momyer stressed their importance in "develop[ing] tactics and techniques for the penetration [of an IADS]."[209] By providing both stateside and USAFE personnel with the opportunity to fly realistic combat sorties, the Air Force would avoid having fighter wings be required to train inexperienced personnel under combat conditions. Unlike Vietnam, Momyer cautioned, a European conflict would provide neither the time nor safer environments (e.g., Route Packages 1-2, Laos, and South Vietnam) for aircrews to be gradually exposed to increased threats. Although the CORONET ORGAN exercises were a good beginning, the lack of live ordnance ranges and limited number of Aggressors meant that conventional training was still not as pervasive as it needed to be. Finally, Momyer simultaneously stated that care needed to be taken lest increased conventional ACM and ordnance delivery training detract from the critical mission of tactical nuclear delivery.[210]

On the topic of developing doctrine, Momyer acknowledged the importance of suppressing enemy defenses in strong terms. He first asserted that "[t]he need to destroy the enemy['s] missile and radar systems at the outset of hostilities is mandatory," and then he stated explicitly why this was true.[211] First, establishing a "permissive aerial environment" was necessary for USAFE to employ CAS in support of its NATO mission.[212] Unlike Vietnam (according to Momyer), where "tactics were effective, but restricted the type of formations and employment of both strike and CAP forces," USAFE and other USAF units deployed in support could expect increased SAM capability from low to medium (~35,000 feet) altitude.[213] Therefore, "[i]t [was] highly unlikely that strike packages the size of those used in Vietnam will be suitable for a larger scale war," since the NATO forces would face "a quanti-tative deficiency" versus the Warsaw Pact.[214] To counter this, it was absolutely essential that TAC (at a minimum) develop a common language and methodology to ensure "maximum flexibility in employing [tactical aircraft] to offset the imbalance in numbers."[215] More explicitly, the entire Air Force needed to direct changes in strike tactics, to include the employment of Wild Weasels both with heavy bombers and TAC fighters.[216] Although Momyer wanted the Air Force include SAC future doctrinal, tactical, or operational developments with regard to SEAD, he took great pains to tell Ellis that all attempts to integrate TAC's sister command had been rebuffed.[217]

Conflict Between General Momyer's Thoughts and Air Force Practice

As a whole, Momyer's memo reflects an author who is intellectually struggling with a changed paradigm in air warfare. In conjunction with General Momyer's post-retirement work *Airpower In Three Wars*, it shows that his reputation as being a cerebral officer willing to change existing practices was well-deserved.[218] Unfortunately, there were several conflicts between the changes he proposed and the actual activities he had supported. For example, with regard to fighter development, as head of TAC, General Momyer had continued to support the development of the F-15 *Eagle* as a single-role, air-to-air fighter.[219] Indeed, so strongly did TAC initially resist the development of air-to-ground capability in the F-15, that McDonnell Douglas' initial attempts to demonstrate this capability were strictly limited to a handful of sorties that proved the *Eagle* could indeed carry and drop standard Air Force conventional bombs. However, when TAC began to prepare and circulate the *Eagle*'s proposed training syllabus in late 1973, Momyer did not direct that *Eagle* pilots be required to maintain proficiency in air-to-ground ordnance delivery.[220]

In this same vein, Momyer's fierce abstract support for the continued development of Wild Weasel platforms and technology was matched with tepid execution. While calling for an expansion of Wild Weasel capability in the Ellis memorandum Momyer refused to authorize expanding Wild Weasel academic instruction or flight training.[221] As with the *Eagle*'s air-to-ground capability, Momyer did not formally request that the F-15 be tested for the ability to deliver Wild Weasel weapons or to carry the necessary electronics to hunt radars. Nor were any steps taken to ensure that this capability was included in the LWF's initial requirements. With regard to the existing F-4C, Momyer did not make fixing that airframe's wiring or ordnance difficulties a priority. As a result, that program continued to languish in its incomplete state through the end of 1973.[222]

Compounding the above issues, Momyer did not provide the same level of guidance for SEAD aircraft that he had for ACM. Therefore, both F-4Cs and F-105Gs were rarely seen during regular TFW evaluations, meaning that most TFW officers' first exposure to Wild Weasels came during major exercises such as CORONET ORGAN. Even in these cases, the lack of reliable radar signal emitters, dearth of ranges capable of allowing the employment of *Shrike* or *StARM*, and TAC's continued risk averse culture meant that Wild Weasel maneuvers were often restricted to the point of uselessness. When combined with the Air Force's haphazard organization and constant transfer of Wild Weasel squadrons from normal TFW wings to consolidated SEAD organizations then back again throughout 1973, these choices greatly degraded the service's conventional capability.[223]

Other Influences on Air Force Doctrinal Development through October 1973

One explanation for General Momyer's reticence could easily be found in the Air Force's numerous competing schools of doctrinal thought after Vietnam. Jokingly called "mafias," USAF's fighter, attack, bomber, and missile communities all formed blocs within the Pentagon, TAC, and SAC headquarters. Of these, one of the most strident, vocal, and successful was the "Lightweight Fighter Mafia (LFM)" led by Colonel John Boyd. A fighter pilot, Boyd had earned most of his fame during his time at the Fighter Weapons School developing ACM tactics and decision theory.[224]

The Air Force's performance during Vietnam

had convinced Boyd and those who believed as he did that the Air Force had become too slow and unresponsive at the tactical, operational, and strategic levels. In everything from a top-heavy command structure to increasingly complex, expensive, and heavy fighters, the USAF had ossified almost to the point of ineffectiveness. Accordingly, at least to the LFM, the solution was to make the Air Force more agile in every way. At the tactical level, the Air Force should reduce its purchase of F-15s and instead increase the procurement of the Lightweight Fighter. Vietnam, after all, had proven that expensive missiles and complex radar sets could easily be bested by properly handled "daylight only" fighters in sufficient numbers and the correct conditions. With the Warsaw Pact enjoying a massive numerical advantage, it was imperative for the Air Force to at least try to match these numbers. Otherwise, the small contingent of sophisticated, costly F-15s would be gradually overwhelmed by an enemy that could simply generate more sorties than the *Eagles* could shoot down. Similarly, SEAD would be accomplished by a large number of these same fighters employing relatively simple, autonomous anti-radar missiles built with off the shelf components. With proper ground control interception or, even better, an airborne command post, larger groups of LWFs, backed by the small number of *Eagles* already purchased, would quickly wrest control of the skies in any foreseeable European scenario.[225]

The Air Force Turns to Central Europe, 1973

The European scenario's centrality in General Momyer's view of an increasingly sophisticated, better equipped TAC, and Colonel Boyd's adherence to a lightweight solution was not coincidental. Since 1949, one of the United States Air Force's primary missions had been deterring and, if needed, preparing to win a conflict against the Communist bloc in Central Europe. Beginning with the Berlin Blockade and continuing through the Korean War, the era of Massive Retaliation, and even the intense combat of Vietnam, the Air Force had always maintained at least part of its focus on stopping the Warsaw Pact.[226]

This concentration on a particular theater reflected the United States' larger Cold War strategy. NATO, with its guarantee of collective security, had been begun as a means to maintain the United States' involvement in Europe. Although the cynical commentary that the purpose of NATO was to "keep the Germans down, the Americans in, and the Russians out" perhaps took things a bit too far, in reality the alliance provided a military backstop to the Marshall Plan's economic investment. This was reinforced by the Eisenhower administration's commitment of surplus equipment, training, and economic investment in Western Europe's military industry as a complement to Massive Retaliation. [227] By President Eisenhower's departure in 1961, NATO had developed long-term plans for its conventional deterrence to supplement the United States' nuclear umbrella. Although no fixed date had been given, the Alliance generally accepted that these plans would be implemented throughout the subsequent decade as funding became available.

The United States' involvement in Vietnam disrupted many of these plans. Contrary to the repeated assurances given to NATO allies, first by President Johnson and subsequently President Nixon, both the United States Army and Air Force began using United States Army Europe (USAREUR) and USAFE as a reserve bank to pay the fiscal, equipment, and personnel bill for operations in Vietnam. This practice first began with individual personnel, then grew to unit reductions, and finally culminated in increasing congressional pressure for the military budget to be balanced by reductions in force in Europe prior to 1968.[228] This pressure greatly increased with the March 1968 economic crisis, as congressional leaders of both parties began to question openly whether the United States' NATO allies were honoring agreements on mutual defense spending made during the Eisenhower and Kennedy administrations.[229] Subsequently, both the House Ways and Means and Armed Service committees recommended that American ground and air forces be reduced as part of the FY 69–FY 72 budgets.[230]

President Nixon embraced this viewpoint at

the start of his first term in 1969. It was not, however, as well received by the United States' NATO allies. In early 1968, it appeared to NATO's European members that the Communist bloc was liberalizing many of its hardline policies towards the West. The subsequent events of the Prague Spring, elucidation of the Brezhnev Doctrine, and aggressive Soviet foreign policy in the Middle East and Asia swiftly reversed this view. Indeed, the rapidity with which the U.S.S.R. was making inroads internationally gave the appearance that the Soviet Union was growing more capable as the United States was becoming increasingly distracted by Vietnam. Thus, when President Nixon increased the rate by which the military was demobilized in FYs 70, 71, and 72, the NATO allies balked at the withdrawal of additional tactical fighter wings as well as consolidation of ground forces. In order to appease some NATO members' concerns, President Nixon relented by providing funds for USAFE to retain two more TFWs than the USAF had originally intended through 1973. [231]

Deterrence on the Wing

The fact that President Nixon considered two TFWs sufficient enough to restore a balance of forces reflected the ways in which the USAF's capabilities were a key part of the United States conventional policy from 1968 through the end of the Cold War in 1991. The Pentagon, in *Joint Publication 1–02 Department of Defense Dictionary of*

Military and Associated Terms, defines deterrence simply as "the prevention of action by the existence of a credible threat of unacceptable counteraction and/or belief that the cost of action outweighs the perceived benefits."[232] Luttwak and Kohl, in the *Dictionary of Modern War*, provide a more complex variation:

> Measures designed to narrow an opponent's freedom of choice among possible actions by raising the cost of some of them to levels thought to be unacceptable to that opponent."
>
> *Active deterrence* describes a threat specifically intended to prevent a specific move on the part of an opponent, i.e., latent deterrence is the norm.
>
> *Extended deterrence* applies to a particular third party or parties.
>
> *Minimum deterrence*, politically plausible but technically dubious, is a concept based on the recognition that even a small number of nuclear weapons can be sufficiently destructive to inflict damage deemed unacceptable by almost all opponents in all circumstances.[233]

Both of these definitions are somewhat problematic when applied to the United States' conventional military strategy from 1973 to the end of the Cold War. For example, by the Pentagon's current definition, NATO did not have any *conventional* deterrence in 1973. Although far from Massive Retaliation's immediate hair trigger employment of nuclear attacks, NATO's defensive plans relied heavily on the use of tactical nuclear weapons to reduce any potential Warsaw Pact breakthroughs in 1973.[234] Given the obsolescence of most members' conventional equipment, this was the primary manner by which NATO sought to deter the Warsaw Pact. The Soviet Union, in response, repeatedly stated that it did not recognize the West's delineation between "tactical" and "strategic" use of nuclear weapons.[235] In effect, if we use either the DoD or Luttwak and Kohl's definition and apply them to 1973, the sole "unacceptable counteraction" would have been the possibility that a conventional attack against, say, West Berlin would likely be met with tactical nuclear weapons.

In reality, NATO's conventional deterrence was multi-faceted and had three primary outcomes. First, rather than convincing the Soviet Union it would face an unacceptable counteraction (e.g., invasion, unsustainable casualties, destruction of the Warsaw Pact), NATO's conventional forces' primary mission was to persuade their adversaries that they could not achieve a *coup de main*. Or put another way, NATO's conventional forces had to provide a physical presence that was simultaneously competent, modern and, most importantly, *publicly visible* in a manner that made Soviet military adventurism an infeasible method for achieving Moscow's foreign policy goals. In addition, this conventional capability had to be constructed in such a way to convince NATO's European members that it was sustainable fiscally, socially and, should war break out, militarily in the face of its Warsaw Pact counterpart. Finally, NATO's conventional posture had to convince the United States' president, Congress, and public that it was a worthwhile investment of American resources.

NATO CORPS SECTORS, 1973-1991[519]

It was this last aspect of NATO conventional deterrence that made the USAF's ability to penetrate an IADS critical. Even before the Nixon Doctrine, Central Europe's geography and the alignment of NATO's sectors meant that USAF forces were expected to play a pivotal role in any potential conflict.

For many Americans of a certain age, much of the talk about a potential World War III had focused on the so-called "Fulda Gap," i.e. the salient bulging from Eastern Germany that was held by the US V and VII Corps (a.k.a., Central Army Group, or CENTAG). This was viewed as the most dangerous attack route from a NATO perspective, as analysts expected a successful attack west through this terrain to seize first Frankfurt, then Bonn in possibly less than three weeks. In the case of Frankfurt, seizing the city and the area around it would not only have disrupted most of the German autobahn system but also hindered the United States' ability to move personnel rapidly from North America to fall in on prepositioned equipment in Germany. Subsequently taking Bonn, in turn, would have either displaced or removed the government of West Germany and would likely have lead NATO to sue for peace. Thus, at least from the United States' Army and Air Force's perspective, the Fulda-Alsfeld avenues of approach were the most critical in all of NATO.[236]

Although the U.S. Army and Air Force had not wholly ignored their mutual responsibilities pertaining to NATO during Vietnam, by mid-1973 the two services' coordination efforts in Europe had shown the effects of being neglected during the war in Southeast Asia. The Warsaw Pact's advantage in military forces in Eastern Germany meant that NATO's war plans assumed CENTAG's forces would be heavily outnumbered within the first 48- to 120-hours.[237] With the United States' post-Vietnam demobilization still ongoing, the U.S. Army also realized that, given planned 1975 force structures, this situation would be far worse within two years. Therefore, the Army began to consider how it would attrit follow on Soviet forces as they moved westward from their cantonments in the Ukraine, Belorussia, and Poland.[238] The answer, at least to the Army, was clearly USAFE airpower employing either conventional or nuclear ordnance.

Similarly, the European members of NATO expected USAFE to be a force multiplier in the Northern Army Group (NORTHAG). Whereas American analysts and military officers were quite insistent the Warsaw Pact would come through the Fulda Gap, European analysts believed the terrain and lines of communication in CENTAG precluded the employment of massed Soviet armored formations. Given the relative weakness in numerical strength and obsolescence of equipment of most NATO members, the North German Plain seemed to be the path of least resistance to both the Warsaw Pact and NATO's military planners. Thus, instead of short, massive strike into the American sector,

British, French, and German military officials expected a maneuver reminiscent of World War I's Schlieffen plan with several mechanized divisions penetrating NATO's initial defensive positions. This would be followed by Warsaw Pact second echelon forces penetrating to the Rhine River then executing a north to south wheeling maneuver that would sever West Germany from the remainder of NATO.[239]

Due to fiscal, political, and social constraints present in the early '70s, NORTHAG's European forces lacked the ability to fully prepare to meet this threat. However, much like the U.S. Army in CENTAG, NORTHAG expected airpower to serve as an equalizer for their ground forces' inadequacies. This was not mere wishful thinking, as the same terrain that made the NORTHAG sector ideal for mounted forces would also facilitate the use of massed airpower. Furthermore, unlike CENTAG's short distance to Frankfurt, a wheeling offensive through NORTHAG would greatly extend the Warsaw Pact's lines of communication. This would make resupply and reinforcement operations much more difficult provided NATO could achieve air superiority. [240]

That such an event would occur in either the NORTHAG or CENTAG sectors was considered almost a given. In the north, the NATO allies had organized their collective air arms into the Second Allied Tactical Air Force, or 2 ATAF, to complement USAFE. From 1965 through 1973 these two headquarters conducted several staff exercises to increase cooperation. As a result of these interaction, their commanders had agreed on certain standards with regard to air force's communications, refueling operations, ordnance requirements, and targeting. If the attack was in the center, 2 ATAF elements were prepared to shift to the network of United States and *Luftwaffe* (the air arm of the West German *Bundeswehr*) in southern Germany. Should the attack fall in the north, it was understood USAF TFWs from North America would immediately reinforce 2 ATAF rather than USAFE. In this manner, NATO saw airpower's flexibility as a viable substitute for attempting to shift ground combat power against the Warsaw Pact.[241]

The Warsaw Pact

The forces that NATO's airpower was expected to help counter were both more and less capable than the alliance believed in 1973. While the United States was easily the most powerful partner within NATO, it understood that its European allies would develop their own doctrine, equipment, and training standards. By contrast, the Soviet Union fully dominated the Warsaw Pact's processes of procurement, training and, most importantly, doctrine from the alliance's inception in 1955 to its eventual dissolution in 1991. This control of the Warsaw Pact was seen as both a counter to the West's military power in Central Europe and a check on nationalist movements within the Soviet Union's near abroad.[242]

Therefore, in 1973 studying Soviet military doctrine was the key to understanding how the Warsaw Pact expected to function in wartime. Much like their American counterparts, the Red Army and Soviet Air Force (SAF) had gone through a period when organizational leaders believed nuclear release was certain. This had started a period of both doctrinal revision and unit reorganization called "The Revolution in Military Affairs," during which the Red Army and SAF wrestled with how to operate on a nuclear battlefield. Furthermore, unlike the United States Army, the Red Army had experienced the trauma of operating under enemy air superiority for long periods of World War II. Both of these circumstances had led to a force that was similar yet quite different than what Western defense officials had expected to deal with in 1973.[243]

The first contradiction was that the Red Army was not organized into staid, rigidly maintained "echelons" intended to attack on a firm timetable. Soviet military literature had recognized that such forces, in addition to being operationally clumsy, were highly susceptible to conventional aerial weapons and nuclear attack. Instead, by 1973 the Red Army began experimenting with what it termed the operational maneuver group (OMG). Consisting of 3–5 divisions, an OMG was task organized from existent Warsaw Pact forces in Germany or eastern Poland. Upon the onset of war, OMGs were expected to move closely behind the initial breakthrough forces along either or *both* the NORTHAG and CENTAG avenues. In any case, the attack that appeared most likely to succeed would then have an OMG immediately committed along its axis. In this manner, the OMG would have the best chance to rapidly close with NATO forces, complete a breakthrough, and conduct a subsequent exploitation operation before a NATO corps commander was granted nuclear release by higher headquarters. Although in its infancy in 1973, this revision of Soviet doctrine had already been taught at the Frunze military academy for several years to both Red Army and client states. In short, the offensive NATO thought it would face was significantly different than what the Warsaw Pact had planned. [244]

Warsaw Pact IADS

To defend this form of attack from NATO airpower, the Soviet Union depended on an IADS that had advantages and disadvantages with North Vietnam's. As with NATO, the establishment of a fixed boundary and known foe allowed the Warsaw Pact to develop extensive infrastructure to support command and control of the Warsaw Pact–IADS. WP–IADS radar sites were often hardened against aerial attack, meaning that near misses might temporarily disable a site but were unlikely to destroy it. Command posts were also sealed against attack by chemical weapons and radioactive fallout, with the side effect being that they were even harder to destroy with most common ordnance.[245] All sites were linked not only with radio but also telephonic interchanges, albeit with the limitation of only having 2-3 operators speaking at a time per open line.[246]

In theory, this arrangement meant that the Warsaw Pact, from the Inter-German Border (IGB) in the west to the Soviet Union in the east and the Baltic in the north to the Adriatic in the south, operated under the same command network. Although each country maintained nominal independence, their air defenses were all coordinated by Soviet field marshals and could be shifted by these officers to meet potential threats outside their national borders. Using the same equipment, this also meant that Bulgarian interceptors could ferry to East German airfields to reinforce the latter's combat air patrols. In reality, differences in language, rigidity of sectors, and variance of aircraft models would have made such shifting difficult.[247]

Warsaw Pact Fighters

By 1973 the SAF's fighter aircraft were organized into Frontal Aviation or Air Defense (*PVO Strany*). Frontal Aviation was responsible for both defensive and offensive operations in the Central European area of operations. In addition to the same MiG-21 flown by the NVAF, Frontal Aviation fighter regiments were also equipped with the MiG-23 *Flogger*. The *Flogger*, first tested in 1968, was flown by a single pilot, had a variable geometry wing and, most importantly, a powerful radar that allowed BVR engagements. Fast enough to catch any western aircraft at low altitude and roughly as maneuverable as the F-4 *Phantom*, the MiG-23 was a potent stablemate to the MiG-21. More importantly, the *Flogger* gave Soviet pilots the ability to conduct interceptions at greater range and with more flexibility than North Vietnamese pilots had enjoyed during Linebacker Operations in 1972.[248]

Beyond Frontal Aviation units, the East German Air Force (EGAF) and Polish Air Forces (PAF) also operated the MiG-17 and -19 in addition to less capable variants of the MiG-21. In time of war, the SAF planned to supplement Warsaw Pact forces in East Germany and Poland with missile-armed Su-15 *Flagons* from *PVO Strany*. Within 30 to 60 days of a potential conflict, the Soviet Union also planned to reinforce Frontal Aviation in East Germany with an additional 500-600 reserve fighters (*Fresco*, *Farmers*, and *Fishbeds*) from storage. In all cases, these fighters would be less effective than Frontal Aviation units due to lack of training (EGAF and PAF), separation from the U.S.S.R.'s advanced radar network (Su-15s), or obsolescence of the reserve aircraft.

Warsaw Pact Ground Defenses

Whereas western forces expected their fighters to be the primary means of preventing enemy air attack, the Warsaw Pact considered the fighters to be secondary to their primary defensive weapons: SAMs and AAA. Much of this stemmed from the Red Army's experience in World War II, where most of the Soviet Air Force was destroyed on the ground in June 1941. Even with replacements from Lend Lease, increased domestic Soviet production, and the Allied Bombing Offensive's attrition of the *Luftwaffe*, German ground attack aircraft remained a significant threat to massed Soviet armor through the end of 1944.[249] With this common institutional experience in mind, the Red Army had invested heavily in research on fire control radars, heat-seeking and radar-guided SAMs, and air defense assets' mobility after World War II. This decision was reinforced by Soviet observations of Vietnam and, in the Middle East, the Six Day War (June 1967) and subsequent War of Attrition (March 1969– August 1970) between Israel and most of her neighbors. By 1973 the Red Army had developed an impressive and formidable array of weapons as a result of this focus.[250]

At the battalion level, Soviet motorized, mechanized, and armored formations each possessed an anti-aircraft platoon. As a command and control effort, this organization passed along warnings of hostile aircraft in the area to include type, likely time of arrival, and expected direction of approach. With regard to weapons, each platoon was equipped with two or more SA-7 *Grail* teams. A heat-seeking missile with limited range, long preparation time, small warhead, and an easily decoyed guidance system, nonetheless the SA-7 was more accurate than a manually-aimed machine gun or cannon. Moreover, as demonstrated in Vietnam and several other conflicts in sub-Saharan Africa, the weapon was extremely deadly to helicopters and propeller aircraft.[251]

At the regimental level, anti-aircraft defense was provided by a battery consisting of two four-vehicle platoons. In 1973, this was initially a total of eight ZSU-23-4 *Shilka* anti-aircraft guns. With four 23mm cannon, a radar dish, and a fire control computer all mounted in a turret on a tracked chassis, the *Shilka*'s primary purpose was to interfere with dive-bombing or rocket-firing aircraft. Shortly before October 1973, the second platoon of *Shilka* had been replaced with a platoon of SA-9 *Gaskins* in most Soviet formations. Combined, both systems were intended to prevent the low-level ingress, dive-bombing, low-level egress model practiced by most western air forces.[252]

These regimental units would usually be reinforced by divisional assets when on the offensive. The typical Warsaw Pact division in 1973 was equipped with three SAM battalions. Each SAM battalion, in turn, had three firing batteries of three launchers apiece for a total of nine launchers, plus a control battery with 2-3 radars. The tank and motorized division batteries, in 1973, were usually equipped with the SA-4 *Ganef* or SA-6 *Gainful* SAMs. Like the SA-2 used by the North Vietnamese, these missiles were designed to engage aircraft from 1,000 through 70,000 feet. Unlike the *Guideline*, both the *Ganef* and *Gainful* were mobile. This feature allowed the commander of a Warsaw Pact division to shift his medium- to high-altitude missile defenses with advancing forces in order to better protect them, and the division staff practiced it regularly during exercises. With ranges of 35 (SA-4) and 12 (SA-6) miles respectively, the duo of missiles were intended to force attacking aircraft to either jettison their weapons in order to evade or approach at low level.[253]

Beginning in 1972, the *Ganef* and *Gainful* were supplemented by the SA-8 *Gecko*, a mobile system whose guidance radar and missiles were collocated on the same chassis. The *Gecko* and the *Shilka* were both intended to defend mechanized forces on the march, with the gun vehicle covering the SAM launcher's "dead zone." With a battery of *Gecko*s added to the previously assigned SA-4 and SA-6 units, a division's internal SAM and AAA assets could move forward, detect their own targets, and begin engaging them well before the NATO aircraft could employ their own weapons. Furthermore, the divisional assets' mobility made detecting, targeting, and destroying them before they opened fire problematic. Finally, given that USAF TFWs, to say nothing of their NATO counterparts, lacked their own electronic warfare aircraft, jamming or spoofing the radars that cued these weapons onto target would have been difficult.[254]

Complicating NATO's EW options were the systems available at the Warsaw Pact's front and army level. These consisted of additional battalions of the same SAMs and AAA present at the division level along with the front- and army- controlled SA-3 *Goa* and SA-5 *Gammon* missiles with their associated radars. The *Goa* and *Gammon* were relatively immobile compared to the *Gainful, Gecko*, and *Ganef*, as they were mounted on trailers rather than self-propelled. Before firing, both the *Goa* and *Gammon* were usually towed to a given position, dug in, then oriented in the direction hostile aircraft would most likely attack. The *Goa* was a relatively slow missile that was a more maneuverable alternative to the earlier *Guideline*. The *Gammon* was a large, long-range missile intended for use against high-altitude targets such as bombers, jammers (e.g., the EB-66), and airborne early warning (AEW) aircraft. Acting in concert, the paired weapons were intended to force a strike package to change its path of ingress or only approach with heavy ECM and SEAD support.[255]

Warsaw Pact IADS and Deterrence

The Soviet Union believed that these systems gave it an effective counter to NATO airpower. This was based on their advisors' observations of the United States' efforts in Vietnam, actual limited participation by Soviet military personnel in Middle Eastern conflicts, and extensive live fire exercises conducted in Siberia and Kazakhstan.[256] By 1973, Soviet doctrine and published articles considered their air defense to rest on three expected events. First, although they were not wholly capable of independent action or besting their NATO counterparts in air combat maneuvering, Frontal Aviation pilots were fully capable of disrupting western flights by using slashing attacks against NATO attackers in East German airspace. Second, these heavily-laden NATO flights would then have to ingress and egress through a gauntlet of highly maneuverable, radar-guided SAMs in order to reach attack range. Finally, at short range the attackers would have to contend with the *Shilka*, *Grail*, and dozens of machine guns and cannon wielded by the attacked units. [257]

The goal of this combined network was not necessarily to destroy a large number of the attacking aircraft. Instead, much like its North Vietnamese predecessor, the Warsaw Pact intended its IADS to force pilots to jettison their ordnance, degrade the accuracy of their attacks when they were still delivered, and force increased fuel consumption by necessitating low-altitude ingress and egress from the target area. Frontal Aviation and the Red Army, in short, simply intended to deny NATO the air superiority the latter considered necessary for a successful defensive action.[258]

Defining Effectiveness

The complexity of the opposing doctrines, tactics, and equipment of both NATO and the Warsaw Pact makes discussion of their relative effectiveness in 1973 (and the remainder of the Cold War) somewhat problematic. The lack of a general European conflict precludes a direct historical assessment. However, historical analysis is supported by three other avenues of inquiry. First, there were discussion of how the United States' president, Congress, and the other services viewed the Air Force's conventional capabilities in general and with regard to the European area in particular. This can be gleaned from public statements, funding decisions, interservice agreements, professional journals, and General Accounting Office (GAO) documents. Second, foreign civilian authors, other countries' military analysts, and decisions by foreign governments also present a prism through which one can view contemporary perceptions. Finally, although NATO and Warsaw Pact forces did not engage in combat, nations aligned with either the United States / NATO or the Soviet Union employed their systems in other conflicts. For purposes of understanding SEAD doctrine development, the most important of these took place in October 1973.

The War of Atonement

Like most conflicts, the Yom Kippur War did not occur in a vacuum. As the fifth Arab-Israeli War, its causes were rooted in the outcome of the previous conflicts. Having achieved independence in 1948, Israel aligned itself with France and Britain during the Suez Crisis in 1956. In that conflict's aftermath, Israel faced an increasingly bellicose and nationalist Egypt under Gamal Abdel Nasser. Over the subsequent decade, Egypt and Syria, Israel's northern neighbor, grew increasingly bellicose and belligerent in their actions towards their smaller adversary. This culminated with the Six-Day War in 1967, a conflict that saw Israel's Air Force completely annihilate its Egyptian, Syrian, and Jordanian counterparts within a matter of hours on June 5th, 1967, followed by a rapid ground offensive that seized the Sinai Peninsula, Golan Heights, and West Bank territories by June 10th. For many military observers, the Israeli preemptive strike and the IAF air-ground coordination gave a textbook example of how airpower could facilitate rapid maneuver.[259]

For their part, by the conclusion of the Six-Day War, the Israelis came to look on the aircraft and the tank as war winning weapons in and of themselves. Behind the IAF and the Armored Corps, the Israeli government's thinking went, the Israeli Defense Force (IDF) could strike with sufficient speed that future conflicts would be concluded within one or two weeks. Aircraft and tanks required minimal manning compared to infantry and artillery organizations. Nominally, this meant that Israel could maintain more active aircraft squadrons and tank units to achieve their desired decisive effects, instead of investing in mechanized infantry or self-propelled artillery. Furthermore, in case of conflict, the IDF could rely upon its air superiority and well-trained tank crews to provide sufficient time to mobilize reserves and thus counterattack. As the IDF began to transition from French and British equipment to employing what was built by the United States, its leaders came to believe that the new equipment's technological superiority more than offset the numerical superiority of Israel's Arab neighbors.[260]

Of those neighbors, Egypt and Syria remained Israel's most implacable foes. Egypt's economy had suffered with Israel's seizure of the Sinai and subsequent closure of the Suez Canal. As a result, it was forced to rely on Soviet military aid to begin replacing the aircraft lost during the Six Day War. The Soviet Union, for its part, aided Egypt as part of its Third World foreign policy and so that Moscow could have an additional testing ground for its SAMs. As the Egyptian military launched a series of attacks that eventually became known as the War of Attrition (March 1969–August 1970), this air defense system gradually grew into what the IDF dubbed "The SAM Belt." [261]

Running the length of the Suez Canal, the SAM

Belt initially consisted of SA-2s supported by anti-aircraft batteries. After the IAF initially exploited the SA-2's limitations in height and maneuverability in the War of Attrition's early stages, the Soviets provided the Egyptians with SA-3s, a large number of *Fire Can* radars, and advisors. These new missiles immediately restricted the IDF's ability to retaliate against the Egyptian Army's attacks on Israeli forces in the Sinai. Despite the United States' provision of ECM pods and chaff dispensers, the SA-3 proved worryingly effective against heavily-laden Israeli strike aircraft. As a result, the IAF began to use the Mediterranean and southern Nile Delta to outflank the SAM Belt and strike at Egyptian infrastructure rather than artillery positions and military bases. This punishing counteroffensive, combined with international pressure and the death of Abdel Nasser, gradually led to Egypt ending the War of Attrition with the Sinai still in Israeli hands.[262]

Publicly, the Israeli government and IDF's leadership claimed they had achieved a victory over the Egyptian air defenses and their Russian patrons. This confidence was not shared by Israeli regular force pilots, especially those who flew the older *Mirage* and less advanced A-4 *Skyhawk*. Like their contemporary American counterparts struggling with the NV-IADS, many Israeli squadron commanders also noted that the IAF lacked a general doctrine for dealing with air defense networks. Even though superior pilot training and equipment largely eliminated interceptors as a threat, most of these commanders realized that in a general conflict they would not have the option of attempting to fly only where the SAMs were absent. These feelings of professional disquiet grew as the SAM Belt was complemented by mobile SA-6 *Gainful*s and ZSU-23-4s.[263]

The situation was similar on Israel's northern front. Although Syria did not fully participate in the War of Attrition, that nation also sought Soviet aid to replenish its losses. This aid was primarily geared towards conducting an armored offensive using Soviet doctrine to regain the Golan Heights. Emphasizing mobility, by October 1973 the Syrians had acquired a proportionally larger number of SA-6 *Gainful*s, ZSU-23-4s, and SA-7s than their Egyptian allies. More critically, the Syrian Army began to train in night operations, intending to use darkness to protect themselves against the Israeli Air Force. Though a limited number of SA-2s and SA-3s were emplaced along the road between Damascus and the Purple Line, as the 1967 ceasefire line between Israel and Syria was called, the Syrians mostly eschewed the fixed SAMs in favor of the *Gainful* or *Grail*. The IAF, having limited to no exposure to the SA-6, believed their primary threat to be Syrian fighters (which they regularly defeated) and anti-aircraft artillery. As with the Egyptians, the IDF's leaders did not feel that there was much of a need for a dedicated SEAD doctrine. Squadrons, operating as complete units, were expected to simply task a flight to perform the Iron Hand /

Wild Weasel operations as necessary.[264]

The IAF Versus the Egyptian and Syrian IADS

At 2:30 PM local time on October 6th, 1973, Syria and Egypt simultaneously initiated the Yom Kippur War by attacking the Golan Heights and Sinai Peninsula. On the Southern Front, the Egyptian Army breached the sand wall erected by the IDF as part of its Bar Lev line. On the Northern Front, the Syrian Army launched an armored offensive against the IDF's 7th and Barak Armored Brigades with a force that enjoyed over 3:1 superiority in tanks, artillery, and infantry. These ground attacks were supported by attacks on Israel's airfields and headquarters by both the Egyptian and Syrian Air Forces. Although the latter were ineffective, they did serve to disrupt and delay the initial IAF response to the ground incursions by at least an hour. Rather than conducting their prior plans, Israeli squadrons were expected to conduct *ad hoc* attacks by flights since the IDF's Northern Command considered the situation desperate.[265]

The result of these choices was a debacle for the IAF. On both fronts, the SA-6 *Gainful* forced Israeli A-4s, *Phantoms*, and *Mirages* to descend to low altitude. Once there, the ZSU-23-4, previously unused in active combat, caused great losses among attacking Israeli fighters. More importantly, they forced attacking Israeli aircraft to adopt ingress and egress methods that prevented them from efficiently acquiring and striking targets. For their part, Egyptian and Syrian interceptors were mainly kept away from the front lines to prevent fratricide, but still played an active role in harassing Israeli flights as they approached and departed previously established air defense zones. [266]

The Arab nations' tactics were effective insomuch that they denied the IAF the air superiority it had grown accustomed to in previous conflicts. On the Southern Front, this meant that the Egyptian Army was able to establish a strong foothold across the Suez Canal and conduct resupply operations across hastily erected pontoon bridges under the SAM Belt's protection. This subsequently allowed Egypt to attain a strong military position on the east bank of the Suez Canal and defeat initial Israeli counterattacks. It was only when the Egyptian Army unsuccessfully attacked to seize the Mitla and Gidi passes on October 14th that the Israelis were able to reverse the situation. Having moved beyond the SAM Belt's range, the Egyptian attack first suffered the depredations of the Israeli Air Force, then was soundly defeated by dug-in Israeli tanks. The ensuing Israeli counterattack not only crossed the Suez Canal in the south, but allowed the reduction of the SAM Belt by ground attack. Beginning on October 15th, the arrival of updated ECM pods from U.S. war stocks previously earmarked for use in a Central European conflict also reduced the SA-6's effectiveness. It was only at this point that the IAF once again enjoyed freedom of action over the battlefield, a situation that continued until the ceasefire on October 25th. [267]

On the Northern Front, desperate Israeli close air support missions initially did little to affect or disrupt the Syrian offensive. Battlefield air interdiction missions launched against the Syrian supply lines and second echelon forces were only marginally more effective over the first 48 hours. Rather than the actions of the IAF, it was a combination of Syrian miscues and heroic defenses by the IDF's ground forces that prevented the Syrians from regaining the Golan Heights. As on the Southern Front, Israeli ground counterattacks and new ECM pods disrupted the Syrian air defense network beginning on October 10th. By the ceasefire on October 25th, Israeli aircraft were able to fly over Syrian territory almost at will.[268]

Western Analysis of the War of Atonement

Despite the conflict's seemingly positive outcome for the IAF, the Yom Kippur War was a major shock for not only the Israelis, but the USAF as well. First, it was readily apparent that the newest Soviet air defense systems were extremely effective. Publicly, air power proponents in the United States and NATO countries pointed out that the Israeli loss rates overall were not much heavier than those suffered by the USAF over North Vietnam. Professionally, the USAF realized that the *initial* loss rates in the first 72-hours of the war were so prohibitive that they would have led to the IAF's destruction within two weeks of combat had they continued. Indeed, the IAF had required the USAF, USN, and USMC to divert F-4E *Phantoms* and A-4 *Skyhawks* as well as the aforementioned ECM pods from NATO war stocks in order to remain operational. Inversely, the Soviets' failure to anticipate how rapidly the Syrians and Egyptians would deplete their missile stocks had forced the latter to be far less profligate in their engagements after October 10th. This had contributed to the IAF's success in supporting Israeli counterattacks, which in turn had allowed close air support to have a freer hand on both fronts. It was unlikely, analysts observed, that such a supply shortfall would occur in a Central European scenario.[269]

USAF and NATO military observers also recognized that the Arab air defenses had forced marked changes in IAF mission planning and tactics. On the Northern Front, the IAF had been forced to violate Lebanese and Jordanian airspace in order to outflank the Syrians' extensive air defenses. On the second day, an attempt to hunt the mobile SA-6 batteries had led to the loss or damage of most of an Israeli F-4 *Phantom* squadron, with the remaining aircraft jettisoning their ordnance to little effect. *Skyhawk* squadrons, lacking effective internal ECM, suffered so many losses that the Israelis temporarily restricted their use on the Northern Front. In the South, having to fly circuitous routes over the Mediterranean in an attempt to outflank the SAM Belt led to reduced ordnance loads and increased fuel consumption. On both fronts, strikes against headquarters, infrastructure, and oil facilities had little effect on the battlefield even if they reduced the IAF's losses.[270]

It was the IAF's ineffectiveness on the battlefield that was most ominous of all to the USAF and NATO. Although the Israelis were themselves not provided with the exact same versions of fighters flown by American and NATO forces, they were similar enough. In any case, Western intelligence agencies were aware the Soviet Union had provided Egypt and Syria with the same "export" versions of their systems employed by the Warsaw Pact. Therefore, the relative disparity in capabilities combined with superior Israeli training should have been decisive. That the Arabs had not only neutralized Israeli air superiority but had been able to do so while conducting twenty-four hour operations was a capability that Western military observers had not believed either the Soviets or their clients possessed. [271]

Operationally, the Syrians and Egyptians had employed a reasonable facsimile of Soviet doctrine against well-trained Israeli regular forces on the defensive. In the case of the Syrians, that doctrine had been mostly effective, with battlefield friction, poor decisions, and inexplicable delays in deploying their forces the main reason for their defeat. The Egyptians had achieved their initial war goals, but had taken a strategic and operational gamble in an attempt to relieve pressure on Syria as the IDF counter-attacked. Neither of these outcome bode well for a potential NATO defense that relied a great deal on air power as an equalizer. As the United States dispatched several military missions to Israel in an attempt to find out what happened, there were questions as to whether modern air defense systems had made the manned jet aircraft obsolete.[272] It would be up to the United States Air Force to begin answering this question in the negative over the next seven years.

WEASELS, WARTHOGS, AND THE SECOND ECHELON

The State of the Air Force, 1974-1980

In the aftermath of the conflict in Vietnam and the Yom Kippur War, the United States found itself in a far different situation than at the start of Operation Rolling Thunder. In January 1974, the Air Force was doctrinally adrift, had a force that was experiencing a dramatic drain on personnel as experienced pilots were lured away by airlines, and possessed obsolescent equipment that seemed decidedly ill-suited for the threat it faced. The Yom Kippur War had seemed to indicate the service's ideas on training, its purpose and, most tellingly, its foundational guidance were flawed with regard to destroying an IADS as part of a larger campaign. In short, there were valid questions both within the Pentagon and outside the Department of Defense on whether the Air Force was capable of carrying out its designated responsibilities.[273]

Within six years, this situation was dramatically changed. By 1980, the Air Force not only had a new foundational doctrine that acknowledged enemy IADS as a holistic tactical system, but also joint agreements with the Army on how to defeat the IADS pursuant to facilitating close air support and battlefield area interdiction. It would apply this new way of viewing SEAD to the development of individual, flight, wing, and theater training regimens. This development of personnel was matched with the development of

new equipment, ordnance, and airframes specifically targeted at disrupting or destroying SAMs
and MiGs influence on the modern battlefield.
The Air Force developed Red Flag, a training site
intended to develop conventional capability to a
level equivalent to the first ninety-six hours of
combat in a military conflict. Although doubts
would remain among analysts and external
observers as to the Air Force's capabilities in
1980, within the service it was readily apparent
that great strides had been made with regard to
crews' ability to achieve conventional air superiority.[274]

Views on Military Force in the Presidencies of Gerald Ford and Jimmy Carter

A Demi-Presidency: The Ford Administration

By the time Richard Nixon resigned and
gave way President Gerald Ford on August
9th, 1974, the 38th President was well aware
of the United States' military and diplomatic
limitations. Internationally, South Vietnam's
stability continued to decay while an Arab oil
embargo impacted America and NATO's military
readiness. Domestically, stagflation, racial

tensions and, most of all, the continued political fallout from the Vietnam War and Watergate all served to limit President Ford's ability to shape policy. In addition to inheriting much of Richard Nixon's national security team, Gerald Ford had been bequeathed his predecessor's military and strategic shackles. The nation, the presidency, and the military had all been chastened by their experiences in Southeast Asia.[275]

Despite these experiences, President Ford considered military force to be a viable component of his national policy. However, this power would not be used based on ideological grounds but rather because of a cold blooded assessment of national interest and chances of success. Furthermore, given the military's need to refurbish both its equipment and personnel after the Vietnam War, and Secretary of State Henry Kissinger's views that a "multipolar" world better served the nation's interest, the Ford administration sought ways to employ military power with minimal long-term investment and precise violence. In NATO, given Western Europe's increased economic power, this meant that Ford continued to expect the Air Force to be the United States' major contribution to the alliance's conventional deterrence. This stance enjoyed bipartisan support as part of the broader policies of Détente, and seemed the best path forward in Vietnam's aftermath. [276]

Overall Ford, while not as bellicose or willing to skirt Congressional authority as Nixon, firmly considered it within his purview as Chief Executive to direct and control military action. In April 1975, Ford's White House initiated the necessary deployments to respond to North Vietnam's invasion of the Republic of Vietnam. While the War Powers Act, public dissatisfaction with Vietnam, lack of Congressional approval, and the rapidity of South Vietnam's collapse precluded American action against Hanoi, Ford had every intent of using military force. When Khmer Rouge forces seized the *Mayaguez* two weeks after Saigon's fall, this intention was carried through to a military response. In both cases, airpower played a prominent role in the Ford administration's method for employing the military. Although the circumstances of his term precluded development of a strategy truly independent of Nixon's, the small number of examples (e.g., South Vietnam's implosion and the *Mayaguez* incident) indicated a belief in deploying either USAF or USN fixed-wing assets in the national interest rather than ground units.[277]

The Carter Administration

President Jimmy Carter defeated Gerald Ford primarily due to the impact of a stagnant economy, anger at the latter's pardon of Richard Nixon, disgust with the Nixon and Ford administrations' *realpolitik*, and the Democratic Party's promise to reform Washington. When President Carter was inaugurated in January

1977, he became the first president since Lyndon B. Johnson to enter office without a major war or crisis affecting his administration. Furthermore, through President Nixon and Ford's efforts in establishing Détente, Carter inherited a national security situation in which the United States enjoyed far better relations with the Soviet Union and the People's Republic of China than had been the case in 1968. Despite Republican (and some Democrat) claims that Soviet power had eclipsed that of the United States, neither country enjoyed an objectively overwhelming advantage in strategic nuclear weapons in 1977. Carter's party controlled Congress, which ostensibly meant that his administration would find it far easier to shape the Department of Defense's priorities as it saw fit.[278]

President Carter initially intended to minimize military commitments and interventions in order to facilitate trimming the Department of Defense's annual budget. This fell in line with his personal beliefs that, with the exception of the nation's NATO obligations, the United States should minimize its military commitments elsewhere by applying other elements of national power. Carter fully believed that the United States could achieve military advantages through modernization of individual weapons systems and the leveraging of technology. Despite many concurrent and subsequent claims that Carter was "dovish" or "weak on defense," there was little evidence to support these accusations. In reality, President Carter, like Dwight Eisenhower, believed that out-of-control defense spending was a threat to the United States' economy. Therefore, whereas the latter had attempted to achieve military overmatch through the use of nuclear weaponry, President Carter and Secretary of Defense Harold Brown intended to achieve the same effects through purchasing fewer systems that were technologically superior to their Soviet counterparts.[279]

This belief was also reflected in how President Carter approached the arming of nations friendly to the United States. Although not openly espousing a stance similar to the Nixon doctrine, President Carter continued Nixon and Ford's policies of arming non-NATO allies with advanced weaponry in hopes of promoting regional stability, deterring hostile aggression, and facilitating U.S. efforts should military action be necessary. This mirrored Secretary Brown's efforts within Western Europe, where Carter intended for the nation's European allies to also purchase weapons systems that were compatible with the United States' own programs. In aid of the latter, Carter's administration simplified the process by which European nations could obtain American weapons systems such as the F-16 *Fighting Falcon* or advanced ordnance (e.g., *Paveway* laser-guided bombs). This then lowered the overall cost of these items for the USAF. Unfortunately for his administration, both domestic economic realities (e.g., inflation) and foreign events (e.g., aggressive Soviet activity and the Iran hostage crisis) denied Carter's Department of Defense the ability to fully realize any of his overall defense plans before his loss in the 1980 election.[280]

The Air Force's Changing Mission

Given this strategic backdrop, the United States Air Force found itself in a time of transition from 1974 through 1980. At the strategic level, the Air Force continued to develop intercontinental missiles while maintaining a manned bomber fleet. The *Minuteman III*'s deployment and initial development of the *MX* missile absorbed a significant portion of the Air Force's budget, but, otherwise, intercontinental ballistic missiles (ICBMs) had little effect on SEAD doctrine. In contrast, developments in manned bomber doctrine reinforced the USAF's desire to develop tactics, doctrine, and air frame to penetrate IADS at low level and high speeds. Recognizing the losses suffered during Operation Linebacker II, successive Air Force Chiefs of Staff General George S. Brown, General David C. Jones, and General Lew Allen all pushed for the replacement of the B-52 *Stratofortress* with a more advanced, supersonic low-level bomber. To meet this need, the Nixon and Ford administrations directed the purchase of the shorter-ranged FB-111 (a variant of the F-111) and development of the B-1 *Lancer*. Although the Carter administration cancelled the *Lancer* in 1978, SAC's embracement of low-level penetration implicitly recognized that the days of overly cautious training were drawing to a close throughout the entire Air Force. Furthermore, training and facilities for electronic countermeasures developed in support of SAC were also tasked to begin supporting TAC training.[281]

Army–Air Force Initiatives and Agreements

While SAC decided to ingress at high speeds and low altitudes in order to defeat an IADS, TAC moved to formalize close cooperation with the United States Army. This process had formally begun with the mid-1973 meeting of Major General Leslie W. Bray, USAF Chief of Doctrine, Concepts, and Objectives, and Major General John H. Elder, United States Army, as the representatives of their respective Chiefs of Staff, General Brown and General Creighton Abrams. Bray and Elder, studying the problem of CAS, BAI, and the frictions that had arisen during the Vietnam War, decided that a European scenario would require strict "primacy" that established areas of control for their respective services. These decisions would reduce fratricide, prevent duplicate targeting of high priority Warsaw Pact systems, and ensure unity of command in combat. Moreover, it would allow the Army and Air Force to "reduc[e] the costs of weapons research, development, and acquisition" while "eliminating Air Force and Army duplication of capabilities."[282]

With this in mind, Bray and Elder decided that the Army should have control of all operations along the forward edge of the battle area (FEBA), a line defined by the point where ground troops were in direct fire contact, and for 25 miles into enemy territory. In the proposed Bray-Elder system, the Air Force provided a given number of CAS sorties to a designated Army corps or division. The supported Army commander would determine into which subordinate sectors these fixed-wing sorties would be directed. The corps would also be responsible for controlling NATO air defense assets in the given sector in order to prevent fratricide from friendly SAMs or AAA systems such as *Hawk*, *Chaparral*, or *Vulcan*. The division commander receiving air support would then determine where to assign these aircraft to best support his offensive or defensive scheme of maneuver. The brigade and battalions in contact would mass direct and indirect fires against Warsaw Pact air defense assets in an attempt to suppress them. Army attack helicopters would support this SEAD mission, thus removing the Warsaw Pact's air defense assets at the regimental level and below as the Air Force CAS attacked the designated hostile ground forces. In order to ensure this complicated process was carefully coordinated, the Army would start requiring it to be trained in all staff exercises.[283]

The United States Air Force, as the provider of

these close air support sorties, ensured that CAS sorties would be second only in air defense/air superiority missions when the Air Staff allocated resources. Furthermore, in contrast to what it had done the last two decades, the Air Force would prioritize the acquisition of a single-role attack aircraft (the "A-X") as opposed to carrying out the mission solely through multi-role aircraft such as the F-4 *Phantom* or forthcoming F-16 *Falcon*. All aircraft would require ordnance specifically tailored to CAS, and existing USAF ordnance (e.g., the *Maverick* missile, optical glide bombs, and laser guided weapons) would need additional funding for development. Under the Bray and Elder proposals, the USAF would also treat training for the CAS mission as being equal in importance with air-to-air training. The Air Force would also ensure that at least a third of its tactical aircraft performed air-to-ground missions as their primary role. Air Force pilots would be slated to serve a two- to three-year tour as air liaison officers (ALOs) with designated Army units, with the expectation these officers would serve as forward air controllers if war broke out. In peacetime, they would enhance the Army's understanding of Warsaw Pact air defense tactics in order to facilitate targeting by that service's artillery and rocket battalions around the FEBA.[284]

Bray and Elder also conducted an analysis of how the Army and Air Force could cooperate in attacking the Warsaw Pact's second echelon, the so-called "Deep Fight." It was in this role that the Air Force's F-4s, F-16s, and F-111s were expected to penetrate the regimental and division air defense assets rather than deal with the entire IADS from west to east. The likely routes for such an attack would employ the "open flank" provided by the Baltic or the hillier terrain in the southeastern Germany in order to penetrate the WP-IADS. Once through the defenses, NATO and USAF aircraft would attack Warsaw Pact fuel depots, bridges, railyards, and command posts in addition to conducting air interdiction (AI) / BAI. Geographically, these attacks would be conducted from the expected FEBA to the eastern edge of the Polish and Czech borders. Due to their depth, they were expected to be almost wholly USAFE affairs, since at this time NATO 2 ATAF lacked the requisite aircraft types, training, and tanker assets to conduct attacks at such long range.[285]

The Bray-Elder papers were a massive departure from the Air Force's way of war prior to its experiences in Vietnam. Unsurprisingly, resistance to these ideas from within the Pentagon was immediate. There were those within the Army who believed their service needed internal organic close air support assets just as the Marines possessed. These individuals pointed out that the Air Force had paid lip service to CAS before the Vietnam War as well. Many senior Army officers recalled that the Air Force had been forced to develop CAS capability through many painful trial and error experiences in the initial stages of the war in Southeast

Asia. Such development had been almost wholly due to the USAF's neglect of conventional weapons training. Within the Air Force, senior and mid-level officers expressed concerns that enacting the proposed reforms would be the first step towards dissolution of their separate service. The Bray-Elder framework seemed like a dangerous precedent to set for U.S. Army control of air assets in a European conflict. It also called into question several of the agreements between USAFE and NATO's 2 ATAF regarding operational control of Alliance aircraft in a conventional war.[286]

Concerns about aircraft control were not limited to NATO. Neither the United States Navy nor Marine Corps had forgotten the Air Force's attempts to eliminate the sea services' air component in the 1950s and early 1960s. This initial source of friction had been exacerbated by USAF actions regarding controlling CAS during Vietnam and conduct of the Route Pack system over North Vietnam. As a result, USN and USMC officially refused to consider the Bray-Elder procedures or provide input on their enactment. Although TAC was able to conduct a series of joint service exercises in which Bray-Elder suggestions were employed, these were done more though General Dixon's machinations than any official directed activity.[287] The Navy, in the midst of its own doctrinal renovations and modernization program, wanted no official part of what seemed to be an Air Force-Army circumvention of established Pentagon roles and functions.[288]

The Army and Air Force's next steps did nothing to assuage those who disagreed with the Bray-Elder suggestions. General Brown, having formerly worked for General Abrams when the latter was commander of all U.S. forces in Vietnam, asked the Army Chief of Staff if he would mind TAC and the Army's Training and Doctrine Command (TRADOC) initiated direct coordination to further the Bray-Elder developments. This process began initially with phone calls then culminated with General Dixon visiting General William E. Dupuy, head of TRADOC throughout 1974.[289] As General Dixon recalled, General Brown had told him the purpose for this face to face coordination at the Army headquarters was:

> [To avoid engaging] the doctrinaires; we won't engage the JCS we won't engage those people who jealously guard their narrow strips of turf. We will move forward, if you like, under the guise of procedures, and we will let doctrine get altered by the procedures instead of trying to alter doctrine which we have been trying to do for years and failed.[290]

Put another way, General Dixon, with the explicit support of General Brown, specifically arranged a meeting with his Army counterpart to circumvent previously established Air Force, Army, and Joint Chiefs of Staff methods for establishing doctrine. It was understood by both General Brown and Abrams that any procedures stemming from this meeting would then have the weight of Air Force and Army manuals guiding the employment of tactical airpower. The meeting paid immediate dividends:

> We established ALFA [Air-Land Forces Application agency], which is the Army-Air Force get together. Our staffs had regular and frequent meetings, and we started writing joint procedures. I worked very hard with General [William] DePuy on that subject. There is no more accomplished tactician in the world. Nobody understands the battlefield the way he does. He understands it from A to Z, perfectly. He is as close as you can get to having an open and receptive mind like Abrams had. He joined wholeheartedly, though both of us were limited by our resources. While it was easy to say we will work procedures, it was hard to do that because, although we were doing it away from the Pentagon, the Pentagon was watching us; the rest of the Army was watching him, and the rest of the Air Force was watching me.

> There were people who criticized what we were trying to do, but we hoped to make enough progress during his [General DePuy's] tenure and mine to institutionalize the process so when we left it wouldn't be just us; it would be a way of life.[291]

Although it is debatable whether either service realized Dixon's lofty goals, it is inarguable that the efforts yielded change. For the Army, General DePuy ensured that the discussions on employing fires were inculcated throughout the 1974 draft edition of FM 100-5 *Operations of Army Forces in the Field*.[292] In a similar effort, Generals Dixon and Brown, with the enthusiastic aid of Major General Bray, set about to make a major revision to how the Air Force viewed its basic doctrine, AFM 1-1.

January 1975 Edition of AFM 1-1

There were five major changes between the September 1971 and January 1975 editions of AFM 1-1 *United States Air Force Basic Doctrine*. First and foremost, General Bray's authors did not devote over one third of the document to the conduct of nuclear war. Détente and the Strategic Arms Limitations Talks (SALT) treaties made it apparent neither President Ford nor President Carter wished to expend the resources necessary to make a nuclear war even notionally "winnable." Therefore, unlike the September 1971 edition, the 1975 edition stated that the "deterrence of strategic nuclear war is the highest defense priority of the United States." It then proceeded to expound upon the virtues of the Strategic Triad for two paragraphs, and spent only four paragraphs directly discussing employment of nuclear weapons throughout the remainder of the document.[293]

This lack of emphasis on nuclear combat was not the only major change. In the 1971 edition of AFM 1-1, close air support was an operation that was "centrally directed at the appropriate level for effective management and overall efficiency," but with "detailed control...decentralized to provide flexibility, rapid response and adjustment to local requirements and conditions."[294] Further discussion strongly implies that said control, regardless of decentralization, would remain with an Air Force headquarters and be subservient to the air commander's overall plan for conventional warfare. In contrast, the 1975 edition explicitly states that "close air support operations require detailed integration with the fire and maneuver of friendly forces" in order to "limit the enemy's capability to directly engage friendly forces in close combat."[295] In light of the TAC-TRADOC discussion, either implied or explicit discussions of which service will control CAS is conspicuously absent from the 1975 manual. In similar fashion, air interdiction operations (including BAI) transition from being implicitly planned and executed by an air component headquarters in 1971 to being explicitly responsive to the changing needs of the ground component.[296]

In undertaking these subtle changes, Generals Dixon and Bray ensured that the bulk of their planned changes to tactical and operational missions would still be well within the spirit of Air Force doctrine. While not explicitly spelling out tactical SEAD within the vicinity of the

166 | JAMES L. YOUNG JR.

FEBA, AFM 1-1's choice to tie both air interdiction and CAS to the ground maneuver force
echoed the Bray-Elder suggestions and Dixon
and DePuy's ongoing dialogue. When AFM 1-1
is read in conjunction with the January 1976
edition of the U.S. Army's capstone manual, FM
100-5, *Operations of Army Forces in the Field*, it
becomes clear that the Army understood their
portion of the SEAD mission. Corps and division
commanders fully intended to employ their assets
to destroy or suppress the ZSU-23-4, SA-8 and,
where feasible, the SA-6 on the Central European
battlefield.[297] Although less clear regarding major
theater operations elsewhere (e.g., the Middle
East or Korea), General Abrams and General
Jones felt the interlocking doctrine of FM 100-5
and AFM 1-1 was sufficiently flexible to be
employed elsewhere. Although far from perfect,
the cooperative efforts of DePuy and Dixon were
sufficient to provide an intellectual foundation
for tactical SEAD.[298]

Operational SEAD

The Air Force's close cooperation with the Army
on tactical operations in support of close air
support still left the issue of operational-level
SEAD. The Air Force recognized that in local
conflicts, allies would "often lack adequate air
power, and the Air Force is likely to play the key
role in any future US response for support."[299]
Moreover, the allied nations supported by the
Air Force were likely to have placed "major

emphasis upon developing and maintaining the capabilities of their ground forces."[300] Therefore, the Air Force clearly expected that, both in the expected NATO scenario or an unplanned international contingency, it would be responsible for establishing and maintaining air superiority. Furthermore, the Yom Kippur War had demonstrated that such air superiority may require overcoming a sophisticated IADS such as those fielded by Egypt and Syria in 1973.[301] Unfortunately, while the manual's authors had built in doctrinal flexibility with regard to tactical SEAD that supported CAS and BAI, the 1975 edition of AFM 1-1 still provided very little instruction on how to reduce an IADS at the operational level. Indeed, the only guidance on attacking enemy air defenses was implied in one sub-paragraph in Chapter 3:

> (1) Offensive counter air operations are normally conducted throughout enemy territory to seek out and destroy those targets that constitute or support the enemy air order of battle. These operations are the most effective means for achieving air superiority and are essential for gaining air supremacy.[302]

These two sentences were the lone reference to establishing air superiority and air supremacy over hostile territory in AFM 1-1. In 1971, the Air Force's basic doctrine had directly stated that air superiority would be determined solely by air-to-air combat only to have this thesis disproven by Vietnam and the Yom Kippur War. The 1975 edition did not overtly restate this incorrect belief on the primacy of enemy fighters within an IADS. Instead, the manual once more mentioned enemy fighters, then seemed to imply an IADS's ground components were not worthy of being individually named. Instead AFM 1-1 collectively described SAMs, AAA, and IADS C² centers as "targets that constitute or support the enemy air order of battle."[303] The refusal to explicitly outline these components is curious given the amount of discussion dedicated to tactical SEAD in the Bray-Elder papers, TRADOC-TAC ALFA discussions, Air Force professional journals, and fighter pilot's observations regarding this era.

Despite this decision to omit hostile ground systems in Air Force's basic doctrine, General Dixon personally took several steps to ensure that TAC was prepared to conduct operational SEAD. First, Dixon directed ALFA to write a field manual that established airspace control. Published in November 1976, AFM 2-14 / FM 200-42, *Airspace Management in an Area of Operations,* formally established the policies by which the Air Force and Army would control movement of friendly rotary and fixed-wing aircraft to the FEBA. It also charged the air component commanders at all levels (i.e., squadron through numbered air force) with responsibility for "[c]oordinating the operations of his forces, aircraft, and weapons with other Service components, as required."[304] The manual listed both friendly and enemy air defense assets among the items that were to be covered during this coordination. Combined, these two facets provided a means through which Army division and corps commanders were compelled to discuss SEAD with their Air Force group and wing counterparts within a given operational area.

Second, Dixon established two additional numbered air force headquarters underneath TAC. These organizations, the 9th and 12th Air Forces, ostensibly had a peacetime function of overseeing training throughout TAC. Dixon, however, also used them to test new staff methods for planning and conducting aerial campaigns using different operational scenarios. In this manner, they began to develop the methods by which TAC expected to engage and defeat a modern IADS, with the primary focus being on European operations. Through his previously established relationship with Admiral Isaac C. Kidd, Commander of the Navy's Atlantic Fleet, Dixon ensured that staff from both headquarters were able to conduct unofficial exercises in which USN carrier aircraft provided SEAD assets for Air Force exercises. These were often conducted in conjunction with "Blue Flags," i.e., TAC-designated staff training events. Finally, Dixon ensured that the two organizations conducted liaison with their PACAF and USAFE counterparts in order to provide wartime redundancy and shared dissemination of developed procedures across the Air Force. In the same manner by which fighter pilots gained experience with additional air combat maneuvering sorties, these numbered headquarters began to increase their efficiency as TAC forced them to go through planning and exercises.[305]

New Roles, New Equipment: The Air Force Modernizes

In 1974, the Air Force consisted primarily of aircraft either purchased directly for or inspired by the need to conduct Massive Retaliation. The ubiquitous F-4 *Phantom* was still being purchased in its F-4E variant for frontline service and to replace the obsolescent "C" and "D" models. The F-111 had evolved from being the fighter that the USAF had never wanted to serving as its primary long-range, all-weather strike aircraft. Close air support and battlefield air interdiction were considered the province of the F-4D / F-4E and Vought A-7D *Corsair*, another USN aircraft that Secretary McNamara had forced upon the USAF. SAM and radar suppression missions were performed either by aging F-105G aircraft or the problematic F-4C *Wild Weasel IV* variants. Reserve units continued to fly the F-100 and F-105 in various roles, and air defense units continued to operate the F-106. Airborne command and control was executed by a small number of EC-121 *Constellation* aircraft, while there was no electronic warfare craft capable of penetrating hostile airspace in company with a strike formation.[306]

General Jones and General Dixon both recognized the Air Force's obsolescence in light of how they planned to conduct a future conflict. In a 1974 memorandum, General Dixon stated his intent to have two thirds of these obsolescent aircraft replaced by 1981.[307] The Air Force did not quite meet this goal, but still achieved a marked increase in capability that belied its numbers. By 1980, of USAF's 41 active and reserve fighter wings, roughly half of them were equipped with the F-15 *Eagle* or F-16 *Falcon*. In Europe, the first A-10 *Warthog* wings had been established, thus vastly increasing USAFE's ability to conduct CAS. Finally, the EF-111 *Raven* had completed acceptance trials and was going through its final upgrades before assignment to USAFE and CONUS-based F-111 wings. As Massive Retaliation drove the weapons acquisitions of the Air Force that fought in Vietnam, TAC's support of Flexible and Measured Response guided USAF procurement and organization through the Carter and Ford administrations.[308]

The Means of Air Superiority

Whereas the Century Fighters had their genesis in an apocalyptic view of warfare, the USAF and USN's post-Vietnam fighters embodied many of the lessons learned from that conflict. A comparison of how both services examined the same problem (destroying MiGs) and came to vastly different solutions helps show

how doctrine drove design. Unlike the Air Force, the Navy had conducted little official coordination with its fellow services with on how to conduct conventional operations in case of a general European conflict. However, as an instrument of American national policy, the Navy was ostensibly bound by the same guidelines that spurred the Air Force's doctrinal changes. Although the Air Force considered itself the service of first choice for striking hostile countries, in reality this was often not the case. Air Force fighters required long runways and support facilities, neither of which were certainties in a given conflict. On the other hand, the proximity of international waters to most potential crises had historically made presidents far more likely to rely on carriers to as an instrument of military force than USAF squadrons.[309]

Like the Air Force, the Navy had learned a great deal from Vietnam. When attacking North Vietnam, the Navy's plans for attacking the NV-IADS was relatively simple. Carrier air wings (CAWs), unlike their USAF counterparts, were inherently heterogeneous. A typical CAW had consisted of 2-3 attack squadrons of 10-12 aircraft apiece, a detachment of 4-6 EW aircraft, and two fighter squadrons with an organization similar to that of their attack brethren. Whether attacking with another CAW or with only their own assets, a USN carrier strike's solution to SEAD was to arm 1-2 flights (usually from an attack squadron for that mission) and occasionally reinforce with a dual-armed F-4 flight from the strike's fighter escort. In this manner, a strike consisting of 20 bombing aircraft would be escorted by 4-8 aircraft equipped for suppressing SAM/AAA, with another 4-12 tasked with defeating any MiGs.[310]

Despite its relatively dynamic CAW, the USN found itself woefully deficient in conventional warfare capability through 1968. After Operation Rolling Thunder, the USN conducted a thorough review of its tactics, training, and equipment. Some of these (e.g., Top Gun, additional fleet wide ACM sorties, ordnance modernization) were implemented in the lull between Rolling Thunder and Linebacker. During this review, the Navy found that the F-4 *Phantom* was reaching obsolescence based on the observed performance of the MiG-21 and the expected capabilities of the MiG-23. Furthermore, with its dedicated attack community, the Navy did not feel it was necessary for its next fighter to be a multi-role aircraft. Instead, in July 1968 the USN decreed that the F-4's replacement, currently being sought in the Naval Fighter Experimental (VFX) Program, would concentrate solely on the air-to-air mission. [311]

Issuing this decree was far easier for the Navy than delineating what the mission was. Many Navy aviators believed that the *Phantom*'s poor performance against NVAF MiGs was proof that the next USN fighter needed to be much lighter. This mindset had been reinforced by the relative success the smaller, lighter F-8 *Crusader* had enjoyed during Rolling Thunder. Although Top

Gun graduates' success in 1972 had somewhat undercut this argument, the Navy's equivalent of the "Lightweight Fighter Mafia" still strenuously advocated for smaller aircraft. [312]

However, unlike Colonel Boyd's acolytes in the Air Force, the Navy's lightweight fighter advocates' desires for the VFX fell on deaf ears due to one major reason: fleet defense. The *Phantom*'s genesis had begun in response to the Soviet Union's development of anti-ship missiles with range in excess of two hundred miles. As the USN had been conducting operations against North Vietnam, Soviet Naval Aviation had continued to develop its anti-ship missiles and had fielded the *Backfire* bomber to carry them in 1967. So the VFX would now have to possess the means to engage and destroy Soviet bombers more than three hundred miles from a carrier's flight deck with onboard armament. It would also need the ability to launch from the flight deck, accelerate supersonically to a loiter point, then remain on station for several hours. Last but not least, the new aircraft would have to carry the powerful, but heavy, AWG-9 radar developed for the failed F-111B. [313]

When purchased in 1970, the F-14 *Tomcat* capitalized on advances in computer technology, ergonomics, metallurgy, and systems design to markedly improve on the *Phantom*. The combination of the AWG-9 and the Hughes AIM-54 *Phoenix* missile allowed it to engage multiple targets at over one hundred miles.

In order to facilitate a beyond visual range engagement, the *Tomcat* was also equipped with an onboard camera that allowed it to confirm a fighter-sized target's identity at over forty miles. For close range dogfights, the *Tomcat* was armed with the *Sidewinder* and designed from the outset with the M-61 Vulcan. Finally, the F-14 was aerodynamically designed to allow the large aircraft to be fuel efficient, with low wing loading that made it relatively maneuverable for its size.[314]

The F-14's negative traits demonstrated how even specialization was no guarantee of the optimal design. The *Tomcat* was underpowered, with engines that were unreliable and prone to shut down during air combat maneuvering. Its primary weapon, the AIM-54, was a heavy missile whose carriage rails limited the *Tomcat*'s flight envelope in an ACM environment. Due to its weight, it accelerated sluggishly in and out of turns. With regard to vertical maneuvers, its thrust-to-weight ratio was better than the *Phantom*'s but not by a large margin and only in afterburner. The *Tomcat* was also prohibitively expensive, with the cost precluding any attempt to purchase a possible strike variant for the Marine Corps.[315]

Combined, all these factors indicated that the Navy, by virtue of attempting to satisfy several needs, had purchased an interceptor rather than at true air superiority fighter. As performance at Top Gun demonstrated from 1972-1979, the

Tomcat was far from hapless in ACM. However, its size and preferred weapons suite made it an aircraft that was better suited to destroying an IADS's interceptors from long range before closing to ACM. Furthermore, unlike the *Phantom*, the F-14 lacked an advanced bomb computer, limiting its ability to be used in air-to-ground operations. Its size, cost, and limited capabilities would contribute to Iran being the only other nation to fly the *Tomcat*.[316]

The Air Force Path

The Air Force faced the same difficulties with gaining air superiority in a conventional conflict, but chose a different path than the USN. This was based in large part on their underlying assumptions of what a future conflict would be like after Rolling Thunder. When the Air Force selected the *Eagle* in 1969, the difficulties of integrating the *Phantom* into USAF service earlier in the decade were still fresh in the Air Staff's mind. Rather than the MiG-23 or similar aircraft that the USN expected to face attacking from the ocean, the Air Staff was greatly concerned about the MiG-25 *Foxbat*. In addition, the *Tomcat*'s early engine problems were so profound that the Air Force did not believe it would prove to be reliable enough to meet TAC's operational readiness standards. Therefore, the Air Force made every effort to avoid any direct comparisons between the two fighters during the design process, expedited the F-15's procurement, and placed a moratorium on any official ACM between the two fighters during the *Eagle*'s initial entry trials. The end result was that the Air Force obtained a single seat fighter that, while similar to the *Tomcat* in size, performed the air superiority mission in a much different manner.[317]

From Left to Right: F-16A *Fighting Falcon*, **F-15A** *Eagle*, **and F-14** *Tomcat*
(Author's Collection, taken at U.S.S. *Alabama* **Battleship Park)**

When placed into production, the *Eagle* offered an airframe that, while not truly multi-role, at least had a modest air-to-ground capability. In addition, the F-15A had been modified from its prototype to reflect the need to escort strike groups as far away as western Poland, intercept and destroy the Warsaw Pact's new generation of supersonic fighter bombers (e.g., the Su-17 *Fitter* and Su-24 *Fencer*), and also loiter for extended periods of time as escorts for NATO's AEW and tanker aircraft in case of a conventional conflict. Although the F-15 was 3-4,000 pounds heavier than the *Phantom* and had a larger airframe, its engines provided sufficient thrust to allow the *Eagle* to conduct sustained maneuver in three dimensions when carrying its standard air-to-air load. Furthermore, its large fuselage served as an additional lift surface, with an extremely low wing-loading for an aircraft of its size. Consequently, the *Eagle* was surprisingly nimble, being far more maneuverable than the *Phantom*, and arguably superior to the *Tomcat*. Its battery of eight air-to-air missiles matched the *Phantom*'s firepower, while its onboard radar allowed it to track and engage multiple targets with 'look-down / shoot-down' capability. [318] When compared to the design of the *Phantom*'s twin cockpit, the *Eagle* enjoyed a great deal more visibility:

> Once airborne for the first time in the F-15 I noticed, with a great deal of satisfaction, that a fighter aircraft again had been built with that most valuable of characteristics, visibility out of the cockpit. You can look back over your shoulder and actually check the six o'clock position by looking between the twin tails. In a 60° bank turn it is possible to look over the canopy rail and check the belly area for bandits. This was one of

the first of many pleasant surprises for me during my checkout.[319]

To the *Eagle*'s detractors, however, these improvements over the *Phantom* were more than balanced by the F-15's major flaws. First, its size made it visible almost at the extreme limit of human eyesight, i.e., 10-12 miles. By contrast, a *Fishbed*-sized aircraft was often only visible at eight miles, and the difference in visible range was even greater if the *Eagle* was in a bank. Seemingly trivial, this shortcoming grew in importance when one considered that the overwhelming majority of air-to-air encounters in Vietnam and the Middle East had been within visual distance. In addition, electronic warfare conditions during a European conventional conflict would likely greatly reduce the range and reliability of the *Eagle*'s radar. Thus, to those who opposed the *Eagle*, one of the fighter's most expensive components would be rendered an accessory of little to no use against the Warsaw Pact.[320] Even if the radar functioned as advertised, it seemed optimistic to expect a single pilot to effectively control and manage the radar, fly the aircraft, and maintain situational awareness. From a maintenance perspective, the radar, the airframe, and the electronics within seemed to be too sophisticated, as from 1976-1980 the *Eagle*'s maintenance costs per flight hour and operations readiness rate were both below TAC's expected targets. Finally, and most importantly, the *Eagle* was so expensive that the Air Force could not afford to buy F-15s in the initially expected numbers.[321]

The F-16 Falcon

Despite initial *Eagle* production beginning in 1973, the F-15's shortcomings provided an opportunity for the Lightweight Fighter Mafia to persuade the Air Force staff to explore other options. It was clear, from Air Force doctrine, that the service would need far more fighters to carry out its obligations with regard to BAI and CAS. Put bluntly, no matter how capable the *Eagle* was at air-to-air combat, NATO allies of the United States could not afford to purchase the aircraft. Nor could the USAF procure it in sufficient numbers to meet the service's projected need given the USAF's budget.[322]

The fact that NATO allies needed an alternative was not in dispute. Smaller NATO countries such as Belgium, Norway, Denmark, and the Netherlands entered the mid-70s still flying obsolescent F-104 *Starfighters* and utterly outclassed F-5 *Freedom Fighters*. After the Yom Kippur War, none of these nations' defense ministries expected these aircraft to be able to fulfill their designed role in concert with USAFE platforms. With their own aircraft industrial base as limited as their defense budgets, these NATO allies could not develop a domestic, modern replacement for these aircraft. Nor did these countries believe the purchase or French or British alternatives would meet their needs despite pressure from the United Kingdom and France to do so. Both the Ford and Carter administrations moved to fill this gap by proposing a common airframe that would provide a modern fighter for their allies while simultaneously driving down the USAF's costs to purchase the same.[323]

F-16 and F-15 In Formation (Courtesy NC Bateman via Dreamstime.com)

The F-16, as the eventual winner of the Lightweight Fighter Program, reflected a vastly different technological approach than the *Eagle* yet was still influenced by USAF views on air combat. Unlike the *Eagle*, the *Falcon* was conceived and initially developed purely as a daylight, clear-visibility fighter that would be able to destroy Warsaw Pact aircraft in the vicinity of the FEBA. In this vein, the *Falcon* lacked the expensive radar necessary to employ AIM-7 *Sparrow* missiles as well as the associated electronics. Instead, the F-16 was expected to be vectored in the vicinity of a target and achieve kills using the AIM-9 *Sidewinder* or, if necessary, its internal M-61. With this in mind, everything in the *Falcon*'s design was optimized for conducting high energy dogfighting at low to medium altitudes. Conceived, developed, and pushed through the Pentagon by acolytes of Colonel Boyd from 1972 to 1977, the *Falcon* was expected to be the Century Fighters' antithesis with regard to aerial warfare.[324]

At the operational level, the Air Force expected to purchase sufficient F-16s to meet a portion of its CAS needs as well as contribute to the gaining of air superiority. Chosen in part because of its extended range over its Northrop YF-17 competition, the F-16 was also expected to support battlefield air interdiction via the delivery of "dumb" bombs or the employment of *Maverick* missiles. In order to meet this task, it was equipped with a bombing computer, a solitary nod towards sophistication that facilitated its eventual purchase. However, its proponents were adamantly opposed to the development of any F-16 variant that had ground attack as a primary mission. So deep was this antipathy that the F-16 program manager and his superiors refused to consider a 1975 General Dynamics proposal for a SEAD variant of the F-16. The *Falcon*, according to those who supported it, would support SEAD by being present in sufficient numbers to allow the establishment of air superiority near the FEBA, not by gaining weight and size in an attempt to replace the F-4.[325]

Like the *Eagle*, the *Falcon* had its proponents and detractors. The former pointed out that the *Falcon* was, bar none, the most lethal dogfighting aircraft in the world when it entered official service in 1977. In exercise after exercise, the nimble *Falcon* was able to use its small size and high agility to gain a position of advantage against larger NATO aircraft.[326] This often occurred before the fighter was visually acquired, seemingly proving Boyd's theories on future air combat correct. Unlike the larger F-15, the *Falcon* was a true multi-role aircraft that performed the air-to-ground mission almost as well as dedicated strike aircraft (e.g., the A-7 and F-111).[327] As with the F-15, the *Falcon* was relatively easy to control for neophyte and experienced pilots alike. In the words of Dan Hampton, experienced F-16 pilot:

> [The ease of control] was largely due to a computerized, modular concept that permitted easy expansion as technology and weapons advanced. A lethal dogfighter, the F-16 can only fly by using computers to offset its aerodynamic instability. This designed instability is like starting a fistfight with your first swing nearly complete.[328]

To those who opposed the *Falcon*, this virtuosity came at the cost of low expected survivability. First and foremost, the new jet had a single engine, which seemingly ran counter to the operational experiences from both Vietnam and the Yom Kippur War. Although a European environment was not expected to have a civilian populace performing the "Mad Minute" found in Hanoi, there would be enough manually aimed anti-aircraft fire at low level to be a concern. Next, the initial F-16A design had only limited electronic countermeasures. The *Falcon*'s program managers had been so zealous about saving weight that initially the F-16A had been expected to have no internal ECM capability, but rely on external pods. Overruled by the Air Staff, the officers of the Lightweight Fighter Program had provided the F-16 with only a limited ECM suite that was arguably vulnerable to SAMs and the *Shilka*'s gun radar.[329]

Other F-16 opponents (of which F-15 pilots were often the most vocal) pointed out that the *Falcon*'s lack of BVR capability would be a marked disadvantage in either a European or Middle Eastern contingency. To these experts, the proliferation of modern fighters such as the *Mirage* F1 and the Soviet Union's export of the *Flogger* to friendly nations meant that eventually the F-16 was going to find itself facing enemies that could engage it at over twenty miles before it was in visual range. At that point, the F-16 would be analogous to the world's greatest knife fighter attempting to kill a man armed with an assault rifle while charging across a wide open football field.[330] Moreover, the *Falcon*'s initially poor acceleration compared to the *Flogger* at low altitude meant that the latter would ostensibly be able to disengage rather than dogfight.[331]

Despite these negative views, the F-16 was a major improvement to the USAF's SEAD capability, with an impact arguably greater than the *Eagle*'s. Almost immediately, the fighter's agility and dual-role capability led to USAFE employing it in hunter-killer teams with that command's *Wild Weasels*. Initially, this was an unofficial, "habitual relationship" between the F-4C *Wild Weasel III* squadrons based at Spangdahlem and F-16 squadrons assigned to USAFE beginning in 1978.[332] As the F-4G was introduced to USAFE in 1978, this arrangement became much more frequent, with F-16s often replacing the 52nd's own integral F-4Es in "hunter-killer" packages.[333]

The F-4G

As the "hunter," the F-4G *Wild Weasel V* leveraged advances in computer processing and electronic warfare technology to be arguably the best defense suppression aircraft the USAF produced in the Cold War. The impetus for producing a new Wild Weasel variant sprung both from the poor performance of the modified F-4Cs and the USAF's analysis of the Yom Kippur War. With mobile SAMs and the lethality of the ZSU-23-4, the Air Force's EWOs determined that tactical fighters required the capability to acquire enemy ground-based air defense assets, track their movements and, most importantly, direct other aircraft to attack them. Almost as importantly, the new airframe needed to be able to employ the full range of USAF ordnance, from the *StArM* to the new *Maverick* guided missile. Finally, the new airframe needed to be maneuverable enough to operate at low level, unlike the F-4C *Wild Weasel* or F-105G.[334]

In order to expedite production and with the expectation that the airframe was a stopgap measure, the USAF chose to use the newest model F-4E as the basis for the new *Wild Weasel*. Although the Air Force did not consider it as sophisticated as the F-15 or as nimble as the F-16, the slatted-wing F-4E was maneuverable enough, fast enough, and sufficiently spacious in the fuselage to allow the introduction of computer-based electronic warfare equipment. Rather than modifying existing airframes, the Air Force purchased new F-4E *Phantoms* as part of its defense budget beginning in 1974. The USAF then directed McDonnell Douglas to replace the fighters' nose mounted cannon with the APR-38, a radar acquisition system, and other internal systems that would facilitate targeting enemy ground-based air defenses. With deliveries beginning in 1975, the first squadron of F-4Gs became operational at Spangdahlem in 1978.[335]

The difference in capability between the F-4G and all other aircraft that preceded it was marked. Although it did not possess the same straight-line speed and acceleration as the

F-105G, the *Wild Weasel V* was more maneuverable at low level. At medium to high altitude, the F-4G not only possessed greater speed but had a longer range. Unlike the F-4C, the F-4G could carry *StARM* as well as *Maverick* missiles, and was a more survivable aircraft. Finally, the F-4G retained the ability to carry up to four AIM-7 missiles without detracting from its SEAD capability. This meant the *Wild Weasel V* and the F-4E that usually accompanied it could provide some of their own escort, if necessary, during ingress and egress.[336]

F-4G Wild Weasel (Courtesy Don Despain via Dreamstime.com)

Despite these improvements, the F-4G was not the best means of meeting the Air Force's commitments to the Army. Much like the F-4E on which it was based, the *Wild Weasel V* could not loiter near the FEBA for extended periods. As an air-to-air platform, it had inherited all of the *Phantom*'s faults while also reverting to lacking a gun. In order to accompany penetrating aircraft to distant targets, the *Wild Weasel V* had to carry three external fuel tanks, which limited the aircraft's speed, maneuverability, and ordnance. Finally, as first the F-15 and then the F-16 began replacing the F-4E, the F-4G became increasingly dissimilar to the other aircraft in USAF strike groups. This made it easy for air defenses, both those in exercises and potential Warsaw Pact systems, to differentiate the *Wild Weasel V* from other aircraft in the strike package.[337]

The E-3 Sentry

General Dixon, as the commander of TAC, felt that developing a means of controlling a strike group and its associated escort, as well as any other fighters in the area, was as important as developing modern aircraft. The Air Force had begun developing this aspect of aerial warfare during Vietnam by using EC-121 *Warning Stars* as airborne command posts. Realizing these aircraft's limitations and, once again, taking advantage of both computerization and Doppler technology, the Air Force began developing a successor. Designated the E-3 *Sentry* under the Department of Defense's joint naming convention, the Air Force more commonly referred to this new airframe as the Airborne

Warning and Control System, or "AWACS." Built on the same modified 737 airframe as most USAF tankers and electronic reconnaissance aircraft of the period, the *Sentry* was designed to operate in an orbit that allowed its radar to track airborne contacts for a radius of 2-300 miles depending on various target variables (e.g., size, speed, relative altitude, and ECM).[338]

Although pitched to Congress primarily as a defensive aircraft, like the *Eagle, Falcon,* and *Wild Weasel V,* the *Sentry* was a major facilitator of all Air Force operations within a given theater. Unlike ground based radars, the *Sentry* could see over the Earth's curvature out to its full range. Moreover, its Doppler radar was far less susceptible to the "ground clutter" that plagued radars such as those in the EC-121 or F-4 *Phantom.* Finally, using computers housed in the aircraft's fuselage that projected contacts' heading, speed, altitude and (after later upgrades) probable aircraft types, the *Sentry* presented its controllers with as much information as their ground-based IADS counterparts.[339]

This capability was a major advance in command and control. USAF (and later NATO) staff aboard the *Sentry* could alert a strike group to hostile interceptors and, if necessary, vector escort flights to attack these same aircraft. When dealing with a friendly strike group equipped with the proper IFF, the *Sentry*'s controllers could also clear the escort to engage with BVR missiles. Indeed, once the E-3 received upgrades in the late 1970s, its radar could reliably track even SAMs once these missiles were airborne. Although not responsive enough for *Wild Weasel* targeting in real time, the AWACS' ability to record what its radars had detected would ostensibly aid in pattern analysis of Warsaw Pact or other hostile actors' SAM deployment patterns in a full-scale conventional conflict.[340]

A Symphony of Destruction— Training to Defeat the IADS

There are many different viewpoints on what sparked the revolution in training that greatly enhanced the United States Air Force's conventional capabilities by the end of the 1970s. In his work *The Air Force Way of War: U.S. Tactics and Training After Vietnam*, Air Force historian Brian Laslie credits Generals Disosway, Momyer, and Dixon with "pav[ing] the way for subsequent commanders to train pilots realistically."[341] Laslie goes on to discuss the fact that all three successive TAC commanders decentralized training, empowered wing commanders to change tactics, and attempted to change USAF training programs to better reflect what would occur in potential conflict. While Laslie does not argue that the transition from staid, pre-packaged exercises to dynamic, fluid training events was wholly driven from above, he does present senior leaders as being the primary impetus of changes to TAC training during the latter stages of Vietnam through 1979.[342]

This viewpoint contradicts the memoirs of Air Force junior and field grade officers during this same period. According to F-4 / F-105 pilot Ed Rasimus, TAC pilot C.R. Anderegg, Brigadier General Robin Olds, and future USAF general Charles Horner, Disosway and Momyer were openly hostile to recommendations proposed to improve training presented in the aftermath of Rolling Thunder. Horner, in his memoir *Every Man A Tiger*, further suggests that Dixon initially did not wish to change the Air Force's methodology for training pilots on its merits but was basically outsmarted by junior officers.[343] To these men and historian Marshall L. Michel III, the changes in TAC during the 1970s were due to a "revolt of the majors," i.e., field grade officers who outright demanded that they never be sent into a conflict without proper training again.[344] Given this approach, rather than directing change, senior officers reluctantly acknowledged it was inevitable and then tried to control the field grades' impetus rather than let it disrupt the Air Force.[345]

Much of the available evidence supports both these disparate viewpoints and thus explains some historical confusion. By January 1974, it was not only clear that the USAF's training methodology was insufficient, but also that the entire service required a massive change in its training mindset. It is true, as Michel points out, that "'[a]cerbic

[was] a charitable way to describe Dixon."[346] In person and when writing correspondence, Dixon was blunt, to the point, and not one to be overly concerned with the feelings of peers or subordinates.[347] These traits were often taken by his staff and subordinates as dismissiveness or outright anger at their suggestions. However, reviewing his memoranda, directives, and policies, makes it clear that General Dixon's initial pugnaciousness often masked a driven, concerned commander who feared that his organization could not perform its wartime mission. In his five years as TAC's commander, Dixon took many explicit and implicit steps to set the conditions within which the "iron majors" would operate and also provided the senior officer "top cover" that protected their efforts from interference. Although General Momyer initiated some of the measures that helped TAC enhance its conventional capability, it was General Dixon who shepherded these and other changes critical to his command's enhanced conventional capabilities through the Pentagon.

The DOC System

General Dixon, like his predecessor, had determined that TAC's training did not properly replicate the modern combat environment. Unlike General Momyer between Rolling Thunder and Operation Linebacker, Dixon personally ensured that the TAC staff developed a plan to change this state of affairs and then enforced it. Building on the discussion of the December 1972 Tactical Fighters Symposium, Dixon developed policies that assigned each tactical fighter wing within TAC a particular wartime mission based on weapons platform and location. Called the Designed Operational Capability (DOC) training system, this new plan reflected the reality that the Air Force was constrained by both the ongoing oil crisis of the mid-70s and the budgetary constraints exacerbated by inflation.[348]

The assumption underpinning the DOC system was that almost no Air Force pilots, including those who were veterans of Southeast Asia, were fully proficient in the skills necessary for modern combat. A baseline of academic knowledge regarding the realities of air combat over both Vietnam and the Middle East was the initial building block for success. This school instruction occurred concurrently with a classroom curriculum that emphasized a pilot's assigned aircraft and mission. For example, a pilot assigned to an F-4E or F-15 and tasked for an air-to-air mission would spend a set number of hours learning the proper employment of the AIM-7, AIM-9, and M-61 cannon in aerial combat. This would include actual operational experiences gleaned from the Red Baron program, USAF and IAF pilot interviews and, where possible, intelligence gathered regarding NVAF, EGAF, and SAF tactical operations. In this manner, fighter pilots became academic experts in their particular field, be it defense suppression, air superiority, or ground attack.[349]

The reason for this rigorous academic training became readily apparent when the TFW's assigned pilots began the next two phases, basic and air combat maneuvers. Basic combat maneuvers were, as the name implies, a selection of drills in which a pilot performed the most common operations used in aerial combat. The drills were first performed alone, but at the end of the training phase the pilot was faced with an adversary (usually from within the wing) who flew a predictable, pre-arranged path. In this manner, the pilot was able to transfer academic learning to practical exercises in a low threat environment.[350]

It was in the final phase, air combat maneuvers, where Dixon's influence and that of the "iron majors" most directly intersected. ACM training, especially with the Air Force's initially inexperienced pilots, was inherently dangerous. When training against aircraft of the same type, i.e., "similar ACM," pilots could become easily disoriented as to which aircraft was a wingman and which was an adversary. Moreover, even with its numerous improvements, the F-4E remained a very unforgiving aircraft when pressed to the edge of its flight envelope. Although much more tolerant of pilot mistakes, the F-15's and F-16's capabilities encouraged pilots transitioning from the *Phantom* to overestimate the limits of their new mounts. The *Falcon*'s single engine, the same Pratt & Whitney F100 as used in the

F-15, showed a disturbing tendency to flame out due to the smaller fighter's greater agility and different design.[351]

The combination of all these factors meant that TAC's accident rate climbed alarmingly from 1974 to 1977, with 1976 being the worst year for crashes in the command's history. The high number of losses in aircraft and corresponding rise in aircrew deaths caused great consternation both within and outside of the Air Force. Officers of the Air Staff and members of Congress openly questioned the utility of ACM training in the modern combat arena. Rather than listening to those who believed the training was excessive, Dixon *increased* the directed amount of ACM training in 1977. He also directed that this training be conducted year round, at low altitude, and at night. Moreover, in collusion with the Navy, Dixon conducted unsanctioned joint dissimilar ACM training between USAF F-15s, F-4s, and USN F-14s off the Virginia coast during this same period. In all cases, Dixon stressed that these sorties were necessary for the USAF to carry out its wartime mission according to its new doctrine.[352]

In this environment, the "iron majors" became critical to success. While TAC conducted regular operational inspections, forced wings to practice "wartime surge" operations, and performed all of the myriad administrative tasks of a major combatant command, majors and lieutenant colonels oversaw daily flight operations. These same officers, in conjunction with their wing commanders, ensured that captains and lieutenants did the necessary academic work. Finally, and most importantly, the field grades began to conduct impromptu meetings and discussions, both in person and via professional journals. The *Fighter Weapons Review* was the most prominent of the latter, but field grade officers also discussed the Air Force's role in national policy, conventional deterrence, and weapons development within the pages of *The Air University Review*.[353]

Win Every Fight: Individual Pilot Training in ACM

These formal and informal discussions of SEAD doctrine led to a gradual, but revolutionary change in how the Air Force viewed the destruction of hostile airpower. Throughout Vietnam, the USAF had clung to its World War II / Korean mindset that air superiority was gained through either smashing the enemy on his airfields or shooting down large numbers of his fighters in the air. The former had been reinforced by the Israelis' success in the Six Day War, and seemed relatively straightforward. The latter was more difficult, but was usually achieved by virtue of determining which pilots were the best at destroying enemy aircraft, then giving said individuals every possible chance to do so. Until the end of the Vietnam War, Air Force senior leaders maintained that this was how American forces had achieved air supremacy World War II

EAGLES, RAVENS, AND OTHER BIRDS OF PREY | 197

and Korea.[354]

By 1974, General Dixon and most of the TAC community began to consider this construct irrelevant. The Warsaw Pact, having seen the contrast between the IAF's relative ineffectiveness in striking Egyptian and Syrian Air Force airfields in 1973 compared to 1967, began to emphasize hardening its own aircraft shelters in the 1970s. Although hostile runways remained a vulnerable asset that both NATO and the USAF targeted, airfields were also heavily defended by SAMs. Over North Vietnam, attempting to emphasize an elite "ace culture" had certainly not worked for the USAF, and was actually considered detrimental by many of F-4 escort pilots during Operation Linebacker. During the Yom Kippur War the Egyptian and Syrian MiGs had effectively operated as "disruptors" rather than attempting to seize air supremacy in any meaningful way.[355]

In this instance, the Air Force's field grades led the push for change. By 1975 the *Fighter Weapons Review* began to emphasize that Warsaw Pact fighters would have to be destroyed in the air. More importantly, articles by the "iron majors" emphasized that this would have to be done by *all* USAF pilots, not only those tasked with air-to-air as their DOC specialty. According to these formal articles as well as the informal professional circles created in the aftermath of Vietnam, *all* TAC aircrews had an obligation to prepare to defeat enemy aircraft from the first day of a potential conflict. Indeed, according to the *Fighter Weapons Review*, the only way the Air Force (and by extension, NATO) was going to win a potential Central European fighter was if all of TAC's pilots prepared on a daily basis for ACM. Furthermore, this admonition applied to every officer in TAC, from the most junior second lieutenant flying A-7s to an F-15 wing commander. Although the *Eagle* was far more likely to have an opportunity to destroy MiGs, numbers and expected roles meant the *Corsair II* pilot could not expect to simply hope he would never have to defend himself against enemy aircraft.[356]

Expressing this opinion in the *Fighter Weapons Review* was one thing, but many mid-level officers knew these opinions had been voiced before under General Momyer. However, in the aftermath of the Yom Kippur War and constant losses to Aggressors, the Fighter Weapons' School's field grade officers decided to take matters into their own hands. The first step was to simply rewrite their organization's training curriculum to introduce the Navy's "Loose Deuce" system as the "Double Attack" formation. Rather than outright copying the Navy's tactics, the Fighter Weapons School actually made the formation *more* aggressive. This was done by emphasizing that if either the #2 or #4 were the first to sport an enemy aircraft, they were to report it and then *immediately* attack. The #1 and #3, while ostensibly more senior, were in turn to support the offensive maneuver until either the enemy aircraft was destroyed or the situation let them resume leading their pair or flight. [357]

This upending of the previously established Air Force system was not done with official sanction. Indeed, no flag officer was tacitly consulted, nor was the decision staffed through normal channels before implementation. However, once he was made aware of it, General Dixon defended it against any outside interference or attempts to reverse it. The new "Double Attack" method, as well as realistic air-to-air training, was codified in 1976 with the publication of TACM 51-50. Provided with regulatory sanction, iron majors at the squadron and wing levels ensured their commands vigorously practiced the new tactic. Although not quite a full scale "revolt," this was a prime example of how change was sparked from below and underwritten by above.[358]

The effect of the change on ACM capability was marked. The USAF Aggressor squadrons, in 2 versus 2, 4 versus 4, and full squadron versus squadron fights initially had their own way when first introduced in 1973. By 1977, DOC air-to-air pilots were beginning to become proficient in spotting, engaging, and "destroying" the smaller F-5s / T-38s in ACM by the second or third day of a week-long Aggressor visit. In the same time frame TAC pilots specializing in air-to-ground operations, while not gaining the same level of proficiency, were certainly not as hapless as their Operation Linebacker predecessors had been. When General Dixon turned over command of TAC to General Wilbur Creech in 1978, the Aggressor squadrons noted that they were often defeated by the F-15 and F-16 air-to-air squadrons on the first day in full squadron engagements and had mixed results when conducting flight and pair ACM maneuvers. Externally, when facing NATO or other allied aircraft in exercises, DOC air-to-air units were consistently besting their friendly counterparts in a lopsided manner. Thus, by 1979, it was clear to internal USAF observers and allies alike that the DOC system and its supporting doctrine had succeeded in increasing the Air Force's capabilities against the expected Warsaw Pact MiGs.[359]

The Construction of Red Flag

After Vietnam, the Air Force had begun to understand that modern aerial warfare was roughly analogous to a symphony of destruction. Although new equipment and the changing of the Air Force's training system were important, these were the equivalent of giving talented musicians new instruments and a chance to play in their respective sections. What CORONET HARVEST, the Red Baron reports, Blue Flag, and other exercises seemingly indicated was a need for the proverbial "concert hall" in order to achieve the necessary synergistic effects in a training environment. In the aftermath of Vietnam, many Air Force officers, both relatively junior field grades and senior flag officers, believed that the key to lower losses in any contingency operation was for pilots to perform their wartime tasks in as close a simulation of wartime as possible. Only in learning how to coordinate aerial refueling, electronic warfare, fighter escort, SEAD and finally, ordnance delivery in real time would flight, squadron, and wing commanders gain the necessary experience in peace to avoid costly casualties in a conflict's initial stages.[360]

The concept for developing this training area, designated "Red Flag," is usually credited to then Major Richard "Moody" Suter. Captain John Vickery, an F-4D pilot, is listed most often as the officer who turned the concept into the information paper circulated amongst the Air Staff. Various other Air Force officers, civilians, and veterans played a crucial role in conducting the coordination to bring together disparate pieces to make Suter's concept a reality. To replicate the Warsaw Pact's SAMs, Suter recommended that Army air defense units use both their own systems and SAMs captured by the Israeli Defense Forces. Defense industry manufacturers were asked to provide material solutions to eventually develop range instrumentation that would track, evaluate, and record engagements in order to provide a higher fidelity than human umpires. Various Department of Defense intelligence organizations and the Central Intelligence Agency (CIA) were asked to provide the most accurate information available on Warsaw Pact systems. Preparations complete, Major Suter briefed General Dixon on the final plan in May 1975.[361]

The TAC commander immediately took to Suter's proposal. So strong was Dixon's support, he reallocated funds allotted to other operational inspections and requirements in order to rapidly initiate of Red Flag exercises. In addition, Dixon made it known that none of the senior officers at Nellis Air Force would have their careers adversely affected if there were a high number of crashes in the first few exercises. To ensure continued Army participation, Dixon personally invited General DePuy to observe Red Flag as his guest in early 1976.[362] Dixon set in motion the development of Tonopah Air Force Base, Nevada, as a facility for the most realistic training aids the Air Force had: its very own MiGs. Through these and various other methods, Dixon signaled his support of Red Flag and protected it against members of the Air Staff and SAC who considered it to be a dangerous, wasteful use of Air Force resources.[363]

This combination of field grade preparation and flag officer support culminated in Red Flag's first exercise in December 1975. Dubbed "Red Flag 75-1," the training event involved only a single squadron of F-4 *Phantoms*. From these austere beginnings, Red Flags grew to multi-squadron events by 1976. Red Flag 78-2, flown in December 1977, became the first iteration to add night missions.[364] By 1979, the Royal Air Force (RAF), West German *Luftwaffe*, and Royal Canadian Air Force (RCAF) had all participated in Red Flags. Although the general consensus by 1980 was that Red Flag's capabilities remained several years behind the actual Warsaw Pact's, it was seen as a vast improvement over what had come before it. Slowly but surely, TAC had begun realistic training that would help demonstrate its growing capability to NATO allies.[365]

The Air Force Publishes New Doctrine

When General Dixon relinquished command of TAC to General Wilbur Creech on May 1st, 1978, he provided his successor with a far more capable force than he had inherited. Despite having a budget crippled by inflationary pressures, increased system costs, and sharply disparate guidance from the Ford and Carter administrations, General Dixon had accomplished a great deal with TAC. In support of the service's primary mission, he had strengthened coordination between TAC and USAFE in preparation for reinforcing the latter should a Central European conflict arise. He had also used his own personal connections to coordinate interservice training and doctrine development with the United States Navy and Army. In Red Flag, General Dixon had developed a training facility that served both to develop USAF combat capability in a realistic environment and also emphasize to allies the service's ability to perform its wartime mission. Finally, in conjunction with the Army's General DePuy, General Dixon had done much to erase the schisms caused between the services during Vietnam. Throughout all these steps, TAC's commander had explicitly and implicitly insisted that his subordinates and staff solve the problem of the Warsaw Pact IADS. Although he did not wholly succeed in all of these endeavors, his influence on the topic would be seen in the final edition of AFM 1-1 published before the Cold War's conclusion.

February 1979 Edition of AFM 1-1

The February 1979 edition of AFM 1-1, according to its authors, was designed to answer four questions (emphasis, centering, and spacing as per the original):

Why do we need military forces?
Why do we need an Air Force?
How do we build an Air Force?
How do you best use an Air Force?[366]

The subsequent pages after these four questions were, in stark contrast to previous editions of AFM 1-1, direct and simple answers to these questions. The military existed to provide the National Command Authority with "a clear and unmistakable capability to apply force to meet any known or potential threat, and to win the military objectives that support[ed] national policies."[367] This was accomplished by maintaining a "dual triad" of forces at the strategic and theater level to "meet possible military threats throughout the spectrum of warfare."[368] Primarily, the intent of these forces, in conjunction with allied forces, was to deter threats so that conflict was not necessary.

Within this framework of military force, the USAF was expected to execute several responsibilities related to aerospace operations. Tellingly, the first listed purpose for the Air Force was to "[c]onduct prompt and sustained combat operations in the air to defeat enemy airpower."[369] This was listed separately and distinctly from, "[p]rovide forces for strategic air warfare."[370] In other words, for the first time since its inception, the Air Force clearly considered the defeat of enemy airpower to be a separate and distinct mission from the execution of strategic air warfare. The document continued to emphasize this fact by outlining the Air Force's responsibilities in theater conflict and discussing how theater air superiority would be achieved in subsequent chapters. Strategic bombers were cast as an aspect of the strategic triad and thus part of the "nuclear umbrella," thus implicitly indicating that B-52s and FB-111s would only be used in times of extreme national peril.[371] The Air Force, at least in doctrine, seemed to have abandoned the concept of strategic attack against the Warsaw Pact or other major theater opponents.

In contrast to deemphasizing strategic bombing, support of the Army and allied land forces was given increased primacy throughout the new AFM 1-1. In everything from tactical close air support to strategic airlift, the Air Force codified most of the tentative agreements reached between General DePuy and General Dixon during the TAC–TRADOC initiatives. AFM 1-1 emphasized the coordination of Air Force efforts with the land commander's operational concept when planning CAS or BAI. Whether cutting enemy lines of communication or directly attacking their formations, USAF assets were to shape their operations towards achieving the land component's tactical and operational gains. The Air Force, it seemed, had abandoned thoughts of achieving operational victory solely through the application of airpower. While not a full subordination to the Army, the February 1979 edition of AFM 1-1 was an acknowledgment that modern warfare and the Central European mission both required success by conventional land forces.[372]

Another acknowledgment that much had changed in the past decade was AFM 1-1's discussion of what was necessary to achieve air supremacy. Innocuously entitled "Counterair Operations," the section devoted to "gaining and maintaining air supremacy" specifically acknowledged the role of defense suppression in modern operations.[373] Indeed, rather than implying that SEAD was a tactical task of secondary importance, AFM 1-1 stated that defense suppression tasks "must be fully integrated" in order to achieve air supremacy and enable the support of ground maneuver.[374] After the travails of Vietnam, the Israeli experience during Yom Kippur, and four years of exercises, the Air Force had finally directed that SEAD be planned for in order to achieve its other tasks. This was a watershed moment in Air Force doctrine, and it would shape the following decade in ways that greatly enhanced USAF training, procurement and, in at least one case, combat operations.

FROM THE VALLEY
TO THE CANYON

The Air Force made no significant changes to its SEAD doctrine between April 1979 and January 1980. However, the doctrine espoused in the February 1979 edition of AFM 1-1 had far reaching effects on how the Air Force trained to execute its SEAD mission. These training methods, concurrent improvements in airframes and weapons and, finally, combat experience were indicative of the Air Force's increased capability. In January 1980, military analysts, NATO military leaders, and domestic American observers all questioned the Air Force's ability to project power, indicating a lack of conventional deterrence. By December 1985, not only did the Air Force's projected capabilities have improved, but its weaponry and methods would have been proven in combat operations.

State of the Air Force, January 1980

Organizationally, the Air Force had shrunk to three major commands from the four with which it had begun the 1970s. With the absorption of the fighters from the Air Defense Command into Air Defense, Tactical Air Command (ADTAC) in 1979, TAC became the sole controlling headquarters for developing fighter combat doctrine. Given the Soviet Union's increasing reliance on ICBMs and low number of strategic bombers, ADTAC began to be seen as an Air National Guard and Air Force Reserve mission rather than one conducted by the Air Force's regular component. Still, ADTAC continued to be funded and equipped with modern fighters, with the latter continuing to provide support to Red Flag exercises.[375]

Operationally, in 1980 the standard unit remained the Tactical Fighter Wing with its usual organization of 2-3 squadrons of 16-24 fighters. European TFWs continued to be modernized, with the F-4D being phased out of USAFE service and replaced by F-4Es as the latter was in turn replaced by new *Eagles*. Within the United States, F-15 production increased as President Carter's final defense budget increased the number of *Eagles* purchased. Israel and Saudi Arabia also began taking deliveries of the big fighter, with the IAF conducting its first combat operation on June 27th, 1979. As for the F-16, the Air Force's plan to expedite the *Falcon*'s introduction by replacing two wings in USAFE by 1980 was delayed by the Carter administration's decision to allocate fifty of the new fighters to American allies in the Middle East. Even with this diversion, however, the Air Force had managed to field its first F-16 wing in January 1979 at Hill Air Force Base, Utah.[376]

The doctrine espoused in AFM 1-1 continued to drive the training for the employment of these new fighters. This was supplemented by local unit tactics, techniques, and procedures and TAC manuals published or updated in the first two years of General Creech's stint as TAC commander. The Air Force also found new areas to train in and allies to exercise with. In addition to Red Flag, TAC squadrons were regularly invitees to the RCAF's biannual Maple Flag exercises. Complementing these two sites in North America, USAFE squadrons and their NATO counterparts were given access to several of the RAF's range complexes in northern Scotland, while PACAF

forces conducted Cope North in the vicinity of
Guam. Although none of the European or Pacific
exercises replicated the full panoply of an IADS
as Red Flag did, they still provided opportunities to develop techniques for evading interceptors, dropping live ordnance, and conducting
dissimilar ACM.[377]

Strategically, the Air Force's stance and posture
had not changed from relying on both strategic
bombers and ICBMs. However, SAC began to
increase its participation in Red Flags beginning
in 1978. These exercises led to B-52 cell
commanders growing increasingly independent
in their planning and execution of missions.[378]
Additionally, the development of new nuclear
capabilities (the AGM-88 Air Launched Cruise
Missile) and further refinement of old technol-
ogies (the AGM-69 SRAM) within SAC supported
concurrent conventional weapons capabilities.[379]
Despite this, the Carter administration's attempts
to update ICBM basing, upgrade the missile fleet,
and modernize the B-52 all suffered from a lack
of congressional support.

On the other hand, TAC benefited from President
Carter's negative foreign policy experiences, the
Soviet Union's perceived bellicosity, and the
increased attention the American electorate gave
to military strength. Compared to the first two
budgets Carter presented to Congress, the FY
79 and FY 80 budgets both requested increased
outlays to purchase more tactical fighters
and conventional weaponry for the Air Force.

However, these attempts to strengthen the Air Force did not seem to cause a commensurate reassurance of domestic or foreign military analysts' opinions of the United States' military ability. Both within the Pentagon and its foreign counterparts, there were grave doubts about the U.S. Air Force's ability to support anticipated treaty obligations in wartime.[380]

Deterrence at the End of Détente

It is easy to assess both allies' and domestic observers' views of the USAF's conventional capability due to the plethora of articles and books published between 1976 through 1981. The most well-known work that presents NATO allies' opinions is Sir John Hackett's *The Third World War, August 1985*. A former commander of NORTHAG, Hackett gathered together NATO senior officers who had all held major commands in their respective nations' military to evaluate a potential Central European conflict occurring on the eponymous date. Basing the outcome on several wargame sessions, Hackett intended his work to be more a cautionary tale than one of popular fiction. Hackett's scenario established a possible casus belli, which involved Soviet excesses in Eastern Europe leading to what is intended as a limited war. Hackett then posited that only the West's timely purchase of sophisticated weaponry in sufficient numbers allowed it to win the subsequent major conflict. Lest the reader believe that *The Third World War,*

August 1985 was meant to imply that enough is already being done, Hackett dispelled this notion in his afterword. Stating "[t]here is also a very high probability that unless the West does a good deal within the next few years to improve its defences a war with the Warsaw Pact could end in early disaster," *The Third World War* concludes by outlining that then current defense plans and expenditures were hopelessly insufficient.[381]

The belief that NATO was inferior in conventional forces was especially telling in regard to airpower. Prior to publication of *The Third World War*, NATO had established Commander Allied Air Forces Central Europe (COMAAFCE) in 1974 to exert centralized control of the alliance's airpower and also reorganized its subordinate aerial headquarters. 2nd Allied Tactical Air Force remained established in support of NORTHAG, with German *Luftwaffe* units in southern West Germany joining the bulk of USAFE as the 4 ATAF. In Hackett's opinion, 2 and 4 ATAF would be able to complete their missions only if they were provided with "area-denial and cluster weapons...in abundance." Given the Warsaw Pact's air defenses, Hackett believed NATO's aircraft would not be able to employ precision guided munitions in sufficient numbers to affect the battlefield.[382] In Hackett's estimation, only investments in human capital, sophisticated platforms, and increased pilot training would allow NATO's air arm to influence a ground war. Even then, it would be a near run thing which would require stripping NATO forces from

Southern Europe and a wholesale commitment of reinforcements from TAC. Failing any of these, the air arm would not be able to influence the ground battle, leading to the eventual need for release of tactical nuclear weapons or to Western Europe's subjugation to a Soviet military threat.[383]

An even grimmer estimate than Hackett's was the similarly titled *World War 3*. Edited by Shelford Bidwell, a former British brigadier, *World War 3* gathered a similarly esteemed panel of analysts and experts to provide their viewpoint on a potential war in Central Europe. Like Hackett, Bidwell and his group believed that the increased sophistication of NATO's weapons did redress the numerical imbalance in 1978. However, *World War 3* posited that NATO's parsimony and the overwhelming strength of Warsaw Pact numbers would surely lead to the former employing nuclear weapons. Unlike the limited exchange discussed in *Third World War*, Bidwell and his companions' scenario concluded with a general exchange that resulted in civilization's destruction.[384]

Unsurprisingly, Bidwell's projection concerning aerial combat was also pessimistic. Due to the disparity of training levels among NATO allies and the continued use of obsolescent aircraft by some European nations, *World War 3* assumed that the Warsaw Pact would manage to keep the kill ratio at 2:1 in aerial combat. Furthermore, given publicly available information on weapons procurement, Bidwell's team estimated that the NATO air arms would run out of standoff munitions within the first 48 hours of the war beginning, while the USAF would follow suit less than a day later. In Bidwell's opinion, this meant that all NATO aircraft would have to penetrate into the heart of the Warsaw Pact air defense envelope. Based on the recent wars in Southeast Asia and the Middle East as well as the outcome of exercises such as Red Flag, the expert opinion of Bidwell's team was that the resultant losses would render NATO airpower not nearly as effective as it would need to be to affect the ground war. Only the training and skill of individual NATO aircrews, improvements in the alliance's electronic warfare, and the Warsaw Pact's expected profligate use of ammunition would allow the air attacks to make any headway against the second echelon at all. This failure would, in turn, contribute mightily to the eventual tactical nuclear exchange that would spiral out of control and become a general nuclear conflict.[385]

These grim views of NATO's chances in a conventional war were also held in the United States. In a 1979 report, the Congressional Budget Office stated it could "only acknowledge that air forces (both Warsaw Pact and NATO) could affect the battle" as opposed to playing the decisive role USAF had planned.[386] However, the report's authors proceeded to indicate that these effects would be so negligible that air attacks would basically be ignored when determining force ratios. The report then went on to highlight the modernization of Warsaw Pact forces, including air defense units, and how this negatively impacted NATO's ability to mass firepower of all kinds against Warsaw Pact forces.[387] In professional journals, senior RAF officers and USAF field grades both questioned whether NATO's airpower would be rendered ineffective by a combination of the Warsaw Pact's improved air defenses and Europe's inclement weather.[388] Given that deterrence relied on convincing allies, domestic decision makers, and opponents alike that the United States Air Force could project power, the situation was less than optimal as the United States began turning away from détente.

Transition to the Reagan Administration

Ronald Reagan's victory in the 1980 election signaled a change in the United States' Cold War strategy. Although not the revolutionary paradigm shift often claimed by Reagan's admirers, some Cold War historians, and members of his administration, President Reagan still caused a major change in the United States' strategic guidance. Presidents Nixon, Ford, and Carter had largely decided to accept the Soviet Union as a necessary adversary and spent the majority of their time in office avoiding overt confrontation. President Reagan, on the other hand, ran on the platform of confronting the U.S.S.R. politically, diplomatically, economically and, militarily. Borrowing heavily from some aspects of President Eisenhower's strategic outlook, President Reagan believed that America's path to success lay in invigorating the economy in order to finance increased military strength. Only when relative strategic and conventional parity had been achieved would the United States be able to compel the Soviet Union to step back from the perceived bellicosity of the Brezhnev Doctrine. A less aggressive Soviet Union could then be engaged diplomatically and politically on issues such as human rights, arms agreements, and establishment of a mutually palatable world order.[389]

Strength at All Levels of Conflict

Strategically, the Reagan administration almost immediately began to reverse what they perceived as the Carter administration's miscues. The Reagan administration sought to revive the M-X missile and the B-1 bomber as counters to perceived Soviet nuclear superiority. Simultaneously, the administration asked Congress for increased funding for the *Trident* missile system and further development of the land attack version of the *Tomahawk* cruise missile. Finally, Reagan began to publicly discuss establishing an anti-ballistic missile defense system known as the Strategic Defense Initiative, or SDI.[390]

The sum effect of these strategic initiatives,

contrary to the rhetoric of the time, was to greatly decrease the chances of a thermonuclear exchange. As with the Soviet development of a credible ICBM force, the United States' increased capabilities created a quandary for the U.S.S.R.'s strategic planners. It is arguable whether the U.S.S.R. *ever* possessed the capability to deliver a "first strike" that would destroy the United States' ICBM and bomber capabilities. Thankfully the hypothesis that the Strategic Rocket Forces could do so, held to various degrees by the Nixon, Ford, and Carter administrations, was never put to the test. However, in modernizing SAC and the USN's ballistic missile submarine fleet, publicly renouncing the SALT treaties, and raising the specter of SDI, the Reagan administration successfully negated many of the perceived advances the U.S.S.R. had made from 1972 through 1979. In addition, it served notice to the Soviet leadership that their already strained economy would face additional challenges if they wished to maintain the current strategic balance.[391]

The Reagan Administration and NATO

This strategic impasse affected the development of USAF conventional preparations in general and SEAD doctrine in particular. First and foremost, it increased both the United States and NATO European nations' focus on conventional warfare. The Carter administration's efforts in its last two years had begun an era of increased defensive cooperation. With the outcome of elections in Great Britain (1979), France (1981), and West Germany (1982), the Reagan administration was able to build on this foundation by successfully encouraging its chief European allies to increase spending on conventional arms. In addition, the Reagan administration coordinated with its NATO allies to increase emphasis on deployment exercises, command post exercises, and maneuvers beginning in 1982 and continuing through 1986.[392]

Secretary of Defense Weinberger's Guidance

The intent of these various operations was to demonstrate American resolve and increased capability. The primary architect behind redesigning the United States' conventional forces so that these capabilities seemed credible was Defense Secretary Caspar Weinberger. Secretary Weinberger felt that a strengthened defense was "the most important of [Reagan's] foreign policy" and conducted his conventional modernization plans accordingly.[393] To Weinberger, the United States had already established a qualitative edge in technology due to the weapon systems designed after the Yom Kippur and Vietnam Wars. The problem with the Carter administration, at least from Weinberger's point of view, was that these systems had not been purchased in sufficient *quantity*. Nor had the military in general, and the Air Force in particular, been given enough money to adequately train on their new systems. Although the Air Force's new systems (e.g., the *Eagle*, *Falcon*, *Sentry*, etc.) all had, at the time of purchase, the ability to be modified and made even more capable, the Carter administration had consistently refused to request funds for upgrades from Congress.[394]

Weinberger's plan to reverse these short-comings was simple. First, one of President Reagan's first acts was to ask Congress for more funding for FY 81 and FY 82. Second, Weinberger loosened the restrictions on the transfer of military technology among the United States, Great Britain, France, and West Germany. Finally, although a significant portion of this increased funding would be put towards strategic weapons, Weinberger directed that the majority of the Air Force's increased budget be devoted to weapons and training that would support conventional operations.[395]

General Creech and Modernizing TAC

The officer who set in motion most of this modernization was General Dixon's successor at TAC, General Wilbur L. Creech. A former fighter pilot, General Creech had been selected as TAC's commander after serving time as a

EAGLES, RAVENS, AND OTHER BIRDS OF PREY | 221

flag officer in USAFE. Creech had also overseen the Air Force's development of command and control systems, electronic warfare, and long-range communications as the head of Systems Command. During his time there, Creech had initiated a procedure through which the Air Force set a cost cap for a given system, asked Congress for that amount of money, then ensured that the program came underneath that budget. First used during the E-3 *Sentry*'s acquisition process, this methodology would serve Creech in good stead as head of TAC.[396]

Although General Creech and General Dixon shared much the same mindset about the Warsaw Pact's conventional threat, the two men differed on what aspect of it held primacy. General Dixon's experiences and analysis had caused him to fear the WP-IADS's capabilities with regard to the SAM and MiGs ability to destroy aircraft or force them to jettison their ordnance. General Creech's own time in USAFE and other staff positions led him to be concerned more with the Warsaw Pact's advantages in electronic warfare. Specifically, Creech firmly believed that the USAF and its NATO counterparts were woefully unprepared to deal with Soviet jamming of radars and communications equipment. In Creech's mind, the finest weapons in the world were going to be useless if they could not communicate during a conventional conflict. After spending the first two years of his tenure focused on decreasing TAC's number of crashes without compromising realism, by 1981 Creech had decided to make marked changes in the way tactical fighters prepared to defeat an IADS.[397]

Electronic Warfare

Creech's initial steps in convincing the service of the need to pay attention to EW had been to ensure its inclusion in AFM 1-1.[398] The next step was to provide hard evidence of the threat's seriousness to the fighter community. This was done by creating an exercise called "Green Flag" in 1981. Occurring concurrently with Red Flag, Green Flag was based on the employment of jammers against the participating USAF and allied aircraft's radios. This was a particularly brutal introduction to the effects of electronic warfare, as "[s]eventy-two percent of the [training unit] sorties were ineffective." The Air Force had not faced effective EW over Vietnam and thus simply assumed that they would always be able to communicate over their radio networks. The initial Green Flag, followed by subsequent iterations, proved just how dangerous this assumption was.[399]

Defensively, this caused the Air Force to "get religion," especially as Creech directed that Green Flags continue to be conducted biannually with designated Red Flag exercises. [400] This also caused SAC to support the development of anti-jamming radios, as continued exercises demonstrated that

EAGLES, RAVENS, AND OTHER BIRDS OF PREY | 223

the heavy bomber fleet's tactical communications were also vulnerable. After the Navy had a strike package crippled during a joint exercise, the USN also lent their support to obtaining congressional authorization to acquire anti-jam radios as well. Both services began fielding the new radios by 1986, with immediate improvement being seen in subsequent Green Flags.[401]

The EF-111 Raven and EC-130 Compass Call

Offensively, the demonstration of EW's effectiveness also led the Air Force to increase production of the EF-111 Raven as well as fund the development of the EC-130 Compass Call. The former aircraft, as suggested by General Momyer, was intended to accompany a strike package into hostile territory. Unlike General Momyer's original vision though, the EF-111 was not an additional Wild Weasel aircraft. Although the Raven could be armed with Shrike and, later, AGM-88 HARM missiles, this was not an optimal use of the airframe due to its poor maneuverability and limited numbers. Instead, the EF-111 was best suited for penetrating the initial band of Warsaw Pact defenses with a strike group, then loitering at a distance from a target to avoid engagement from short-range SAMs and AAA batteries. When used in this manner, the EF-111 could limit targeting radars' effectiveness during the final stages of weapons delivery, then rejoin the strike group as it egressed out of hostile territory.[402]

EF-111 Aardvark

**(Courtesy Mark Stephens via Dreamstime.com—
Taken at USAF Museum at Wright-Patterson AFB)**

Like the Vietnam-era EB-66 *Destroyers*, the EC-130 *Compass Call* lacked the performance to penetrate hostile territory. However, due to it being based on the Air Force's C-130 *Hercules* cargo aircraft, the *Compass Call* traded its relatively slow speed for a large cargo bay, carrying capacity, and loiter time. These abilities meant it could perform several critical SEAD functions simultaneously. First, in acting as a "barrier jammer," the EC-130 could prevent the Warsaw Pact's radars from acquiring the E-3 *Sentry* and tanker aircraft at long range. Offensively, the *Compass Call*s antennae array allowed it to triangulate fire control radars, thus providing their location for later targeting by *Wild Weasel* hunter-killer flights. Finally, due to the EC-130 having more room for jammers than the EF-111, the *Compass Call* could perform these missions while also interfering with Warsaw Pact communications networks. This helped negate the interceptor portion of the triad by preventing communication between interceptors and ground control stations or command nodes who were trying to prevent SAM batteries from committing fratricide against interceptors.[403]

When first introduced, these electronic warfare capabilities were unfamiliar to TAC. Creech firmly believed that the electronic warfare systems, although they were not as directly destructive as ordnance delivered by *Wild Weasels* or as immediately measurable as a kill made by a F-15 or F-16, would greatly reduce the WP-IADS's effectiveness if properly planned and employed. To deal with the former, General Creech increased the role of EW during Blue Flag command post exercises. To solve the tactical issue, Creech not only increased the number of Green Flags, but also required EF-111 participation in Red Flag exercises. Even if the *Ravens* were not always allowed to use their full EW capabilities due to U.S. government regulations, planning geographical spacing, navigational timing, and actually flying with the *Ravens* in formation served to help develop strike group tactics and procedures. In turn, these procedures were disseminated through the Fighter Weapons School's professional publication and bulletins, then formally codified into doctrine by TAC. [404]

Tactics, Ordnance, and Airframes,

Electronic warfare procedures were just one facet of SEAD training that General Creech sought to adjust. General Creech made several other changes based on his own interpretation of how future conflicts would unfold. In a sharp departure from his predecessor, General Creech directed that TAC increase its percentage of night sorties by up to 70 percent depending on the weapons platform. This directive seemed counterintuitive given Creech's increased insistence on aircraft safety and contemporary Air Force views that night flying was inherently dangerous. From the Air Force's continued analysis of the Yom Kippur War, NATO assessments of Warsaw Pact weapons systems, crew after action reviews of Red Flag rotations, and his own operational experience, Creech believed the concealment of darkness would save far more aircraft from destruction in the opening weeks of a conflict than would be lost over several years of training accidents. Red Flag increased the number of night sorties flown and also diversified the type of aircraft employed through 1986. Once solely the purview of F-111s, a few select F-4 squadrons, and visiting RAF all-weather aircraft, nighttime missions at Red Flag by TAC fighters became a regular occurrence by 1984. TAC Manual 51-50, the aircrew qualification "bible," was also updated to increase the number of nighttime crew, flight, and squadron hours required for TFWs to be considered combat ready. Whether the next conflict would come in Europe or elsewhere, TAC (and by extension, USAFE and PACAF) planned to conduct 24-hour operations.[405]

In addition to using night's cloak to reduce the effectiveness of Warsaw Pact anti-aircraft artillery, General Creech was a vocal advocate of lowering vulnerabilities through "stand off," i.e., longer range, accuracy, and the ability to "fire and forget." To Creech, the use of *Paveway* weapons in Vietnam had been merely the first step in a precision guided munitions revolution. As evidenced by the efforts required to protect *Pave Knife* F-4s, laser-guided weapons required a certain set of conditions to be effective. Some of this could be mitigated through better mountings for the designation pod (e.g., the F-111F's carriage of *Pave Knife* in the bomb bay) or *Pave Penny* system that allowed for the reception from ground forces' laser designators. However, even with these advances, battlefield smoke, dust, or other obscurants still made laser guidance a relative dead end.[406]

The Air Force's System Command had spent most of the 1970s working on alternative methods for weapons' guidance. Military technicians were aided by developments in computer technology and modern imaging in the private sector, which in turn allowed for the miniaturization of infrared imaging equipment. This led to what the military designated as Forward Looking

Infrared (FLIR) sensors. Creech believed that placing these sensors on airframes, either inside the aircraft or in external pods, would allow even "day fighters" (e.g., the F–16) to conduct night operations. Furthermore, Creech believed that developing a new strike aircraft with this capability and laser designation was a critical task for Air Force Systems Command. As head of TAC, Creech was a strenuous advocate for both the LANTIRN (as the proposed FLIR pods were known) and a new strike aircraft (based on either the F–16 or F–15) in order to allow USAF strike packages to be as effective at night and in bad weather as they currently were in daylight.[407]

F–117 Nighthawk

Complementing this change to constant operations was an improvement to TAC's basic airframes. While the proposed *Strike Eagle* would only be in the technology development phase by 1986, in 1983 the Air Force began to field the Lockheed F–117 *Nighthawk*, the famous "Stealth Fighter." Capitalizing on decades of research, the F–117 employed special materials and angular construction to deflect hostile radar signals away from their transmitters. In this manner, the aircraft's radar cross section was similar to that of a large bird and was thus ignored by most fire control or tracking computers. In order to achieve this capability, the *Nighthawk*'s designers were constrained in the choices of power plant, ordnance, and fuselage shape. With limited top speed and maneuverability, the F-117 was not a fighter despite its designation. However, in darkness, it was nearly invisible to most contemporary Warsaw Pact radars until it was conducting weapons delivery.[408]

F117 *Nighthawks* (**Author's Collection**)

TAC's planners, in conjunction with USAFE's staff, prepared a list of targets that the F-117 would be expected to strike in the opening hours of a European conventional conflict. Chief among these were the known WP-IADS's command posts and long-range radars located in East Germany. Although concerns for secrecy precluded the USAF from deploying the fighter to Europe, *Nighthawks* were regularly tested against captured Soviet and Western radars over

Tenopah from 1983 into1986. For individuals aware of the project, the F-117 was considered a powerful capability that would allow USAFE and NATO to rapidly degrade the WP-IADS's ability to synchronize its SAMs and interceptors.[409]

In addition to developing the *Nighthawk*, the Air Force also updated the F-111F with improved avionics, an upgraded bombing computer, and increased guided munitions capabilities. These were expected to make the *Aardvark* more lethal against WP-IADS command nodes as well and to facilitate the destruction of fixed SAM sites. To help reduce the threat from enemy interceptors, the Air Force also provided the entire F-111 fleet with the ability to deliver the *Durandal* anti-runway bomb beginning in 1983. Under General Creech, TAC doctrine began to state expressly that one of the F-111's primary missions in the initial stages of war would be counter-airfield strikes, followed closely by attacks on other IADS critical points. Rather than an afterthought supplementing the main aerial effort attacking advancing Warsaw Pact forces, General Creech intended the F-111 to help set the conditions for NATO air superiority. [410]

New Eagles

To improve their ability to defeat airborne Warsaw Pact fighters, USAF fighter wings began to replace their initial F-15As with improved "C" models in 1979. The C models, despite being almost cosmetically identical, were vastly improved by numerous internal modifications. The most important of these was a new radar coupled with a digital fire control unit that allowed the F-15C to acquire, track, and engage a target faster than the original *Eagle*. In addition, the new computer and radar allowed for the rapid sorting of targets from ground clutter, allowing the *Eagle* to engage targets at low-altitude while still maintaining an altitude advantage. Finally, the Air Force undertook a maintenance modernization program that increased both the A and C-model *Eagles'* operational readiness rate. [411]

Missile Development

Complementing the Air Force's improvement to the F-15s airframe were the steps the USAF took to modernize its missiles. As a result of the Red Baron study, General Dixon had made improvement of missiles a priority for TAC. Similarly motivated to increase the *Sparrow*'s lethality, the Navy also aided in this developmental process by focusing on improving the missile's rocket motor. As a result, both services began to field the AIM-7F variant in 1976. With improved electronics, a long-range motor, and larger warhead in 1976, the AIM-7F was a marked improvement over the Vietnam-era E-model *Sparrow*. Almost as important as the missile's internal modifications, the Air Force also developed a maintenance regime that

232 | JAMES L. YOUNG JR.

increased the weapon's reliability. [412]

Despite these advances and the weapon's adaptation by NATO and the IAF, testing and Israeli combat experience made it readily apparent that further improvements were necessary. Most glaringly, the AIM-7F remained highly susceptible to electronic countermeasures and ground clutter. After briefly considering purchasing British (*Sky Flash*) or Italian (*Aspide*) variants, USAF System Command instead began to develop an improved AIM-7F. The improved variant would include an even more powerful rocket motor and further incorporation of solid-state electronics. This missile was designated the AIM-7M *Sparrow*, with the testing phase including extensive engagements against targets protected by captured Soviet jammers and maneuvering drones operating at low altitude. The actual production model incorporated most of the *Aspide* and *Sky Flash*'s improvements while increasing range to over fifty miles. Adopted in 1982, the AIM-7M remained the definitive version of the AIM-7 for the remainder of the Cold War.[413]

For short-range engagements, the Air Force continued to rely upon the AIM-9 *Sidewinder*. The AIM-9J variant used during Operation Linebacker had provided only modest improvement over the *Sidewinder*s used during Operation Rolling Thunder, thus leading to brief attempts to replace the entire missile. These efforts had failed due to cost overruns and budget cuts, so the Air Force was forced to try other avenues of improvement. These resulted in the AIM-9L, or "Lima" being fielded in 1977. Like the AIM-7M *Sparrows*, the AIM-9L took advantage of advances in solid state electronics, computer modeling, and tracker technology to produce the first heat-seeking missile capable of "all-aspect" engagements.[414] This model was succeeded by the AIM-9M, or "Mike" variant in early 1982, with the major improvements being higher resistance to flare decoys, higher speed, and better control surfaces. As with the *Sparrow*, both of the new *Sidewinders* were extensively tested against actively maneuvering drones in realistic conditions. With a maximum range of just over ten miles and a top speed that was a full third faster than the AIM-9E/J, the AIM-9L/M suddenly provided both *Eagle* and *Falcon* pilots with much greater capability in ACM.[415]

Determining how to best employ these new capabilities was the purview of both the Fighter Weapons School and Red Flag. The former began to propagate new tactics, techniques, and procedures for the F-15 community to use against Warsaw Pact MiGs. The initial catalyst for many of these changes was the Air Force and CIA's acquisition of MiG-21, MiG-23, and MiG-25 airframes from both defectors and former Soviet allies. As these aircraft were tested against F-15s and F-16s, USAF intelligence officers began to realize they had vastly overestimated the *Flogger*'s and *Foxbat*'s capabilities. By 1982, this new information led the *Eagle* and *Falcon* communities to discuss ways to seize the advantage against Warsaw Pact fighters, especially near or just beyond the FEBA. For the *Falcon* community, the lack of a radar-guided missile limited just how many changes they could make. *Eagle* pilots, on the other hand, began to discuss conducting repeated "slashing" attacks as a method to rapidly attrit Warsaw Pact interceptors.[416]

Slashing attacks had their genesis during World War II when they were employed by larger, heavier fighters against their lighter opponents. The tactic's name derived from how friendly aircraft, usually with an altitude and speed advantage, "slashed" through a hostile formation without stopping to conduct ACM. This had fallen out of favor with the USAF due to the lack of ACM training, perceived lethality of an IADS's multiple threats, and the Century Fighters' poor maneuverability. As the *Eagle* continued into service with the USAF and IAF, American and Israeli pilots began to grow more confident in the large fighter's agility in both the horizontal and vertical planes. At the squadron level, mid-level officers increasingly thought about how to use these capabilities against the more rigid and staid Warsaw Pact interception tactics. During exercises against Aggressor squadrons, *Eagle* pilots began to realize that their ability to acquire the smaller F-5Es and T-38s beyond visual range allowed them to "perch" above their opponents. When engaged by simulated long-range missile fire, the Aggressor aircraft conducted defensive maneuvers to attempt to break the *Eagles*' radar lock-ons, thus expending energy and gradually losing the ability to maneuver. At this point, if the first flight or section of *Eagles* continued to close with the Aggressors and fire head-on shots with *Sidewinders*, the Aggressors would have to conduct further maneuvers to dodge these additional shots or be ruled "dead" by Red Flag's umpires. The friendly *Eagles*, on the other hand, could continue to pass through at high speed and retain separation from the lighter Aggressors while subsequent flights or sections repeated the process. If the Aggressors attempted to engage the second group of *Eagles*, the first group could then return at high speed from an advantageous angle to engage with their remaining heat-seeking AIM-9Ls.[417]

Initial exercises that employed these tactics revealed that they could be quite successful against smaller opponents lacking all-aspect missiles. However, detractors of these changes to technique questioned the veracity of the *Eagles*'s success in the Red Flag environment and applicability to a real world scenario. The Red Flag training environment relied heavily on ground-based computers to accurately "score" success or failure for both sides. Although the system required both "Red" and "Blue" fighters to carry sensor pods that helped replicate both NATO and Warsaw Pact weapons' effects, it was not the real thing. Second, slashing attacks relied heavily on *Wild Weasels*, electronic jamming, and exemplary C2. Contemporary analysts warned

236 | JAMES L. YOUNG JR.

that if Warsaw Pact SAM systems did not prove as susceptible to EF-111s, EC-130s, or F-4Gs in a wartime environment, even the F-15C's advanced onboard jammers would not prevent subsequent heavy losses. Without either an effective ground control radar network (e.g., NATO's SAGE system) or an AWACS aircraft, the *Eagles* were likely to be surprised by additional interceptors in the middle of their attacks. In exercises after exercise, *Eagles* operating without this support in Red Flag were regularly ambushed by a second Aggressor flight. This led to a subsequent dogfight in which the second group of *Eagles* was unable to employ their *Sparrows*, and the Aggressors were subsequently able to inflict heavy losses either on the escort or strike group.[418]

To the Valley: SEAD Combat Operations, 1981–1982

Ironically, it was not the USAF that proved their new weapons' lethality. The first use of the AIM-9L was by the USN during the August 19th, 1981, Gulf of Sidra Incident. This engagement occurred when two F-14s mounting a combat air patrol were attacked by a pair of Libyan Su-22s. After the Libyan section leader fired an *Atoll* missile from the F-14s' front-aspect, the USN fighters turned the tables and shot down both Su-22s within two minutes. Despite this outcome, the engagement was not considered much of a validation of the AIM-9Ls capabilities because the Libyans were markedly inferior to the USN in both training and capability.[419]

The Falklands War

The new *Sidewinder*'s first full combat test occurred less than eight months later. On April 2nd, 1982, Argentina invaded the Falkland Islands. Despite extensive economic and military ties with the South American nation, neither the United States nor the United Kingdom had any indication of the upcoming operation. Having long claimed the distant, barren islands as Argentinian territory, Argentina's ruling military junta had conducted the operation in order to quell domestic unrest by providing a unifying foreign enemy. In response, the United Kingdom dispatched a naval task force to conduct an amphibious assault to regain their distant possession. Inexplicably for two nations that shared several strong military and economic ties, the dispute quickly devolved into a short, intense shooting conflict.[420]

The Argentinian forces held tremendous geographical advantages in the conflict's initial stages. The United Kingdom's nearest unoccupied possession to the Falklands was Ascension Island. This was far beyond the range of tactical fighters, so the RAF were unable to employ either its new *Tornado* strike aircraft or its remaining F-4 *Phantoms*. For its part, the

238 | JAMES L. YOUNG JR.

Royal Navy no longer had any full-sized carriers like the USN's. Instead, the RN had two smaller carriers, the *Hermes* and *Illustrious*, which could carry a maximum of 26 and 10 *Harrier* jet fighters respectively. Of these 36 fighters, roughly half were Fleet Air Arm (FAA) *Sea Harriers* that were equipped with air-to-air radars with pilots trained in aerial combat. The remaining aircraft were RAF *Harriers* that were optimized for ground attack missions. Although additional *Sea Harriers* were deployed to make up for losses, the British never had more than twenty fighters available for air combat. [421]

Facing the British expedition were the combined forces of the Argentine Air Force (AAF) and Argentine Naval Aviation (ANA). These consisted of roughly 50 A-4 *Skyhawk* attack aircraft, approximately 16 Dassault *Mirage* aircraft, an additional 30 Israeli Air Industries *Dagger* strike fighters, and 5 *Super Entendard* anti-shipping fighters armed with the *Exocet* missile. Counteracting their clear numerical advantage was the fact that all Argentinean strikes required tanker support to cross the open ocean from the mainland to the Falkland Islands. In addition, a lack of maritime reconnaissance aircraft made detecting the British fleet difficult until the Royal Navy committed to landing in San Carlos Bay on May 22nd. However, even with these modifying factors, on paper it appeared to contemporary analysts that the Argentinians would shortly gain air superiority and, subsequently, force the Royal Navy to withdraw. The *Daggers* and

Mirage IIIs were faster than the British *Harrier* and *Sea Harrier*, with the Argentinean aircraft also capable of carrying air-to-air missiles. Furthermore, given their estimation of British capabilities and ability to track FAA patrols, the Argentinians believed their *Skyhawks* were fast enough to penetrate San Carlos Water, drop their bombs, then escape before the *Sea Harriers* could react.[422]

As the subsequent conflict proved, both the contemporary analysts and Argentinians gravely miscalculated both the Fleet Air Arm's capabilities and the lethality of the Royal Navy's air defenses. The British victory's connection to USAF SEAD doctrine stemmed from two of the primary factors in the United Kingdom's success. First, the FAA's wresting of the initiative from the Argentinean Air Force followed by their victories of attacking Argentinean aircraft proved the value of dissimilar ACM training. Many of the British *Sea Harrier* pilots had either attended Red Flag exercises as part of United Kingdom's exchange program or participated in dissimilar ACM exercises against USN, USAF, or RAF interceptors. Therefore, when facing Argentinean *Mirages* on 1 May, the FAA were aware of what steps to take against larger, faster fighters. In contrast, the Argentinean fighters had little understanding of how to engage the smaller, nimbler *Harriers*. Despite being outnumbered, the *Sea Harriers* destroyed two *Mirages* in such one-sided fashion that the AAF refused to conduct fighter sweeps for the remainder of the conflict.[423]

In addition to being better trained, British pilots were better equipped. The Falklands Conflict served as an opportunity for the first use of the new *Sidewinders*, as the United States rushed 200 of the new AIM-9Ls to the United Kingdom in the conflict's first days. In contrast, AAF aircraft were equipped with either the Israeli *Shafrir* or AIM-9B *Sidewinder*s that needed to be launched from almost directly astern. The contrast in performance was stark, as the Argentinians failed to score a single hit while the *Sea Harrier* pilots achieved over an 80 percent success rate.[424] So critical was the AIM-9L to British efforts that both Rear Admiral Sandy Woodward, the British expedition's commander, and Prime Minister Margaret Thatcher would later credit the *Sidewinder* as being the most important weapon in the British arsenal. American missiles, it seemed, were as lethal as the USAF claimed.[425]

In addition to affirming the value of regular ACM training and advances in missile technology, the Falklands War also reaffirmed the lethality of modern air defenses. Both the British and Argentinian forces suffered significant losses from radar-guided gunfire and missiles. For the Argentinians, the rapidity with which the British established *Rapier* missiles and anti-air-craft artillery to support their naval air defense came as an unpleasant shock. For the FAA / RAF attempting to conduct air support operations, the Argentinians' obsolescent early warning and fire control radars still managed to deny *Harriers* and *Sea Harriers* the ability to freely conduct close air support operations. Both the AAF and RAF / FAA fighters had to make extensive use of terrain masking, chaff, flares, and electronic countermeasures to minimize their losses. For the British, it was a particularly sobering lesson given the advances the RAF believed it had made since the end of Vietnam. It would take a conflict several thousand miles away to conclusively demonstrate just how far the pendulum had swung back in favor of a well-prepared attacking force.[426]

The Bekaa Valley

Although the USAF had yet to employ their new fighters in combat, the IAF had already demonstrated the F-15s' and F-16s' capabilities on several occasions. The *Eagle* had scored its first air-to-air kill against the Syrian Air Force in June 1979, while the *Falcon* destroyed a Syrian helicopter in April 1981. This was followed by Operation Opera, the IAF's long range raid against the Iraqi nuclear reactor at Osirak on June 7th, 1981. By 1982, IAF F-15s and F-16s had destroyed over 20 Syrian MiGs in skirmishes over northern Israel, southern Lebanon, and western Syria. Throughout all of these engagements, the Israelis had escaped without loss due to a combination of planning and their opponents' shortcomings. Although the *Eagle* and *Falcon* were found to be clearly superior to the IAF's

F-4s, the feeling within the IDF was that the newer fighters had yet to fully demonstrate their potential.[427]

The lack of opportunity was mainly due to strenuous diplomatic efforts. President Carter's push for peace between Egypt and Israel had culminated in a peace treaty between those two nations in 1979. The subsequent return of the Sinai to Egypt and the movement of Egypt into the United States' sphere of influence largely eliminated the threat of another war between Israel and Egypt. In contrast, Israel's northern border had become even more dangerous due to Lebanon's implosion into a multi-sided civil war in 1975. Although Syrian intervention had briefly reduced the level of violence, by 1979 Lebanon was incapable of enforcing its own sovereignty. This lack of central authority allowed the Palestinian Liberation Organization (PLO) to establish an enclave in southern Lebanon. The PLO then proceeded to use this enclave to strike at northern Israeli settlements and military forces. To counter this, Israel allied itself with Lebanese Christian militias which launched regular attacks against the PLO. In addition to military aid and intelligence, the IAF began to provide increasing amounts of air support to the militia in their clashes. In response, the Syrian Army deployed SAM batteries to southern Lebanon in early 1981. Only intervention by the United States and United Nations, to include direct pressure from the Reagan administration on Israeli Prime Minister Menachem Begin, prevented Israel from immediately launching a ground offensive in response to this action.[428]

Despite this temporary truce, it was quite apparent to external observers that the slightest provocation would lead to an Israeli attack north into Lebanon. Syria's government acted to curtail the PLO's attacks even as the Syrian Army began to reinforce with additional SAM batteries. Having extended their ground defenses into Lebanon, the Syrians began to practice regular aerial interception missions over that country's southern portion. In order to prevent further escalation, these were controlled from previously established IADS command stations in western Syria. Having established an air defense network, the Syrians then increased their ground forces in anticipation of an Israeli attack. Provided the IAF remained neutralized, the Syrian Army was confident a combination of their upgraded equipment, Lebanon's dense terrain, and the IADS neutralization of the IAF would allow them to inflict unacceptable casualties on the IDF's ground forces.[429]

Israeli Preparations

For their part, the Israeli Air Force had spent the nine years after the Yom Kippur War preparing to defeat the Syrian IADS. The Israeli Air Force had conducted dozens of studies on what had gone wrong during the Yom Kippur War and taken measures to prevent being shocked again. This included sending pilots to participate in USAF Red Flags as well as establishing their own training facilities in the Negev Desert. The infrastructure at these facilities included the ability to replicate several types of SAM emplacements and signatures, from the venerable SA-2 through the more modern SA-6. Israeli squadrons repeatedly rehearsed attack runs with live ordnance on these positions, with the geographical arrangements modified as Syrian SAM batteries shifted in Lebanon between June 1981 and June 1982. Although the test sites were not perfect replicas of southern Lebanon, the relative distance and bearings between SAM sites was maintained. This, in turn, allowed IDF squadrons to practice the ingress and egress routes they intended to take when striking the SAM locations as well as deconflict timing between separate squadrons. Electronic and photographic reconnaissance missions were flown using both manned and unmanned aircraft in order to establish a Syrian order of battle. Finally, the IDF and Israeli Army began holding planning meetings in order to coordinate mutually supportive artillery and SEAD strikes.[430]

Doctrinally and materially, the IAF had decided to split the difference between General Momyer's intention to have a *Wild Weasel/Iron Hand* flight per squadron and the contemporary USAF's practice of maintaining specialized SEAD units. Although the IAF did not invest in a specific airframe such as the F-4G, the Israelis modified several of their *Phantoms*, *Eagles*, and *Falcons* with the capability to use the *StARM* and *Shrike*. Israeli ordnance officers modified the anti-radiation missiles with pyrotechnics that would aid visual acquisition of the targeted radar and SAM site. This simple change facilitated follow-on attacks with *Maverick*s, rockets, high-drag bombs, or cluster munitions by other tactical fighters. The IDF also conducted weapons tests on captured SA-3s and SA-6s to determine the most effective ordnance load for aircraft striking at Syrian SAM sites.[431]

Complementing the ground attack plan were similar preparations for dealing with the Syrian Air Force. The IAF modified several Boeing 707s with electronic warfare equipment in order to blind the MiGs' radars and sever communications with ground-based controllers. F-15 and F-16 squadrons rehearsed interception techniques that would exacerbate both MiGs' vulnerabilities while maximizing the *Eagle* and *Falcon*'s advantages. Finally, E-2 *Hawkeye* AWACS crews orbiting over northern Israel began to regularly track and time Syrian MiGs' flight times, courses, and patrol habits. By June 1982, the IAF's fighter pilots were more confident of their ability to shoot down their opposite numbers than any time since 1967. All that remained, in their minds, was the order to execute their plan.[432]

Operation Mole Cricket

After several provocations, the IAF received the order on June 9th, 1982 shortly after the Israeli Army initiated Operation Peace for Galilee, the invasion of Lebanon. The Israeli Air Force's part of the offensive, dubbed Operation Mole Cricket, began with the penetration of Lebanese airspace by dozens of unmanned aircraft. As the IDF had predicted, these contacts caused the Syrian IADS's personnel to begin radiating both their long-range tracking and SAM acquisition radars. The IAF and Israeli Army immediately began striking these while the IAF's 707s initiated jamming of both the communications networks and acquisition frequencies. Syrian MiGs, scrambling as per their doctrine, found themselves airborne in their designated patrol areas unable to communicate with their ground controllers even as the IADS's SAM batteries were being destroyed beneath them.[433]

With the SAMs neutralized, the IAF's *Eagles* and *Falcons* struck. Vectored into initial position by Israeli E-2s, the IAF often used the *Eagles'* superior radars to control *Falcon* flights making the initial interception. If the Syrians survived the F-16s initial passes, the *Eagles* then closed to complete the MiGs' destruction. On June 10th, when the F-16s were often tasked to conduct ground attack in support of advancing Israeli Army units, the *Eagles* validated the proposed slashing tactics by destroying dozens of Syrian aircraft themselves. Within 48 hours, the Israelis had destroyed over eighty MiGs while only losing, at most, three fighters (a pair of *Phantoms* and an Israeli *Kfir*) to Syrian interceptors.[434] By June 11th, the Syrian Air Force had ceded control of Lebanese airspace to the IAF. With the exception of the Syrian Army units' organic, optical-ly-aimed weapons, Syrian forces' ability to defend themselves against IAF attacks had been destroyed. [435]

Effect of the Falklands and Bekaa Valley on USAF SEAD Doctrine

The one-sided nature of the Syrian IADS' destruction came as a shock to most military observers. The *Eagle* and *Falcon* had been considered superior to the *Flogger* since inception, while the MiG-21's obsolescence had been long acknowledged in aviation circles. However, previous analysis of the F-15 and F-16's abilities with regard to their opposite numbers had assumed that pilots flying the MiGs would at least have some warning that they were being tracked by hostile fighters. According to both Syrian and Israeli reports, it appeared many of the MiG pilots had been shot down before they were even aware there was danger. With respect to the ground based SAMs and AAA, the Israelis had shown little difficulty in jamming even the SA-6 or ZSU-23-4's radars. Although a large measure of this had been accomplished by the IAF's modernized Boeing 707s, the self-protection jammers carried by Israeli fighters had also allowed them to operate more freely. Publicly, the Soviet military was quick to point out that a large part of the Syrians' defeat was due to the Syrian Air Force's lack of air combat training, poor equipment maintenance, and predictable tactics. As for the SAM sites, the Soviets also felt the Syrian Army's failure to dig proper emplacements, displace to different locations, or execute any degree of deception contributed to their heavy losses.[436]

Privately, however, the Soviet Union's military leadership was quite concerned over the Syrian Air Force's performance. The Soviet Air Force began to institute training reforms across Frontal Aviation, with more stringent attention paid to ensuring pilots increased their hours of ACM. Although full independence was anathema to Frontal Aviation doctrine, increased emphasis was placed on exercises that ensured pilots could complete limited tasks in the absence of GCI guidance. The development and production of the MiG-29 *Fulcrum* and Su-27 *Flanker* were also expedited, while increased funding was allotted to acquire the next generation of SAMs and air-to-air missiles. The Soviet military had been provided a preview of new USAF capabilities at great cost to one of its client states. Chastened at the results, Soviet leaders began to seriously focus on closing the revealed qualitative gap.[437]

The reaction to the Israeli victory in the USAF and NATO was unsurprisingly positive. There had been concerns in the *Eagle* and *Falcon* professional communities that USAF training had given far too much credit to Third World capabilities in Vietnam's aftermath. It was undeniable that the Aggressor program had increased the ability of individual pilots and flights to perform ACM. Prior to the Bekaa Valley, however, the fighter community had possessed a growing sense that the Aggressor program was creating an unnecessary sense of caution given the *Eagle* and *Falcon*'s superiority to the *Fishbed* and *Flogger*. The decisiveness of the IAF's victory indicated that both fighters were vastly advanced compared to both MiGs. This advantage was exacerbated when pilot training was taken into account. USAF's fighter community noted that the IAF's attention to proper command and control, AEW, and electronic warfare support had played a critical role in the ultimate outcome. However, combined with the AIM-9L's performance in the Falklands, mid-1980s' USAF fighter pilots began to have great faith that their training and equipment would more than counter Warsaw Pact numbers.[438]

For the Wild Weasel community, the Israeli methodology further spurred an ongoing debate on tactics. First, the use of drones to decoy the Syrian radars into revealing themselves was noted with great interest. Second, defense suppression pilots noted that the Israelis had ingressed to attack the SAMs at medium altitude, with a descent into AAA range being required only at the final stages of attacking a SAM battery. Finally, in several instances the IAF had used hunter-killer teams that partnered *Phantoms* with *Falcons*, *Skyhawks*, or *Kfir* attack aircraft. Much as the Vietnam-era F-105s had used *Phantoms* to complete the physical destruction of a SAM site, the Israelis had relied on *Falcons* armed with *Maverick*s, cluster bombs, and high explosive ordnance to perform the same function. This fostered the thought in USAFE that perhaps the F-16 was better suited to be a "killer" aircraft than originally thought. In response, the F-4Gs of the 52nd TFW at Spangdahlem increased the number of mutual training exercises with nearby F-16 squadrons in this role.[439] As with the Yom Kippur War, the Israeli plans, tactics, and doctrine sparked changes that would have long-lasting effects on how the USAF conducted SEAD.

The 31 Initiatives and SEAD

The Bekaa Valley had influenced the USN, USMC, and US Army's views on SEAD almost as much as it had influenced the USAF's. The first two services began to consider how Marine artillery and other indirect assets could assist in the delivery of USMC close air support either during amphibious operations or during a large-scale land operation. The Army began to consider how it could employ its attack aviation helicopters and long-range field artillery to also suppress Warsaw Pact or other likely enemies' air defense systems. All four services brought these different mindsets to the Joint Force Development Group (JFDG), a body formed by the Joint Chiefs of Staff in November 1983. The JFDG's charter was to find ways to increase interoperability across DoD in order to facilitate the United States' ability to conduct military operations.[440]

A great deal of the work on what the Pentagon would designate "Joint-SEAD (J-SEAD)" had been done prior to the JFDG's formation. After the Bray-Elder agreements and the Army's publication of the 1976 edition of FM 100-5 *Operations*, USAF and USA leaders had continued to conduct regular professional discussions. This had resulted in a May 1981 agreement that developed the term "Joint Attack on the Second Echelon" (J-SAK) followed by an additional agreement on Offensive Air Support (OAS). The Army, having begun to review its doctrine as it fielded more advanced weapons systems, eventually settled on a concept entitled "AirLand Battle." Codified in the Army's 1982 edition of FM 100-5, this new operational methodology relied heavily on offensive counterattacks rather than shifting between defensive positions or trading ground for time as the suggested in 1976. For the first time since 1945, the U.S. Army's operational doctrine included an implied threat to conduct operations into East Germany should war occur in Central Europe. [441]

The Army had several reasons for this paradigm shift. First, it signaled to NATO allies that the United States would not simply accept a "separate peace" in the event of a conventional conflict. Second, the change in doctrine was intended to force Warsaw Pact commanders to maintain an operational reserve rather than commit all their forces to a potential Central European offensive. Lastly, American and NATO political leaders privately believed that regaining lost ground in the aftermath of an initial Warsaw Pact offensive would lead to a stronger negotiating position and simultaneously lower the likelihood the conflict became nuclear. As an additional bonus, planners felt that NATO forces entering the Eastern bloc during a conflict might lead to large-scale uprisings in Poland, Hungary, and Czechoslovakia. This, in turn, would possibly lead to the Warsaw Pact's disintegration mid-war resulting in a NATO victory.[442]

Whether it would have actually worked, AirLand Battle doctrine, like the IDF's success in the Bekaa Valley, spurred the Army to act as the USAF's full partner in developing the 31 Initiatives. As its name suggested, the new Army doctrine was unfeasible without Air Force participation. Therefore, in order to achieve success, the Army and Air Force used the 31 Initiatives to shape a common lexicon regarding the Warsaw Pact's IADS. Once this common language was set, the Army (and to a lesser extent, the Marine Corps) also fully invested in teaching their staffs, commanders, and soldiers to target the first echelon's air defense artillery assets. Put another way, the Army began to ensure that every service member, from the enlisted tank gunner determining what vehicles to shoot to a division commander apportioning his artillery assets, was taught the importance of engaging Warsaw Pact air defense equipment as part of their training.[443]

For its part, the Air Force continued to refine its SEAD techniques. Given the Army's participation in suppressing the WP-IADS' tactical array, Air Force SEAD planners developed methods to exploit the expected gaps that would be created by systems' destruction in the so-called "Close Fight." The majority of this planning was conducted once the Air Force and Army had determined ways to model electronic warfare, J-SEAD, and Warsaw Pact air defense systems' performance in simulated environments. During Blue Flags, Air Force staffs employed these models to plan notional air offensives against not only WP-IADS but other hostile nations' equivalents. The Air Force's System Command then applied operational research techniques to improve this doctrine, using the Israeli's operational experiences and their service's own Green / Red Flag events to refine the models' accuracy. This was supported by the Army's own modeling and exercises, all driven by both service's desire to develop hard data that supported their execution of the 31 Initiatives. Belatedly, the USN and USMC EW communities also began to assist in these efforts, albeit in an unofficial fashion.[444]

The State of SEAD in December 1985

The Air Force began 1981 with promising advances in technology, an improved process for distributing intellectual thought, the genesis of training infrastructure and, most importantly, a plan for synchronizing all these elements into a more effective conventional and strategic force. Five years after President Reagan's inauguration, the Air Force had the most technologically advanced training facilities in the world, replaced many of its Vietnam-era aircraft with the more advanced F-15 and F-16, and deployed the EC-130 and EF-111 electronic warfare aircraft. Much of this improvement had occurred due to the implementation of the 1979 edition of AFM 1-1, especially with regard to that document's requirements for SEAD and EW operations. Air Force senior leaders, by ensuring acquisition processes, training events, and personnel training directives reflected their services' doctrinal tenets, forestalled many of the contradictory processes that had contributed to failure over North Vietnam. Although USAF forces did not participate in combat themselves, the success of American equipment in the South Atlantic and Middle East seemed to indicate the service was on the correct path. The Cold War's final years would confirm this hypothesis through combat during Operations El Dorado Canyon and Desert Storm.

FROM THE CANYON
TO THE STORM

B y January 1986, the United States' strategic
situation seemed vastly improved compared
to what it had been January 1981. Having won
a second term in resounding fashion, President
Reagan continued the economic, diplomatic,
and military policies designed to prevent Soviet
expansion abroad, strengthen NATO and other
alliances, and eventually force the U.S.S.R. to the

negotiating table to stop the strategic arms race. These actions were largely successful, although the desired outcomes were often as much the result of other international actors' decisions as the Reagan administration's. At any rate, this continuation of policy allowed the Air Force to further develop its capabilities against the same predictable WP–IADS.[445]

The continuation of President Reagan's foreign policy in regard to the Soviet Union ran concurrent with the United States' increased bellicosity to smaller, less traditional enemies. In his first term, President Reagan's foreign policy advisors firmly believed in the limits of American power. In October 1983, American intervention in Lebanon had led to a disastrous barracks bombing that killed over 240 Marines. This then proceeded to a gradually escalating exchange of fire between the United States' forces and various Lebanese factions which culminated in airstrikes and shore bombardments against Syrian forces. By January 1984, the fighting had grown so intense that bipartisan leaders from the House of Representatives and Senate asked President Reagan to either withdraw ground forces or request authorization from Congress to use military force. On the advice of both Secretary of State George P. Shultz and Secretary Weinberger, President Reagan chose to end large-scale United States military participation in Lebanon.[446]

The Reagan Administration and State Sponsored Terrorism

The Lebanon debacle highlighted the United States' difficulty in employing military force in support of national objectives. Although by 1985 the military had largely shaken off its post-Vietnam malaise, the American public was clearly less interested in becoming embroiled in ground wars to support foreign policy goals. From the administration's perspective, the major issue appeared to be explaining to Congress and the American people why the nation's military personnel needed to be placed in harm's way. Led by Shultz, those within the administration who advocated a more robust foreign policy seized upon the issue of "state sponsored terrorism" as a justification for military interventions. Opposing them was Secretary Weinberger, who firmly believed the nation's military forces should only be committed to war in pursuit of clear objectives that the American people, through Congress, had agreed were vital to national interest or the country's survival. For all its horrors, terrorism did not seem to meet this criterion during President Reagan's first term. The Lebanon experience only seemed to strengthen Weinberger's reticence to use military force.[447]

A spate of terrorist incidents in 1985 swung the Reagan administration's opinion back towards Secretary Shultz's more robust views on foreign policy. The first of these incidents was the hijacking of TWA Flight 847 (June 14th, 1985). This was followed in short order by the Frankfurt Airport Bombings (June 19th, 1985), the *Achille Lauro* hijacking (October 7-10th, 1985), and the Rome and Vienna airport attacks (December 27th, 1985). This series of attacks in short succession, in addition to several thwarted attempts, tilted the advantage back towards Schultz's interventionism. Having run for two successive elections on a policy of not tolerating overt attacks against the United States, President Reagan thought that there needed to be an immediate and strong response to the next major incident. As Hezbollah, the PLO, and other non-state actors remained elusive, the Reagan administration would demonstrate its resolve against the next state actor it could tie to a terrorist attack. This, the interventionists believed, would simultaneously demonstrate American resolve abroad and also showcase the military's new capabilities.[448]

From the Air Force's perspective, this change in focus seemed unlikely to involve USAF forces. Most of the named or likely state sponsors of terrorism were located in the Middle East or North Africa. Due to the State Department's inability to obtain basing rights in the region, USAF planners considered SAC's B-52s the only aircraft to have the requisite range and payload capability to attack likely targets throughout the Mediterranean and Persian Gulf regions. Although some planning was given to preparing for possible contingencies against Iran and Syria, many of these exercises were seen by Air Force officers as a means of adding variety rather than sincere Blue Flag exercises. Given the United States' positive relationships with Israel, Saudi Arabia and, increasingly, Egypt, geopolitical factors precluded any thought of basing tactical fighters in any of these countries for an aerial campaign. Nor did it seem likely that there was any possibility of even flying shuttle missions through these nations' more remote airfields.[449] Therefore, Air Force planners believed that President Reagan would continue to employ the United States Navy's carrier fleet to carry out any punitive actions or sustained air campaigns if they became necessary. USAFE and the 48th TFW carried out some contingency planning in the aftermath of the Frankfurt and Vienna attacks, but only in general terms. Specific items such as targeting and SEAD preparations were not done, as it seemed highly unlikely strikes would be conducted by USAF forces.[450]

The Libyan Problem

The Air Force's planning assumptions began to unravel by January 1986. Reliable intelligence indicated that, at a minimum, the Frankfurt and Vienna terrorist attacks had been planned by Abu Nidal, a Palestinian nationalist and wanted terrorist. Nidal had allegedly been able to finance the operations with the aid of Libya. Ruled by Muammar Qaddafi, Libya had also allegedly supported the Irish Republican Army and other terrorist organizations in Europe. In response to these allegations as well as Qaddafi's stated intent to restrict freedom of navigation in the Gulf of Sidra, the Reagan administration had begun to apply economic and military pressure against Libya. In response to this, Libya had requested additional military equipment and technical support from the Soviet Union. The Soviet Union quickly provided Libya with SA-2, -3, and -5 missiles, as well as additional MiG-23 fighters. These were added to Libya's already existent air defense network, with the SA-5 providing Libya with a true long-range ability to enforce Qaddafi's "Line of Death" across the Gulf of Sidra.[451]

Emboldened by the new equipment and feeling increased pressure from the presence of additional American aircraft carriers, Qaddafi directed the Libyan armed forces to engage in a series of skirmishes with the United States Navy. The USN won all of these skirmishes without loss, and this outcome demonstrated the Libyan military's inability to project power outside of its own borders. Qaddafi perceived that the American's success was causing Libya to lose prestige in both the so-called "Arab world" and with the Soviet Union. In response, Qaddafi directed Libyan intelligence services to conduct retaliatory operations against U.S. interests in Western Europe. On April 5th, 1986, Libyan operatives (perhaps aided by the East German Stasi) successfully attacked a West Berlin nightclub in response to this order.[452]

El Dorado Canyon

To the Reagan administration, the nightclub bombing seemed like a textbook example of state sponsored terrorism. As such, it demanded an immediate and robust response to demonstrate the United States military's ability to project military power. Furthermore, both President Reagan and Secretary Weinberger believed such a strike needed to include both USN and USAF elements launched from European bases in order to show Western resolve. Despite this intent, it quickly became apparent to the United States that only the United Kingdom intended to provide any level of support to any American retaliatory strikes. France and Spain publicly and vehemently refused even to allow overflight privileges, meaning that any American aircraft involved would have to fly over 1,000 additional miles. West Germany similarly refused to allow support aircraft to be redeployed to the United Kingdom. Rather than demonstrating a united front, American plans had exposed schisms in the NATO alliance.[453]

The long-term impact on NATO was of little immediate concern to the USAF planners assigned to prepare for Operation El Dorado Canyon. The Pentagon, apprised of the failure to obtain flyover rights, briefly considered either staging the new F-117 *Nighthawks* from England or, due to the long range, employing B-52s. The F117s were considered due to the density of the Libyan air defenses around Tripoli but would require extensive tanker support. The *Stratofortresses* possessed the necessary range and payload capability to strike from bases in the United Kingdom with minimal refueling. In the end, the *Nighthawk* was still considered too important an asset to reveal for what amounted to a punitive action. Strategic Air Command, with organizational memory of how compressed planning had contributed to early losses in Linebacker II, was loath to risk B-52s without extensive tactical fighter support. Ultimately, the Air Force selected the 48th TFW, based at RAF Lakenheath in the United Kingdom, to conduct its part of the strike.[454]

In the years since El Dorado Canyon, there have been allegations that the Air Force's involvement was purely for political reasons. As mentioned, President Reagan and his advisors wished to send a message to states that supported terrorism that they risked retaliation from all of the Western bloc, not just the United States. However, there were at least two prominent military reasons to include the 48th TFW in the strike despite the mission's extended range. First, the 48th TFW was equipped with F-111Fs, the most advanced *Aardvark* variant available in the Air Force's inventory and the sole tactical fighter capable of all-weather operations. With the Pentagon's rules of engagement requiring a night attack in order to limit interference by Libyan interceptors and reduce anti-aircraft artillery's effectiveness, the F-111F and the USN's A-6 *Intruders* were the only options available for precision delivery.

Of the two, the *Aardvark*'s speed and terrain following radar made it far more survivable than the *Intruder* for targets in and around Tripoli.[455]

In addition to being faster, the F-111Fs could also carry a larger amount and type of ordnance than any aircraft in the USN's inventory. According to specifications, the USN's *Intruder*, F/A-18 *Hornet*, and A-7 *Corsair II* could all nominally carry the same 2,000-lb. *Paveway* bombs as the F-111F. However, employing these would greatly complicate carrier launch operations while severely limiting all three aircraft's range and performance. In order to strike the White House's list of targets, three to four additional sorties (aerial refueling, fighter escort, and SEAD) would have been required for each USN aircraft armed with precision weapons. Therefore, even with three carriers within range of Libya, the USN realized it would be hard pressed to conduct all the tasks necessary to properly meet President Reagan's intent with the aircraft available. By April 9th, 1986, the need for USAF support was even more apparent when the number of USN aircraft incapable of flying due to maintenance issues was factored in. As a result, Vice Admiral Kelso, the overall force commander, not only asked for USAF support but tripled the number of F-111s that had originally been included in the strike's contingency plan.[456]

In the flurry of planning that followed this request, the USN and USAF's refusal to fully integrate their SEAD doctrine became problematic. The 48th TFW, in conjunction with USAFE, had developed a contingency plan to attack Libya in the aftermath of the Rome and Vienna attacks. The USN's Sixth Fleet, the primary Navy command that oversaw operations in the Mediterranean, had directed its subordinate carriers to do the same. Although some limited discussions had taken place between USAFE and their USN counterparts, this had been very general and used broad terms. Thus, although the 31 Initiatives had at least established a common SEAD language, it quickly became apparent that the Air Force and Navy spoke different dialects when it came to what "suppression" meant at the operational and tactical levels.[457]

By April 1986, USAF planners had fully embraced the *concept* of rollback even if units differed on how this would be conducted. In short, even with a rapid strike, a robust SEAD package would seek to destroy individual SAM sites as EF-111s jammed the radars that cued these sites to begin looking in a given direction. In contrast, the USN considered each strike to be a separate, distinct contest between an inbound strike group and air defenses in the area. This savage duel was expected to be carried out by individual flights of F/A-18s and A-7s specifically targeting whatever air defense assets presented themselves along a likely ingress route. However, as long as these sites went off the air, they were considered "suppressed" as far as the USN was concerned. Therefore, the USN's SEAD fighters planned to fire anti-radiation missiles at long range rather than closing with and finishing a site with cluster bombs or other ordnance.[458]

The problem with the USN's technique, at least from the 48th TFW's perspective, was that the Air Force's targets required several F-111s to be over Libyan territory for an extended period. This time only increased as the Air Force strike grew from six to eighteen aircraft. While the fighter wing's package involved its own EF-111s and thus would use the same jamming methods honed by repeated Green Flags, the USAF planners were concerned with the USN's less aggressive SEAD techniques. In order to assuage some of these concerns, the USN increased the number of sorties dedicated to SEAD during Operation El Dorado Canyon. This included planning a strike on the airfield which housed the only Libyan fighter squadron trained for night operations.[459]

After an extremely compressed planning process, the actual raid took place over the night of 14-15 April 1986. Also as planned, it began with long-range jamming conducted by both USN EA-6B's and USAF EF-111s. As planned, USN A-6's successfully cratered several fighter runways prior to the F-111Fs crossing the Libyan coast. Simultaneously, the USN's relay of suppressive missile launches and supporting strikes seemed to diffuse and confuse the Libyan air defense efforts. As the 48th TFW approached its targets, the Libyan defenses managed to destroy a single F-111F by either directly shooting it down or causing it to maneuver into the sea. The defenders damaged another aircraft so badly that it had to land at an airbase in Spain. In return, the USN and USAF managed to strike over a half dozen targets, including Qaddafi's main residence. Due to stringent rules of engagement and the use of precision munitions, this was accomplished with minimal collateral damage. The Reagan administration, satisfied that the operation had sent a clear message, hailed El Dorado Canyon as a successful application of American military power to deter hostile activity.[460]

El Dorado Canyon's Legacy

With the passage of time, El Dorado's legacy is slightly more mixed. Strategically, Libyan support of terrorist groups simply became more clandestine rather than significantly declining. Operationally, USAF and USN forces had demonstrated that they could strike a common target at extended ranges. Although it had required a great deal of tanker support and the diversion of two aircraft carriers from the western Mediterranean, the United States had planned and executed a strike by over one hundred aircraft against what was considered one of the better IADS of the world. While some military analysts' comparisons to the contemporary air defenses that surrounded Moscow or those that ringed Hanoi in 1972 were somewhat hyperbolic, the Libyan targets had been well-defended by Soviet-supplied systems. Publicly, it appeared that for the second time since June 1982, Western equipment had easily triumphed in a military contest against their Soviet counterparts.

This perception masked several tactical issues that caused some consternation among the Air Force's tactical leaders. Only four of the eighteen F-111Fs had scored direct hits on their targets as opposed to varying degrees of damaging near misses. Even accounting for aborted attack runs due to the stringent rules of engagement and the rushed planning cycle, this was a far lower percentage than the Air Force had expected when it dispatched the strike. In addition, many of these misses had been due to errors imparted by either major system malfunctions or errors in the F-111Fs' navigational systems. Due to these system failures and battle damage, fewer than half of the launched aircraft could have conducted a follow-on strike by midday on April 15th. This did not build confidence in the 48th TFW's ability to operate in a high-intensity, multi-sortie conflict.[461]

Further complicating an objective assessment of the raid was the fact the Libyans had seemingly made a conscious decision not to scramble any fighters. As noted above, the USN's initial strike had managed to ground the Libyan Air Force's primary night fighter squadron. However, other Libyan units equipped with *Mirage F-1* and MiG-23s were seemingly not even alerted until ten minutes after the USAF departed Libyan airspace. Operation El Dorado Canyon's detractors pointed out that this lack of opposition disqualified the strike as any type of measuring stick for how far the USAF's capabilities had grown since Vietnam. [462]

Supporters of the strike's effectiveness, however, pointed out that the primary reason the interceptors did not scramble was the effectiveness of American electronic warfare. Since the combination of EF-111s and EA-6B *Prowlers* had thoroughly jammed the Libyan long-range radars, there was no opportunity for their operators to sound a timely alarm. In Operation El Dorado's aftermath, senior Air Force officials also pointed out that several Third World dictators were equipped with the same obsolescent equipment that the Soviets had provided to Qaddafi's IADS. The not so hidden threat was that what the USAF and USN had accomplished over Tripoli could be replicated elsewhere, with likely much more lethal results to other supporters of terrorist organizations. Not every dictator, the Pentagon reasoned, would receive a last minute phone call that likely saved their lives.[463]

The allure of this seemingly precise and surgical approach was so strong it became the basis of a new airpower theory. Most commonly attributed to USAF Colonel John A. Warden III, this methodology implicitly differentiated between conflicts with a great power (i.e., the Soviet Union) and application of military force against a regional threat (i.e., most of the "state sponsors of terrorism"). Warden alluded to the fact that the former possessed sufficient redundancy and the means to conduct immediate, direct retaliation against the United States or its allies. On the other hand, the latter were often despotic dictatorships with centralized power structures and minimal ability to retaliate against the continental United States. Warden then posited that, given the difference between the two threats, the Air Force needed to consider a new framework with which it could plan this additional conventional mission. Although the formal encapsulation of what would become his famous "five rings" theory did not take place until 1994, it began to find its genesis in the aftermath of Operation El Dorado Canyon. Regardless of how one viewed its ultimate effectiveness, Operation El Dorado Canyon clearly sparked a change in American airpower and, concurrently, how SEAD was considered.[464]

The Goldwater–Nichols Act and SEAD

While airpower theorists were still processing Operation El Dorado Canyon's importance, Congress provided a more immediate and unexpected boost to the development of SEAD doctrine. Familiar with the impact interservice had on operations from Korea to Vietnam and incensed by more recent issues in Operation Eagle Claw (Iran hostage rescue) and Operation Urgent Fury (invasion of Grenada), Senator

Barry Goldwater and Representative William Flynt Nichols shepherded a military reform bill through their respective legislative houses in 1986. Passed on October 1st, 1986, Public Law 99-433 was dubbed the "Goldwater-Nichols Department of Defense Act of 1986" or, more commonly, "Goldwater-Nichols." Less than a hundred pages long, the law took major steps to force the Department of Defense to comply with the military principle of unity of command while simultaneously seeking to eliminate redundancy across the services.[465]

The Goldwater-Nichol Act's primary purpose was to simplify military command and increase joint service cooperation, and the effect on SEAD doctrine was secondary to this. In the service of the first, Goldwater-Nichols simplified the chain of command by dividing the world into combatant commands by geographical region (e.g., Central Command [CENTCOM], Pacific Command [PACOM], European Command [EUCOM], etc.) or by function, such as Special Operations Command (SOCOM). Each of these entities, in turn, would have a single commander-in-chief, or CINC, whose line of authority encompassed all forces within his or her area of responsibility. Subordinate to this commander would be a component commander who oversaw land, sea, or air operations within each combatant command. Regardless of service or, in the case of combined operations, national affiliation, all units which were employed in a given sphere of operation would fall under the combatant commander's designated representative.[466]

Airpower under Combatant Commands

Strategically, this reorganization of the Department of Defense's combat power immediately served to counter the dilution of effort that had bedeviled air operations in Vietnam. It also provided a level of clarity to the Air Force's operational objectives by simplifying the chain of command. Before Goldwater-Nichols, any communication of strategic objectives and end states flowed from the President, to the Secretary of Defense, then to the services, and on through those chains of command. The new act specified that the chain of command went from the President of the United States, to the Secretary of Defense, and then to combatant commanders. Moreover, once forces were assigned to a given combatant command, they were no longer subject to their service's control or guidance from their providing unit. Thus awkward planning arrangements such as the Route Package system used in Vietnam or the mixed chains of command employed during Operation El Dorado Canyon became illegal, unless specifically directed by the President in writing.[467]

Operationally, this now meant that the air component commander, as the combatant commander's designated subordinate, was responsible for allocating sorties for the accom-

272 | JAMES L. YOUNG JR.

plishment of designated missions. According to the DoD regulations and doctrine quickly developed in response to Goldwater–Nichols, the joint forces air component commander (JFACC) controlled *all* airpower within the combatant command. In effect, this meant that any aircraft not required to defend a United States Navy carrier or carry out the USMC's close air support requirements (protected by law and DoD regulation) was subject to direct control by the combatant commander. This was intended to ensure that all aerial capabilities, from a Strategic Air Command B-52 or a USN F-14, were each operating to satisfy the combatant commander's goals as part of a joint plan.[468]

The actual mechanics needed to execute this intent took several months to develop, but were largely in place by 1988. Services or, in some cases, nations provided a given number of aircraft to a combatant commander based on what the JFACC (in most cases, a USAF general) expected would be needed for an operation. The JFACC would then take the provided aircraft and allocate them against given tasks in support of an air campaign. Once this process was complete, the assignment of sorties, targets, and aircraft would be published as part of an air tasking order (ATO) to subordinate units. These units would then have until midnight of the day the ATO was issued to make corrections regarding available aircraft, ordnance, or aircrew. Using this methodology, the JFACC was expected to use USAF, USN, USMC, and allied aircraft in a manner that gradually overwhelmed an opponent's air defenses with mass.[469]

The Pentagon's interpretation of Goldwater-Nichols' guidance with regard to airpower met immediate resistance from all of the services. For the USN, there were immediate fears that an ATO would not allocate enough fighters to defend their carrier flight decks against Soviet long-range bombers. The USMC, in addition to sharing this view, also pointed out that their ground units were organized with the assumption that fixed-wing aircraft would provide close air support as their "flying artillery." The Army was concerned that, having just completed the 31 Initiatives, the Air Force would consider Goldwater-Nichols a way to escape providing tactical fighters for CAS. Within the Air Force, SAC saw the new JFACC methodology as a way of transferring control of strategic assets to a subordinate flag officer who would likely have a tactical fighter, versus heavy bomber, background. Although these complaints were driven partly by parochialism, as initially presented the JFACC method did little to assuage any of these concerns.[470]

The Air Force Embraces SEAD Doctrine

Regardless of the interservice battles occurring in Washington, the new method of assigning airpower led to immediate changes within

EUCOM's methods of attacking the Warsaw Pact air defense network. Beginning in 1987, EUCOM began to include USN assets from the Sixth Fleet into its targeting plan for attacking fixed radar and SAM sites in Czechoslovakia and Hungary. It also began to include Sixth Fleet EA-6 *Prowlers* in its electronic warfare plan, staging these aircraft through Italy and southwestern Germany in some cases. By 1988 USAFE had stood up the 65th Air Division, a headquarters subordinate to USAFE (which acted as EUCOM's wartime JFACC). This entity was NATO and the Air Force's first attempt to develop a headquarters with the sole purpose to command and control SEAD throughout the entire European theater. After years of disjointed efforts, by 1989 NATO intended to execute a dedicated SEAD campaign against the Warsaw Pact IADS in time of war.[471]

Helping to guide these organizational changes and planning were two major doctrinal documents. The first was Joint Pub 3-01.2 *Joint Doctrine for Theater Counterair Operations*, published on April 1st, 1986. The second was AFM 2-8 *Electronic Combat Operations*. In *Theater Counterair Operations*, an entire chapter (VI) was devoted to the suppression of enemy air defenses. In it, the joint planner was reminded that "[a]ir, surface, or subsurface forces of a joint force may be employed to suppress or destroy enemy air defenses."[472] JP 3-01.2 goes on to give a detailed discussion of what means are available to a joint campaign planner, what facets of an enemy IADS is most susceptible to certain types of disruption, and what steps a campaign planner should take to deconflict available friendly resources. Suggestive rather than prescriptive, *Theater Counterair Operations* concisely condensed the lessons of the Bekaa Valley, various Flag exercises, and the USN's Strike University. For the first time, DoD had a handbook on how *all* of its assets could be employed in disrupting and defeating an integrated air defense system.

AFM 2-8 expounded upon the concepts outlined in JP 3-01.2 for a USAF audience. From the beginning, it explains that it is an operational document to be used in preparing for electromagnetic operations. The document reiterated the offensive and defensive importance of electronic warfare, especially with regard to command and control, air defense, and offensive aerial operations. Most importantly, for the first time in an Air Force document, AFM 2-8 explicitly stated that SEAD and Joint-SEAD were Air Force tasks carried out specifically to neutralize, degrade, or destroy enemy air defenses. The manual went on to explain that this could be done by physical means (i.e., ordnance delivered onto target) or by electromagnetic deception and jamming. In the case of the latter, it established that one of the primary tasks of the Air Force's electronic warfare systems was to "deny enemy commanders effective command and control of their forces."[473] Finally, AFM 2-8 reiterated the need for dedicated electronic warfare ranges and laid out methods for how units could be trained at these facilities.[474]

Having established these doctrinal underpinnings, Air Force Chief of Staff General Larry D. Welch ensured that the Air Force actually followed them. Blue Flags and other staff exercises were modified to include joint assets. To comply with Goldwater-Nichols, the Air Force also assigned its officers to joint staff billets with Navy and Army headquarters. In this manner, Air Force planners were exposed to these services' capabilities. Simultaneously, General Welch also reformed the Air Force's educational programs to make certain the service's field grade and senior officers were well versed in the new doctrine. Lastly, Welch continued the modification and acquisition processes initiated by General Creech during his time at TAC.[475]

F-4G Updates

One of these major modifications was to the F-4G *Wild Weasel V*. Realizing the initial airframe was approaching obsolescence, the Air Force took several steps to increase the F-4G's capabilities by way of a multi-phase performance update program (PUP) from 1983-1988. First, the USAF purchased eighteen additional aircraft to replace F-4Gs lost through attrition and to strengthen the *Wild Weasel* squadrons serving in the Pacific. Second, Air Force Systems Command replaced the F-4Gs' original engines with more fuel-efficient models that did not provide the *Phantom* airframe's characteristic smoke trail. Finally, all F-4G fuselages and wings were inspected and, if necessary, replaced.[476]

Concurrent with these airframe repairs and modifications, F-4Gs underwent a major electronics refit. The aircrew's flight control equipment, previously analog, was replaced with digital upgrades. The PUP also added a new targeting computer, which decreased the amount of time it took to acquire, locate, and engage a hostile radar. Data uplinks capability was added to facilitate communications with USAF, USN, and NATO command-and-control aircraft, as well as accompanying tactical fighters. In order to increase the F-4G's survivability, new electronic jammer capabilities were added for both internal and external carriage. The F-4G was also given the capability to employ the new AGM-88 high speed anti-radiation missile, colloquially known as the "HARM."[477]

The HARM and Hunter-Killers

The AGM-88 was the most potent American anti-radiation missile of the Cold War. Arising from a United States Navy requirement to replace the *Shrike* and *Standard*, the HARM took advantage of the same solid state and digital electronics revolution that had made the newest *Sparrow* and *Sidewinder* so lethal. With the older *Shrike* and *Standard*, hostile radar operators had been able to shut down their systems and enjoy fairly good odds that both weapons would miss. The HARM, however, had electronic memory that allowed it to still home in on the radar's previous location and immediately reacquire if the operators turned the system back on. If a new radar was acquired mid-flight, the HARM could be redirected to this greater threat using the F-4G's new data links. With a wholly new rocket

AGM-88 HARM and HARM Targeting Pod

(Author Collection-Taken At USAF Armament Museum, Eglin AFB, Florida)

motor, as opposed to previously produced items merely adapted to *Wild Weasel* use, the missile was both faster and longer-ranged than most existing or projected Soviet SAM systems.[478]

The new capabilities imparted by the AGM-88 brought a great change to Wild Weasel tactics.

Previously, the F-4Gs either had to either employ the *StARM* at great cost to their fuel consumption and maneuverability, or employ *Shrike* and hope they could close the range with a SAM site. With HARM, *Wild Weasel V* crews believed they could engage and destroy any SAM site long before it could successfully guide a missile onto their aircraft. Given the F-15Cs' demonstrated superiority against contemporary enemy fighters, the F-4Gs were generally unconcerned with being intercepted by MiGs. However, even if a MiG did manage to get past the *Eagles*, the standard F-4G / F-16 hunter killer team was far from helpless. F-4Gs continued to train in air-to-air combat and carried up to four *Sparrows* for self-defense, while their paired F-16s continued to carry up to four *Sidewinders*. [479]

USAFE's 52nd TFW began to employ the new tactics in 1986, with the practice spreading to TAC's 37th TFW in 1988. During training, F-4Gs began training to conduct a medium altitude ingress towards a target area in order to entice hostile radars to illuminate and track them. Once this occurred, the targeted F-4G planned to shoot a HARM at the offending radar to either destroy it or force it to shut down. Whichever course of action the hostile radar operators chose, the F-4G would mark the site's location and transmit it to friendly aircraft using onboard data links. If the hostile site was a system that the JFACC had targeted for destruction in that day's ATO, the F-4G and its accompanying F-16 *Falcon* would continue towards it. If the HARM appeared to destroy the radar, the pair of fighters would resume their orbit at medium altitude. On the other hand, if it did not appear the radar had been destroyed but merely turned off, the pair of aircraft would close to attack the radar and missile vehicles with *Mavericks* and cluster bombs.[480]

This change in tactics supported an operational "rollback" mindset. By 1988, USAFE had fully embraced this method in its war plan. Rather than the previous plan of committing to attacking supply lines and second echelon forces in the opening hours of a conflict, USAFE intended to destroy the WP-IADS with every sortie not providing CAS to engaged ground forces. EF-111s, EC-130s and, under the new JFACC model, EA-6Bs would provide distant jamming support to disrupt WP-IADS communications and surveillance radars. Relying on this support, the F-4G / F-16 hunter-killer teams would approach at medium altitude to begin reducing specifically targeted long- and medium-range SAM sites. With the advantages conveyed to the Wild Weasel hunter-killers by the HARM's performance and electronic support, USAFE planners expected this phase of the engagement to be a near replica of Operation Mole Cricket.[481]

As the Wild Weasel onslaught unfolded, USAFE held that their Warsaw Pact counterparts would commit fighter regiments to the attack. Based on their knowledge of the Warsaw Pact's inventory, USAF and NATO specifically strove to set the conditions for this fight to take place at medium altitude as opposed to decades of planning for low altitude encounters. Whether vectored in by E-3 *Sentries* or conducting fighter sweeps in accordance with *Theater Counterair Operations'* proposed techniques, the *Eagles* would employ slashing tactics to attrit their Warsaw Pact counterparts and gain air superiority. Rather than attack at low level as they had during Operation El Dorado Canyon, USAF strike aircraft would pass through this swirling combat at medium or high altitude as well. Using standoff, they would employ PGMs against critical targets in the WP-IADS. In this manner, the Air Force believed, they would clear the way for joint and allied aircraft to provide the necessary CAS and BAI sorties (again, using precision munitions) to cripple an expected Warsaw Pact offensive by cutting off fuel, ammunition, and resupply. By December 1988, the Air Force was quite public in its belief that, at long last, it had attained complete ascendancy over the Warsaw Pact.[482]

External Evaluations of USAF Capabilities

The USAF's internal confidence was measured by that of external observers. In contrast to Hackett and Bidwell's grim prognostications in the early 1980s, by 1988 many foreign observers believed that NATO's conventional forces, and its air arms in particular, were more than sufficient to defend West Germany. Within the United States, a 1988 GAO report on the conventional forces in Europe found that the Western bloc's air forces appeared to have an overwhelming advantage in quality that offset the Warsaw Pact's quantitative advantages. When discussing airpower, the report specifically stated that its authors could not consider airpower to be a potentially decisive factor in a future European conflict. The contributors then went on to state that there were several factors for their belief. However, many who provided content for the report considered air superiority's advantages as an important offset to the Warsaw Pact's advantage in ground forces. When discussing their reluctance to raise spending on expensive ground warfare systems, NATO governments began pointing to the alliance's perceived advantages in airpower as a reason why further spending unnecessary. Finally, the Soviet Union, when discussing conventional arms reductions, specifically pointed to NATO's airpower as one of the alliance's inherent advantages when discussing mutual concessions.[483]

These factors were the clearest indication that the USAF had come of age. Fifteen years after the Yom Kippur War, it appeared that the USAF and its NATO counterparts had satisfied all three facets of conventional deterrence. First, as evidenced by its arm negotiators in 1987–1988, the Soviet Union considered NATO tactical airpower as threatening to the Warsaw Pact's military capabilities as the latter's tank divisions were to the West. Second, NATO's European members had come to consider airpower to be strong enough to offset ground forces' deficiencies. Finally, by virtue of continued investments and public statements, both President Reagan and Congress considered the Air Force to be a vital component of deterrence not only against the Soviet Union but also other hostile nations abroad. Although not the sole factor in this turn of events, the evolution of Air Force SEAD doctrine had certainly played a major part.

Soviet Response to USAF SEAD Advances

The Soviet Union, while attempting to seek reductions in airpower at the treaty table, was simultaneously pressing forward with the development of new doctrine and systems. In the aftermath of the Bekaa Valley and Libyan experiences during Operation El Dorado Canyon, the Soviet military conducted a thorough review of its equipment and command practices. Having already increased funding and expedited research in support of developing its next generation fighters, both *PVO Strany* and Frontal Aviation asked for an increased portion of the Soviet Union's limited electronics industry's output. Due in part to Premier Mikhail Gorbachev's policies of *glasnost* and *perestroika* but also due to the realization that restricted, staid doctrine made the IADS more susceptible to electronic warfare, the Red Army began to increase battalion and regimental officers' independence. Whereas certain weapons' release (e.g., SA–5 *Gammons*) had previously required approval at the divisional level, Red Army encouraged all battery commanders to use their own discretion when presented with fleeting opportunities. By late 1988, older systems were retrofitted with solid state electronics and new mobile SAMs (e.g., the SA-10 *Grumble*, SA-12 *Gladiator*) were just reaching East Germany. Doctrine was changed to increase mutual support across unit boundaries in an attempt to counter the USAF's "rollback" plans. [484]

As the ground forces sought to find solutions in changing doctrine and procedures, the Soviet Air Force sought to regain parity through material means. In 1985, Frontal Aviation began fielding the new MiG-29 *Fulcrum* and Su-27 *Flanker* to Eastern Europe. Surprisingly, the Soviet Union began exporting the *Fulcrum* to East Germany and Poland before it had completely replaced the MiG-23 *Flogger* in its own fighter regiments. Both of these fighters, contrary to the MiG-23, were equipped with solid state electronics and an infra-red tracking system that was not susceptible to electronic warfare. The aircraft also carried improved radar-guided (i.e., the AA-10 *Alamo*) and heat-seeking (i.e., AA-13 *Archer*) missiles, either of which were comparable to the *Sparrow* and *Sidewinder*. On paper, each of these fighters could easily challenge the F-15C and, given their possession of BVR weapons coupled to an advanced radar, easily defeat the F-16.[485]

Unfortunately for WP-IADS operators, materiel production was only part of the solution.

Although training had increased in the aftermath of Bekaa Valley, by 1988 the strains apparent on the Soviet economy began to preclude regular training for both SAMs and interceptors. For the ground forces, problems with maintenance and parts erased the many gains of the new systems. In the air, fighter regiments increasingly found large-scale exercises cancelled, while flight and squadron training became increasingly *ad hoc* and haphazard. Beginning in late 1987, the SAF attempted to develop a DOC-equivalent. However, even this effort became embroiled in bureaucracy and senior officers' internecine infighting. Training among the other Warsaw Pact air forces was even worse, with many fighter pilots receiving less than 30 percent of the number of flight hours flown by USAF pilots. Although not as inferior as they were portrayed in contemporary Western professional journals and intelligence estimates, the average Warsaw Pact pilot had little experience with night flying, ACM, or independent interception.[486]

United States Air Force SEAD in Desert Storm

Whether or not the Soviet Union's improvements in air defense would have proven a successful counter to the United States' changes in doctrine, equipment, and training remains unknown. In a series of quickly cascading events in 1989, the Eastern bloc seemingly imploded upon itself. Beginning with Hungary opening its borders in June 1989 and concluding with East German citizens demolishing the Berlin Wall in November, the former pro-Soviet regimes of the Warsaw Pact were swept away in mostly bloodless revolutions. Even in Romania, the sole instance where the transition to a non-Communist government became overtly violent, state security forces eventually turned upon their government. Rather than ending in a conventional clash whose likely participants expected the fight to spiral into nuclear holocaust, the "conflict" for Central Europe ended with the Warsaw Pact peacefully forfeiting.[487]

For the United States, the Central European confrontation's sudden end left the Department of Defense seemingly bereft of mission. President George H.W. Bush, Reagan's former vice-president, had run for election with a security plan that generally continued his predecessor's policies. Less than a year after inauguration, the Bush administration found itself with no real adversary against which it could argue for continued strategic modernization, increased conventional capability, and a firmer push for human rights in Eastern Europe. With Mikhail Gorbachev largely agreeing to an overall strategic arms reductions coupled with conventional forces reduction in Europe, the prism through which the United States had viewed the world for over four decades seemed shattered. Pundits and analysts began talking of a "New World Order," in which the United States' military capacity was largely irrelevant to events.[488]

Iraq Invades Kuwait

The invalidity of this opinion was revealed on August 2nd, 1990. Iraqi leader Saddam Hussein, frustrated with negotiations regarding his nation's war debt to Kuwait and believing he had a tacit agreement from the United States to turn a blind eye to his actions, ordered his army to invade Kuwait. Taken by surprise, the Kuwaiti military engaged in a spirited, but fruitless, defense that served little purpose other than to buy time for the royal family to escape. Within 24 hours, over a dozen Iraqi mechanized divisions had advanced south to the Kuwaiti-Saudi Arabian border, halting there to conduct resupply and consolidation operations. From the Saudi perspective, it appeared the Iraqi Army was preparing to continue south to seize the oil production facilities along their nation's Persian Gulf coast. Lacking the internal means to stop the Iraqis, the Saudi government asked the United States for immediate military support.[489]

From the Bush administration's perspective, Iraq's invasion was an act of naked aggression. President Bush had continued Reagan's policy of relatively warm relations towards Iraq due to Saddam Hussein's antipathy towards Iran. Now almost without warning, Iraq had repaid this support by not only invading an allied nation, but also becoming poised to seize enough oil capacity to influence the world's markets. Despite the reticence of Secretary Dick Cheney and his Chairman of the Joint Chiefs of Staff, General Colin Powell, President Bush ordered the deployment of the 82nd Airborne division and a contingent of USAF aircraft. In addition, President Bush ordered General Schwarzkopf, the head of CENTCOM, to act in his role of combatant commander and prepare for the defense of Saudi Arabia. In putting U.S. military forces squarely astride the Iraqi Army's path, Bush intended to buy time for a diplomatic solution and the building of an international coalition.[490]

In 1990, CENTCOM had been considered one of the least likely commands to face a military operation. As had been the case during President Reagan's second term, the Department of Defense lacked basing rights in the Persian Gulf region. Furthermore, although the United States Navy had fought several sharp engagements with Iran and suffered casualties while escorting reflagged Kuwaiti tankers, a major conflict had seemed unlikely prior to the Iraqi invasion. Therefore, the combatant command had no assigned combat power, and its staff elements were undermanned. For this reason Lieutenant General Charles Horner, the CENTCOM JFACC, asked new Air Force Chief of Staff Michael Dugan for assistance in planning an offensive campaign even as his subordinates to prepare for Saudi Arabia's defense. This dovetailed with Secretary Cheney's guidance to General Powell to prepare a plan to strike Iraq itself should the Iraqi Army violate Saudi Arabia's sovereignty. With the Army building defensive combat power slowly due to the distance from its bases or prepositioned stocks, it appeared it was up to USAF forces to deter an Iraqi conventional attack.[491]

Instant Thunder: The Initial USAF Strategic Plan

In a circumstance of a well-trained person being coincidentally in the correct place at just the right time, Colonel John Warden oversaw Checkmate, the USAF's primary strategic planning cell, in August 1990. Having come into his own as a prominent theorist with the publication of *The Air Campaign* in early 1988, Warden had finally codified his "Five Rings Theory" in the summer of that year. In this construct, Warden divided a nation's centers of gravity into five concentric rings. At the outermost ring was the nation's fielded military forces, with the general population the next ring inward. Next was the nation's infrastructure, which was in turn supported by the system essentials such as petroleum, foodstuffs, and strategic materials. Finally, at the innermost ring was a nation's leadership, the paralysis of which would nominally make the outer four rings defunct. Warden's theory held that rather than trying to chew slowly and ponderously through the outer rings to finally reach the center, the United States should use its advantages in airpower, information warfare, and precision munitions to immediately and summarily remove Iraq's leadership. Like a man shot in the base of the skull, the Hussein regime would then collapse upon itself regardless of what the Iraqi Army was doing in Kuwait and Saudi Arabia.[492]

With Warden's guidance, Checkmate's staff quickly came up with a strike plan they dubbed "Instant Thunder," an overt signaling that the strikes would not repeat the gradual increases of Operation Rolling Thunder. After first briefing General Dugan, then General Powell, and following this with a brief to General Schwarzkopf at CENTCOM headquarters in Tampa, Colonel Warden flew to Riyadh, Saudi Arabia to brief Lieutenant General Horner. In a contentious briefing in which Colonel Warden's personality traits quickly incensed Lieutenant General Horner, Warden's plan was turned over to CENTCOM's own staff and the theorist summarily ordered home from Saudi Arabia. Warden, in Horner's eyes, had turned his back on established Air Force and joint doctrine in an attempt to push an Air Force–centric war plan.[493]

After tempers had cooled, the JFACC's staff found several good options in Warden's plan. Unfortunately, the major issue with Instant Thunder was that the resources needed to carry it out were not in CENTCOM's area of responsibility. With under 300 combat aircraft between forces based in Saudi Arabia and USN carriers in the Persian Gulf and Red Sea, Lieutenant General

Horner believed he lacked the airpower to both defend Saudi Arabia and attack Iraq.[494]

KARI: The Iraqi Integrated Air Defense System

Lieutenant General Horner's hesitation in attempting to attack Iraqi leadership targets was well founded. Like Muammar Qaddafi, Saddam Hussein had taken advantage of the Soviet Union's willingness to export weaponry in exchange for possible future access during the 1980s. Unlike Qaddafi, Hussein also had access to Western technology due to his depiction of Iraq as a bulwark against a radical Iran. This portrayal had also stood him in good stead when attempting to obtain funding from his fellow Sunni nations against the potential threat of its large Shia neighbor.[495]

A large part of these resources had been invested in KARI, the French acronym for the Iraqi-IADS. Saddam Hussein, after the embarrassment of the IDF's successful strike against the Osirak reactor, realized that his armed forces' orientation towards Iran was problematic given enemies to the west and south. In response, Hussein directed the establishment of an air defense network that provided for defense against attack from any direction, but especially from the south and west. The heart of this defense was the Air Defense Operations Center (ADOC), a heavily fortified building in Baghdad. Acting as a semi-automated mastermind for KARI was a supercomputer located in the ADOC, which had advanced processors that would facilitate the application of the defense's resources.[496]

Like nerve centers connecting a brain to its limbs, reinforced landlines and fiber optic networks ran from the ADOC to four Sector Operations Centers (SOCs). From the SOCs, radio and landline communications ran to individual SAMs, fighter bases, and GCI centers. Using this system, the ADOC was able to exert centralized command and control over the entire I-IADS in a relatively rapid fashion. Built in 1986-1987, KARI had served the Hussein regime well in the final year of the Iran-Iraq War, and was considered an effective system by JFACC planners.[497]

The Iraqi Army was responsible for conducting KARI's ground-based portion. In 1991, the primary SAMs the Iraqis operated were the venerable SA-2 and SA-3, which were reinforced by mobile SA-6s, SA-8s, French *Crotales*, and the multinational *Roland*. At the tactical level, ZSU-23-4s and various calibers of radar-aimed AAA provided low-level air defense against attacking aircraft. Individual Iraqi forces used a variety of Soviet and Western man portable air defense systems (MANPADS) to provide short-range protection to its mechanized forces. In general, the batteries, battalions, and regiments were organized along the Soviet templates of the late 1970s. In 1990 Saddam Hussein expected his ground-based SAMs to cause heavy casualties among attacking

Coalition air forces, and thus quickly sour American public opinion of the war.[498]

The Iraqi dictator similarly anticipated the Iraqi Air Force (IQAF) to act as a guerilla force rather than to challenge for air superiority in the traditional manner. Although the IQAF had a handful of squadrons equipped with the modern *Mirage F1* and *Mig-29 Fulcrum*, most of its airframes were the obsolescent MiG-23 and wholly outdated MiG-21/MiG-19 variants. In the case of the latter airframes, fighting the Coalition's mix of F-14s, F-15s, F-16s, F-18s, and *Mirage 2000s* directly would be suicidal. On the other hand, even the *Farmer* and *Fishbeds* were dangerous to a heavily laden strike aircraft such as a *Buccaneer, Aardvark*, or *Jaguar,* and could even threaten a more modern fighter if placed in an advantageous position by ground controllers. Furthermore, Iraq's pilots had just finished almost a decade of sustained combat, whereas almost all of the Coalition's pilots were ostensibly untested. As the largest air force in the region, the IQAF could take a large number of losses. If the exchange rate could be kept to 2 or 3 Iraqi fighters for each Coalition aircraft, a potential conflict could rapidly become too costly for Hussein's opponents to bear.[499]

Hussein's assumptions, in a vacuum, were not unreasonable. Unfortunately for the Iraqi defenders, they had three major problems. First, although the Iran-Iraq War had indeed seen the IQAF conduct hundreds of sorties, the overwhelming majority of these had been either air-to-ground or naval antishipping strikes. Second, most of the Coalition's European and USAF / USN pilots had participated in various NATO "Flag" exercises and were thus hardly neophytes. Finally, the C2 evolution initiated by General Creech and shepherded by his successor had almost reached its apogee by late 1990. With the presence of over two dozen E-3 *Sentry* and USN E-2C *Hawkeye* AWACS aircraft, the Coalition's ability to track airborne targets far surpassed that of KARI's in much of Iraq's airspace. Unbeknownst to the IQAF, rather than skulking guerillas skillfully using friendly airspace as a hiding ground, their aircraft would be brightly emblazoned targets whose every move was tracked from the moment their wheels left the runway.[500]

Targeting KARI: The Coalition SEAD Plan

By early October 1990, the CENTCOM staff believed they had enough defensive firepower to fully blunt an Iraqi ground offensive. Furthermore, President Bush had cobbled together a sufficiently large coalition that the forced expulsion of Iraqi from Kuwait would have international legitimacy. Lastly, CENTCOM had established sufficient infrastructure and supplies ashore and naval strength in the Persian Gulf that offensive operations were logistically viable.[501]

Despite his summary dismissal of Colonel Warden, Lieutenant General Horner acknowledged that the Checkmate cell had made several correct choices. First, the use of F-117s and *Tomahawk* cruise missiles to strike targets in the vicinity of Baghdad lessened the risk to Coalition aircrews. Second, the use of precision guided munitions to hit all targets in urban areas would lessen the likelihood of civilian casualties that might fracture the Coalition. By attacking primarily at night, Instant Thunder (as planned) would have limited the effectiveness of Iraqi fighters and anti-aircraft artillery.[502]

What Horner did not like, and expressly told his staff to correct, was the lack of adherence to existing Air Force and joint doctrine. Specifically, CENTCOM air planners were given the directive to consider Iraqi air defense assets to be the primary target of the war's first 48 hours. Once KARI was defeated, the JFACC could both attack the Iraqi Army at will and reduce Iraq's strategic targets such as its biological and chemical facilities, mass communications stations, and regime security apparatus. In addition, Warden's emphasis on possibly killing Saddam Hussein or other senior members of his regime was to be removed from the plan's final iteration. Horner reasoned that if Iraq's leader happened to end up underneath a bomb, it would be an unfortunate incident. However, if CENTCOM was seen as specifically targeting him, it might fracture the fragile alliance that President Bush had managed to collect.[503]

The CENTCOM air planning cell, dubbed "The Black Hole" for various aspects of its personnel's nature and habits, conceived an operational SEAD plan that adhered almost completely to the tenets of JP 3-01.2 and AFM 2-8, with a few additions. The first of these changes was the interweaving of Joint and Coalition assets to achieve desired effects. Rather than opening with fixed-wing platforms, CENTCOM planners chose to use U.S. Army *Apache* helicopters to destroy several Iraqi radar posts located a few miles from the Saudi Arabian border. By using the low flying helicopters instead of the faster, higher-flying jets, the Coalition would poke out KARI's long-range eyes with little warning. Simultaneously, United States Navy vessels would launch *Tomahawk* cruise missiles to begin their journey towards targets in Iraq. With the radar sites destroyed, Air Force F-117s would then pass through the resultant gaps in KARI's coverage on their way to Baghdad.[504]

Phase Two of the defense suppression plan would begin with the advance of dozens of unmanned drones followed closely by EF-111s and F-4Gs. As the drones were detected concurrent with the inbound *Tomahawks*, it would appear to KARI that a massive Coalition airstrike was unfolding. This would spur the computer to begin issuing orders for SAM radars to begin radiating and tracking targets. At this point, F-117s in the vicinity of Baghdad would destroy the ADOC with precision-guided munitions. The ASOCs would also be attacked either by additional F-117s, *Tomahawks*, or AGM-86s launched by B-52s. Given the Iraqis' lack of mid-level initiative, General Horner expected this to result in the radars being left on once the command to illuminate was given. Therefore, once the radars illuminated, the EF-111s would have plenty of opportunity to jam the systems while the marauding F-4Gs began to dispatch them with HARMs. EC-130 *Compass Calls* would facilitate this process by jamming Iraqi radio networks.[505]

With KARI blinded and concussed, the Coalition's dedicated strike aircraft (i.e., F-111, *Tornado*, and F-15Es) would initiate Phase Three of the SEAD campaign. Minutes after the *Tomahawks* and AGM-86s impacted command posts and concurrent with anti-radiation missiles suppressing or destroying area defenses, the strike fighters would approach behind the planned "wall of *Eagles*" at low and medium-altitude. General Horner and his subordinates fully expected the IQAF to be able to scramble despite the confusion sewn by the first two SEAD phases. To facilitate the destruction of the IQAF's few all-weather interceptors, CENTCOM assigned F-15 units to specific ingress and egress routes that would maximize opportunities to employ their AIM-7 *Sparrows* in BVR engagements. After some initial friction with the Navy, additional routes were planned to allow F-14s with opportunities to employ their long-range AIM-54s and AIM-7s. The JFACC's blunt guidance for the opening night was for Coalition fighters to shoot down as many Iraqi interceptor pilots without the defenders even knowing what killed them. Rather than conducting a hit and run campaign, the survivors would hopefully find themselves facing overwhelming numbers of Coalition fighters closing to ACM range.[506]

After the airborne interceptors were destroyed, the Coalition would immediately seek to destroy the remaining Iraqi fighters on the ground. The first step of this process would be USAF and Coalition aircraft cratering Iraqi runways with specially designed weapons. With the IQAF runways cratered, this would be followed by hardened air shelters (HAS) being demolished via guided weapons aimed at weak points on the roofs. Finally, SAM sites would be destroyed rather than suppressed whenever possible. Lieutenant General Horner, as a veteran of the first attempt to destroy a SAM site during Vietnam, was quite adamant that long-range SAMs would be eliminated by aircraft specifically designed for that purpose.[507]

Executing KARI: The First 96 Hours of Desert Storm

As planning concluded, the common language of doctrine had provided a strong, robust framework for SEAD at the tactical level. Hours of realistic flights during various Flag exercises had put actual muscle memory and sinew on the theoretical skeleton of doctrine in the decade preceding Operation Desert Storm. Therefore, despite F-111, F-15, and F-4G mission planners being separated by hundreds of miles, the common experience allowed precise mission planning via secure telephones and, in some cases, physical couriers. This mutual understanding was further solidified by regular rehearsals conducted over the Saudi Arabian desert from late November into early January, with many of the last sorties taking place in a full-scale rehearsal conducted over Oman. After months of feints and near incidents, CENTCOM's EF-111s, F-4Gs, and E-3 *Sentry* aircrews had cooperated to prepare an electronic order of battle of the Iraqi IADS radar and SAM sites. The Air Force, for the first time since 1973, was prepared to employ its full arsenal against a hostile IADS. As the deadline for an Iraqi withdrawal approached, United States Air Forces, Central Command (CENTAF) and its Coalition partners were coiled to strike.[508]

On January 17th, 1991, with diplomatic options exhausted, the Coalition air attack fell upon KARI much as Lieutenant General Horner and his planners had directed. In the opening minutes, the Army's Task Force Normandy destroyed two radar sites in western Iraq before their occupants could sound the alarm. The subsequent F-117 movements, although slightly delayed, still arrived in time to lobotomize KARI by destroying the ADOC with a pair of 2,000-lb. bombs. What followed was a largely one-sided massacre, as the Iraqi air defense units illuminated their radars to find the early morning skies full of USN strike aircraft and USAF F-4Gs all carrying

HARM missiles. At one point in the ensuing engagement, over 200 AGM–88s were airborne at one time heading towards Iraqi SAM sites, with most of these missiles believed to have scored a kill. As SAM sites were being eliminated, the IQAF began attempting to commit interceptors only to find these aircraft rapidly engaged by lurking F–15Cs and USN F/A–18s egressing from strikes. In exchange for one or two possible kills (a USMC F/A–18 and a USAF F–111), the Iraqis lost nine interceptors. Several more IQAF aircraft were forced to disengage and flee away from Coalition aircraft rather than attempting interceptions. Instead of conducting themselves as enterprising guerillas, the IQAF had been forced to stand and fight with disastrous results.[509]

Clipping KARI's Wings: The Destruction of the IQAF

Despite this initial setback, KARI remained dangerous. Even with the ADOC and three of four sector headquarters smoking ruin, over 80 percent of Iraq's SAM batteries and unguided AAA remained operational. Additionally, 75–80 percent of its interceptors remained operational when dawn broke on January 17th, 1991. The C2 of KARI had been severely battered, but the IQAF still attempted to launch over thirty fighters to contest the initial Coalition attacks on January 17th. It was a spirited effort, and given the large number of near misses strike aircraft experienced on the opening night it appeared to

CENTAF leadership they might be in for a difficult air-to-air campaign. Yet by January 23rd, the IQAF's surviving interceptors were huddled in hardened air shelters being destroyed singly or in pairs by Coalition PGMs. Far from the drawn-out guerilla campaign its leaders imagined, the IQAF's interceptors were dispatched in an almost summary fashion.

Lieutenant General Horner's adherence to Air Force SEAD doctrine regarding central planning was the first factor that contributed to this one-sided victory. With personal experience in Vietnam and the Seventh Air Force's diffusion of effort against the NVAF MiG threat, Horner ensured the pressure planned during Instant Thunder was actually applied in the first 96 hours. By constructing tightly regimented Air Tasking Orders, Lieutenant General Horner and the CENTAF staff planned every single sortie that entered Iraqi and Kuwaiti airspace. More importantly, this information was disseminated to every Coalition unit down to the squadron level via physical messenger. From the individual controllers on E-3 AWACS aircraft to the USN F/A-18 *Hornet* pilots launching from carriers in the Red Sea, every allied aircrew had a general concept of how airpower was going to be employed over Desert Storm's first four days. When combined with real time command and control from the E-3s, this basic understanding of where everyone was supposed to be greatly facilitated the initiation of BVR engagements.[510]

By contrast, the IQAF had lost most of its situational awareness on the opening night when KARI's primary C2 was destroyed. Forced to resort to standing patrols, Iraqi interceptors often had little idea where their own forces were located, nevermind the size and composition of Coalition strike packages. For example, on January 19th, when the Coalition made successive USN and USAF strikes near Baghdad, the IQAF attempted pincer operations with a flight of MiG-25 *Foxbats* and supporting MiG-29 *Fulcrums*. Instead of trapping the two Coalition formations between their fighters, the Iraqis themselves ran into a well-executed trap sprung by USAF F-15s. Not only were either IQAF formation able to warn the other, it is unlikely they were even aware of their own peril before the USAF *Eagles* had achieved positions that allowed them to seize the initiative in both fights. Reinforcing *Mirage* and MiG-23s were then bounced by yet a third flight of F-15s held in reserve for just such an event. In less than twenty minutes, the IQAF lost almost half the fighters it launched.[511]

The Coalition pilots' situational awareness advantage was complemented by the Coalition's total dominance of the electromagnetic spectrum. Surviving KARI GCI stations, when allowed to radiate unmolested (more on this below), found it all but impossible to pass pertinent information to airborne Iraqi fighters due to Coalition jamming. As predicted by General Creech, radios incapable of frequency hopping were generally useless. Having constructed an electronic order of battle during the tense months after Iraq's invasion of Kuwait, CENTAF's planners ruthlessly targeted communications down to the individual airframe level. In accordance with SEAD doctrine, EF-111s conducted point jamming of specific nodes while distant orbiting EC-130s filled Iraqi frequencies with a cacophony of general noise. In effect, Iraqi pilots launched alone, attempted to intercept alone, and, if they were in the vicinity of a Coalition strike, often died alone.[512]

The Coalition's relentless attacks on Iraqi airfields exacerbated the morale problems caused by the shocking aerial losses. Beginning with strikes on the opening night, Iraq's major sector airfields were under constant pressure from a myriad of systems delivered from different altitudes. At low level, RAF / Italian Air Force *Tornadoes*, USAF F-111s, USN attack aircraft, and even venerable B-52s targeted runways, infrastructure, and airfield control facilities with both "dumb" iron bombs and specified munitions. From medium altitude, F-111s and F-15Es delivered precision munitions against interceptor ground control stations, hardened C2 facilities and, finally, the numerous HAS that Iraqi had invested in over the previous decade. Instead of being proof to everything short of nuclear weapons as their designers had intended, the aircraft shelters became impromptu crematoriums for IQAF interceptors and their crews seeking refuge from the hail of Coalition ordnance.[513]

By January 23rd, the IQAF had enough. Whether an event planned at the highest levels of the regime or a spontaneous exodus initiated at the mid-levels of the IQAF's command, Iraqi aircraft began fleeing east into Iran. Despite not having planned for the eventuality, CENTAF rapidly shifted its forces to close off even this final respite. For the remaining thirty-five days of the war, the once vaunted IQAF would spend its time split between fleeing for its life or being destroyed piecemeal at its bases.[514]

Flailing In Isolation: The Neutralization of Iraq's Ground-Based Defenses

Although not quite as one-sided as the destruction of the IQAF's interceptor fleet, the reduction of Iraq's medium and long-range ground defenses was another triumph of Coalition planning and execution. On one hand, the massive volley of AGM-88s, free-hunting F-4Gs, and several precision-munition strikes on the opening night of the war were estimated to have reduced Iraqi radar coverage by as much as 30 percent. On the other hand, the surviving radar operators, chastened by the sharp, lethal engagements of the war's first day, became more cautious about how and when they radiated their radars.[515]

Although this lethal game of cat and mouse would persist throughout the conflict, Coalition forces swiftly gained the upper hand through a series of relatively simple steps. First, after a nearly disastrous daylight strike on Baghdad and heavy losses among British / Italian *Tornado* aircraft, CENTAF directed all BAI and operational / strategic operations to fly at medium to high altitude. As expected in pre-war USAF SEAD doctrine, this simple measure took the Coalition's strike aircraft out of most Iraqi anti-aircraft artillery's effective range.

Second, the CENTAF ATO was manipulated to better facilitate F-4G *Wild Weasel* operations. Initial operations confirmed that the venerable *Phantoms* consumed much more fuel than the more modern F-15Es, F-16Cs, and associated Coalition strike aircraft. To alleviate this, CENTAF modified both the ATO and tanker tactics to prioritize the F-4Gs getting more fuel. They also began assigning F-4G sorties to areas (i.e., "Weasel Police") rather than specific strike packages. This increased the *Wild Weasels'* loiter time and helped them actually destroy, rather than just suppress, medium-range systems (e.g., the SA-2, SA-3, and SA-6). Concurrently, CENTAF began increasing the number of F-16 "killers" allocated to accompany the F-4G "hunters" so that the *Phantoms* could carry additional HARM missiles. Once it became clear that the IQAF was a broken force, the CENTAF staff focused EC-130 and EF-111 sorties towards jamming the radio networks of Iraqi air defense regiments and battalions during strike ingress and egress. Finally, CENTAF coordinated with the USN and Coalition forces to better employ their

306 | JAMES L. YOUNG JR.

strike packages' EW capabilities in opportunity attacks that attrited individual SAM batteries.[516]

Although bad weather in the region initially disrupted these changes, their cumulative effects became rapidly apparent. First, Coalition aircraft were largely able to operate with impunity above 15,000 feet altitude over most of Iraq and the Kuwaiti Theater of Operations (KTO). Although AAA barrages were often spectacular and highly visible at night, they were stunningly ineffective as even a deterrent to Coalition strikes at Iraqi strategic and operational targets. Second, Iraqi SAM batteries resorted to launching their SAMs ballistically, i.e., guessing Coalition aircraft's speed and altitude, then attempting to turn guidance radars on at the last minute to increase hit probability. Lastly, in those rare cases where SAM batteries were employed as designed, their operators did so as singular entities rather than as part of a cohesive whole. For almost three-quarters of Operation Desert Storm, Iraqi ground-based defenses were like a blinded, stunned boxer flailing at an opponent whose presence they could only determine from the blows that continued to fall upon them. Although the sheer quantity of short-range, low altitude systems (e.g., MANPADS, SA-8, ZSU-23-4, *Roland*, and 23mm and 57mm guns) meant Iraqi forces were never completely defenseless, by February 1st, KARI was no more. Having achieved air supremacy, Lieutenant General Horner's planners were able to focus almost wholly on operations to set the conditions for the ground campaign.[517]

Apogee and Legacy

If one considers the destruction of Ruby 2 to be the nadir of USAF SEAD doctrine development, dismantling KARI was its highest point. The United States Air Force, in conjunction with the Navy, spent over fifty months total attempting to subdue the North Vietnamese–IADS via direct action. Not only were they unsuccessful, but their shortcomings were dire enough to call into question the United States' capacity to project conventional power. In contrast, the USAF and its Coalition partners planned, rehearsed, then executed the destruction of the KARI system in less than seven days of combat operations.

The difference in outcomes can clearly be traced to the Air Force's doctrinal changes. In 1965, the Air Force had engaged North Vietnam after a decade spent preparing for Massive Retaliation. It employed aircraft whose conception, acquisition, and evolution had been centered around the delivery of nuclear weapons of varying yields. Senior leaders, including Air Force Chief of Staff and head of TAC, had believed that high speed would provide sufficient protection against anti–aircraft guns. Surface–to–air missiles, while a threat, were not expected outside of the Soviet Union. Squadron, group, and wing commanders, without the necessary training against a realistically portrayed enemy, were ignorant of the conditions they would face. The resulting carnage and ineffectual operations spurred reconsideration of what happened and how to prevent it

308 | JAMES L. YOUNG JR.

from doing so again. The October 1973 Arab-Israeli War merely reinforced the notion that the United States Air Force simply had to evolve or cease to be pertinent to the national defense.

The resultant Air Force doctrine drove the evolution necessary for the USAF to remain relevant. General Momyer, dismayed by the events over Vietnam and his own failure to prepare TAC for the Linebacker operations, established the TAC gatherings necessary for mid- and junior-level officers to exchange ideas. General Momyer also found the resources necessary to test these thoughts in conditions that simulated those the Air Force expected to find in combat. Even as he turned over TAC to General Dixon, Momyer had sown a multitude of ideological seeds through the TAC Symposium, subordinates' overhaul of the *Fighter Weapons Review*, and the establishment of the CORONET ORGAN exercises.

These doctrinal seeds were what bore the fruits of victory over Iraq in 1991. Both General Dixon and General Creech, Momyer's successors at TAC, deserve credit for the successful harvest. Dixon, often unheralded and even vilified in subsequent accounts of his term, ensured that the "Iron Majors" were protected from internal and external meddling in the relatively lean years of the Ford and Carter administrations. Additionally, General Dixon's emphatic pursuit of realistic training ensured that Air Force doctrine was tested, often against the very systems the service expected to face in Europe.

With regard to procurement, Dixon was also a strong advocate for the Air Force to purchase what were the right systems, in appropriate numbers, for TAC. The F-15, F-16, F-4G, and E-3s that dominated the skies in 1991 were all examples of the Air Force deciding how it wanted to fight, then ensuring it had the platforms to do so. Almost as importantly, USAF leaders embraced technology and took advantage of the concurrent advances in electronic circuitry, processing, and miniaturization to replace or enhance those systems found wanting during Vietnam. Finally, Dixon's continued insistence on intellectual development led to the Air Force crafting doctrine that, while not perfect, finally shrugged off the dominance of nuclear delivery. In many ways, the publication of the February 1979 edition of AFM 1-1 was Dixon's passing of the intellectual baton to General Creech.

General Creech, for his part, came to embody the Air Force's embracement of technology at the end of the Cold War. It was Creech's resolute pursuit the F-117 that made certain that aircraft was available to lobotomize KARI on the opening night on Desert Storm. His insistence on air defense rollback, electronic warfare, night combat, standoff, and precision-guided munitions helped reestablish the conventional deterrence that was necessary for the United States' foreign policy. With a doctrinal vision, General Creech was able to resist the naysayers who insisted that USAF systems needed to be simpler and purchased in bulk. Instead, Creech helped craft an Air Force that explicitly stated that its quality and chosen realm of warfare would more than counterbalance the Warsaw Pact's greater numbers. Bekaa Valley, the Falklands War, and Operation El Dorado Canyon served as indicators that the Air Force was on the right track. Desert Storm was the final, emphatic confirmation that Creech's doctrinal instincts had merit.

Legacy

The Air Force had not been alone in devising its SEAD doctrine. Desert Storm also served to validate the concepts first discussed in the Elder–Bray conferences, then refined during the 31 Initiatives. Desert Storm was seen as proof that *Joint Doctrine for Theater Counterair Operations* was thematically sound, if in need of acquisition support due to problems with USN / USMC and Allied aircraft's identification friend or foe (IFF) transponders. Goldwater–Nichols had also been validated both through its reorganization into combatant commands and the forced purchase of compatible weapons and electronics systems.

Ironically, the Air Force's success would actually led to a reduction in size for both the electronic warfare and *Wild Weasel* communities. With the Soviet Union's implosion, the United States sought to reduce its military expenditures. Part of this was DoD assigning different roles across the "joint" community rather than having capabilities resided in a single service. Within five years, the EF-111 and F-4G would no longer be part of the Air Force inventory. The former's role was assigned to the EA-6B *Prowler* by the Department of the Defense, with the expectation that any future operations would employ the entire U.S. military. The *Wild Weasel*'s capability was replaced by equipping the F-16 with the HARM Targeting System, an electronic pod that the F-4G community derisively referred to as "Weasel in a Can." Proposals to replace the F-4G with modified F-15E *Strike Eagles* (due to it still being in production) or two-seat F-16s were stalled, then formally rejected within the USAF's hierarchy. Believing that the future lay in low-observable aircraft such as the still in development F-22 *Raptor* and F-35 *Lightning II*, the Air Force made another doctrinal shift towards acquiring these systems rather than building on its already existent foundation. Given the belief that there'd been a "Revolution in Military Affairs" driven by stealth technology and precision munitions, it made sense from the Air Force's perspective to concentrate limited funds on advanced systems rather than legacy technology.[518]

A full accounting of these decisions lays outside the scope of this book. Operation Deliberate Force (1995) and Operation Allied Force (1999) are still recent enough that several operational planning and tactical execution aspects remain classified. Moreover, the effectiveness of Air Force SEAD depends on whom is asked or what criteria is used. At least one F-117 *Nighthawk* was lost during Allied Force, and both the weather in the Balkans and Serbian tactics curtailed NATO aircraft from operating with impunity throughout the campaign. It will be up to other historians to determine whether the Air Force slipped from the perch it had so strenuously struggled to attain in the long climb from Ruby 2's demise to KARI's destruction.

BIBLIOGRAPHY

Primary Sources

United States Government Documents

Department of the Air Force. Air Force Manual 1-3, *Theater Air Operations*. Washington, DC: Department of the Air Force, 1 September 1953.

Department of the Air Force. Air Force Manual 1-1, *United States Air Force Basic Doctrine*. Washington, DC: Department of the Air Force, 28 September 1971.

Department of the Air Force. Air Force Manual 2-8, *Electronic Combat Operations*. Washington, DC: Department of the Air Force, 28 June 1987.

Department of the Air Force. *Mission Employment Tactics and Fighter Fundamentals F-4G*. Langley, VA: Headquarters Tactical Air Command, 15 March 1989.

Forrestal, James, Frank Pace, and Clark M. Clifford. Memorandum for the President of the United States. "Subject: Revision of the National Security Act," February 10, 1949. Truman Presidential Library.

Joint Chiefs of Staff. Joint Pub (JP) 3-01.2 *Joint Doctrine for Theater Counterair Operations*, 1 April 1986.

Momyer, William W., Gen., USAF (ret). Memorandum "SUBJECT: CORONA HARVEST Out Country Air Operations, Southeast Asia, 1 January, 1965 – 31 March, 1968." Albert F. Simpson Historical Research Center Archives (AFS–HRCA).

U.S. Air Force. USAF Operations (Strategic and General Operations) Section, J-3. Unknown briefing location and date. Briefing entitled "The Employment and Effectiveness of Missiles and Guided Weapons in SE Asia." AFS–HRCA.

Unpublished Papers

Whitt, James E., MAJ, USAF. "F-4 Employment of Air To Air Missiles In Southeast Asia: A Special Report." Project CORONA HARVEST, February 1970. Maxwell AFB, AL: AFS–HRCA, declassified 20 NOV 1987. Paper is rough draft copy, with handwritten comments and remarks from the editor. Research center staff indicated published copy remains classified.

Air Force Interviews and End of Tour Reports

Belli, Robert E., Ltc., USAF. Interview by MAJ Lyn R. Officer, USAF, and Mr. Hugh N.   Ahmann,

29 January, 1973. Transcript of interview. U.S. Air Force Oral History Program #645, de-classified 31 December 1981, AFS–HRCA, Maxwell AFB.

Momyer, William W., Gen., USAF (ret.). Interview by Dr. Edgar F. Puryear, Jr., 9 September 1981. Transcript of Part I of Interview. U.S. Air Force Oral History Program. AFS–HRCA, 18 April 1984.

McInerney, James E., Jr., MAJ Gen., USAF (ret.). Interview by Mr. W. Howard Plunkett, 25 January 2006. Transcript of interview. U.S. Air Force Oral History Program. Interview conducted at AFS–HRCA for inclusion in historical archives.

Books

Amir, Amos. *Fire in the Sky: Flying in Defence of Israel.* Translated by Ruvik Danieli. Tel Aviv, Israel: Israeli Ministry of Defense, 2000; Barnsley, South Yorkshire, UK: Pen & Sword Aviation, 2009.

Anderegg, C.R., Col., USAF (ret.). *Sierra Hotel: Flying Air Force Fighters in the Decade After Vietnam.* Washington, DC: Air Force History and Museums Program, 2001.

Blesse, F.C. "Boots," MAJ Gen., USAF (ret.). *Check Six: A Fighter Pilot Looks Back.* Mesa, AZ: Champlin Fighter Museum Press, 1987.

Broughton, Jack, Colonel, USAF (ret.). *Thud Ridge*, Bantam Illustrated Edition. Philadelphia: Lippincott, 1969; New York: Bantam Books, 1985.

_____. *Going Downtown: The War Against Washington and Hanoi*. New York: Orion Books/Crown, 1988; Pocket Books, 1990.

Cobleigh, Ed, Ltc., USAF (ret.). *War For the Hell of It*. New York: Berkely Caliber, 2005.

Cohen, Eliezer "Cheetah." *Israel's Best Defense: The First Full Story of the Israeli Air Force*. New York: Orion Books, 1983.

Halperin, Merav and Aharon Lapidot, Editors. *G-Suit: Combat Reports from Israel's Air War*. London: Sphere Books, Ltd., 1991.

Hampton, Dan. *Viper Pilot: A Memoir of Air Combat*, Kindle Edition. New York: Harper Collins, Inc., 2012.

Handley, Phil, Col., USAF (ret.). *Nickel On The Grass: Reflections of a U.S. Air Force Pilot*. New York: iUniverse, Inc., 2006.

Israelyan, Victor. *Inside the Kremlin During the Yom Kippur War*. University Park, PA: The Pennsylvania State University, 1995.

Marrett, George J. *Contrails over the Mojave: The Golden Age of Jet Flight Testing at Edwards Air Force Base*. Annapolis, MD: Naval Institute Press, 2008.

Peck, Gaillard R., Jr., Col., USAF (ret.). *America's*

Secret MiG Squadron: The Red Eagles of Project CONSTANT PEG. Long Island City, NY: Osprey Publishing, 2012.

Reagan, Ronald. *The Reagan Diaries*. New York: HarperCollins, 2007.

Schreiner, Jim and Braxton Eisel. *Magnum! The Wild Weasels in Desert Storm*. Barnsley, South Yorkshire, UK: Pen & Sword Aviation, 2009.

Sharp, U.S. Grant, Adm., USN (ret.). *Strategy for Defeat: Vietnam in Retrospect*. San Rafael, CA: Presidio Press, 1979.

Sorley, Lewis, ed. *Press On!: Selected Words of General Donn A. Starry*, Volume I. Fort Leavenworth, KS: Combat Studies Institute Press, 2009.

_____. *Press On!: Selected Works of General Donn A. Starry*, Volume II. Fort Leavenworth, KS: Combat Studies Institute Press, 2009.

Spector, Iftach, Brigadier General, IAF. *Loud and Clear: The Memoir of an Israeli Fighter Pilot*. Minneapolis, MN: Zenith Press, 2009.

Toliver, Richard. *An Uncaged Eagle: True Freedom*. Goodyear, AZ: Saguaro Publishing Company, 2009.

Tollini, Rick. *Call-Sign Kluso: An American Fighter Pilot in Mr. Reagan's Air Force*. Havertown, PA: Casemate Publishers, 2021.

Venkus, Robert E., Col., USAF (ret.). *Raid on Qaddafi: The Untold Story of History's Longest Fighter Mis-*

sion by the Pilot Who Directed It, Paperback Edition. New York: St. Martin's Press, 1993.

Warden, John A., III, Col., USAF. *The Air Campaign: Planning for Combat.* Future Warfare Series, Perry M. Smith, General Editor. Washington, DC: National Defense University, 1988; Pergamon-Brassey's, 1989.

Weinberger, Caspar. *Fighting For Peace: Seven Critical Years in the Pentagon.* New York: Warner Books, Inc., 1990.

_____. *In the Arena: A Memoir of the 20th Century.* Washington, DC: Regnery Publishing, 2001.

Woodward, Sandy with Patrick Robinson. *One Hundred Days: The Memoirs of the Falklands Battle Group Commander.* Annapolis, MD: Bluejacket Books, 1997.

Zuyev, Alexander with Malolm McConnell, *Fulcrum: A Top Gun Pilot's Escape from the Soviet Empire.* New York: Warner Books, 1992.

Professional Articles and Personal Vignettes

Anderegg, Dick. "Meeting the Threat: Sophistication vs. Simplicity." *Fighter Weapons Journal*, Fall 1982: 2-6.

Ballanco, Edward M. "Victor" (WW #1774). "Wild Weasel Planning for Desert Storm." In *First In, Last Out: Stories by the Wild Weasels (First Person*

Stories By Wild Weasel Pilots, EWOs, and Their Associates), ed. Edward T. Rock, Col., USAF (ret.), 574-582. Bloomington, IN: Authorhouse Press, 2005.

Baron, Der (pseud.). "Anything Else is Rubbish." *Fighter Weapons Review*, Summer 1972: 32-34.

_____. "Anything Else is Rubbish." *Fighter Weapons Review*, Spring 1975: 10-12.

Cobleigh, Ed. "Top Gun Navy Style." *USAF Fighter Weapons Review*, Spring 1973: 5-7.

Coffey, Kenneth J. "Defending Europe Against Conventional Attack." *Air University Review* 31, No. 2 (January-February 1980): 47-59

Collins, Craig, Capt., USAF. "Air Combat Maneuvering: A Little Help From My Friend." *Fighter Weapons Review*, Winter 1976, 30-36.

Comer, Randy "Pyle" (WW #2521). "Combat Sortie Number One." In *First In, Last Out: Stories by the Wild Weasels (First Person Stories By Wild Weasel Pilots, EWOs, and Their Associates)*, ed. Edward T. Rock, Col., USAF (ret.), 583-586. Bloomington IN: Authorhouse Press, 2005.

Dunn, Peter M. "F-111 Aardvark." In *Flying American Combat Aircraft: The Cold War*, ed. Robin Higham, 153-163. Mechanicsburg PA: Stackpole Books, 2005.

Gish, Donald L., MAJ, USAF. "F-4 Air to Air Training." *Fighter Weapons Review*, Fall 1975: 1-5.

Hamilton, Bill, Capt., USAF. "One vs. Many." *Fighter Weapons Review*, Fall 1977: 1-7.

_____. "Weapons Officer: Air to Air." *Fighter Weapons Review*, Fall 1979: 2-13.

Hampton, Dan, Capt., USAF. "Combat Defense Suppression: The F-4G / F-16C Wild Weasel At War." *Fighter Weapons Review*, Summer 1991: 4-6.

Harwick, Alexander H.C. "F-4 Phantom." In *Flying American Combat Aircraft: The Cold War*, ed. Robin Higham, 305-318. Mechanicsburg PA: Stackpole Books, 2005.

_____. "Thoughts on Flight Leadership," *Fighter Weapons Review*, Summer 1973: 6-8.

Hawks, George W., Jr. "Flying the F-15 Eagle." In *Flying American Combat Aircraft: The Cold War*, ed. Robin Higham, 1-19. Mechanicsburg PA: Stackpole Books, 2005.

Hoag, Robert J. "Symposium 1972." *Fighter Weapons Review*, Winter 1972: 9-11

Hosmer, Bradley C., LTG, USAF. "American Air Power and Grand Tactics." *Airpower Journal* 1, No. 1 (Summer 1987): 9-14

Jumper, John, Capt., USAF. "Air-to-Air—Training to Win." *Fighter Weapons Review*, Winter 1976: 16.

_____. "When You Have to Go Low." *Fighter Weapons Review*, Spring 1977: 55-71.

_____. "Ground Attack Tactics: To Fly and Fight." *Fighter Weapons Review*, Spring 1977: 85–88.

Keys, Ron, Capt., USAF. "Air Combat Tactics: The Run for the Roses." *Fighter Weapons Review*, Winter 1976: 44–50.

_____. "AHC / BFM for Instructors." *Fighter Weapons Review*, Winter 1976: 16–30.

_____. "Air-to-Air Multi-Threat." *Fighter Weapons Review*, Spring 1978: 2–6.

Larson, T. Bear (WW #952). "The F-4G/APR-38/ HARM Evolves as a Weapons System." In *First In, Last Out: Stories by the Wild Weasels (First Person Stories By Wild Weasel Pilots, EWOs, and Their Associates)*, ed. Edward T. Rock, Col., USAF (ret.), 566–573. Bloomington IN: Authorhouse Press, 2005.

New, Larry D. "Reentering the Fight." *Fighter Weapons Review*, Winter 1981: 22–24.

Oliver, Luis, LTC, USAF. "Nellis Tactical Ranges." *Fighter Weapons Review*, Fall 1977: 8–13.

Phillips, Clyde, CPT, USAF. "Air-to-Surface Target Destruction with Force Survival." *Fighter Weapons Review*, Spring 1977: 53–55.

Press, Mike, LTC, USAF. "Aggressor Reflections." *Fighter Weapons Review*, Spring 1981: 2–6.

Roy, Vincent P., MAJ, USAF. "Double Attack Revisited." *Fighter Weapons Review*, Spring 1971: 26–32.

Shoenfeld, Mike W., CPT, USAF. "New Guy on the Street-the AIM-9L." *Fighter Weapons Review*, Spring 1980: 2-6.

Stucky, Paul, CPT, USAF. "Blocking and Tackling." *Fighter Weapons Review*, Winter 1981: 24-28

Turner, Chuck, MAJ, USAF. "Fightergram: RAF Red Flag." *Fighter Weapons Review*, Fall 1977: 36.

Winzell, Jim (WW #1098). "The F-4G Wild Weasel." In *First In, Last Out: Stories by the Wild Weasels (First Person Stories By Wild Weasel Pilots, EWOs, and Their Associates)*, ed. Edward T. Rock, Col., USAF (ret.), 562-565. Bloomington IN: Authorhouse Press, 2005.

Secondary Sources

Department of Defense Documents

Department of Defense. Joint Publication 1-02, *Dictionary of Military and Associated Terms April 2001 (As Amended Through 9 June 2004)*. Washington, DC: Department of Defense, 2004.

Defense Nuclear Agency Documents

Blustone, B.L. and J.P. Peak. "Air Superiority and Airfield Attack: Lessons from History." Technical Report prepared for Defense Nuclear

Agency, Contract No. DNA 001-81-C-0183, 15
May, 1984.

Books

Angelucci, Enzo with Peter Bowers. *The American Fighter: The Definitive Guide to American Fighter Aircraft From 1917 to the Present, First American Edition*. New York: Orion Books, 1987.

Boyne, Walter J., Col., USAF (ret). *Phantom in Combat*. New York: Jane's Publishing Co., 1985; Atglen, PA: Schiffer Publishing, Ltd., 1994.

_____. *The Influence of Air Power upon History*. Gretna, LA: Pelican Publishing Company, Inc., 2003.

_____. *Beyond the Wild Blue: A History of the United States Air Force, 1947-2007*, 2nd ed. New York: Thomas Dunne Books, 2007.

Brown, Archie. *The Gorbachev Factor*, Oxford Paperback Edition. Oxford, UK: Oxford University Press, 1997.

Brown, Craig. *Debrief: A Complete History of U.S. Aerial Engagements, 1981 to the Present*. Atglen, PA: Schiffer Military History, 2007.

Brungess, James R., Lt. Col., USAF. *Setting the Context: Suppression of Enemy Air Defense and Joint War Fighting in an Uncertain World*. Maxwell AFB, AL: Air University Press, 1994.

Budiansky, Stephen. *Air Power: The Men, Machines, and Ideas That Revolutionized War, From Kitty Hawk to Gulf War II*. New York: Viking Books, 2004.

Campbell, Christopher. *Air Warfare: The Fourth Generation*. New York: Arco Publishing, Inc., 1984.

Carter, John R., MAJ, USAF. *Airpower and the Cult of the Offensive*. College of Aerospace Doctrine Research and Education (CADRE) Papers. Maxwell AFB, AL: Air University Press, 1998.

Chun, Clayton K.S. *Aerospace Power in the Twenty-First Century: A Basic Primer*. Maxwell AFB, AL: Air University Press, 2001.

Clancy, Tom with Chuck Horner, Gen., USAF (ret.). *Every Man A Tiger*. Berkley Paperback Edition. New York: G.P. Putnam's Sons, May 1999; Berkley Caliber, May 2000.

Collins, Robert M. *More: The Politics of Economic Growth in Postwar America*. New York: Oxford University Press, 2000.

Coram, Robert. *Boyd: The Fighter Pilot Who Changed the Art of War*, Back Bay paperback edition. New York: Little, Brown and Company, 2002; Back Bay Books, 2004.

Cordesman, Anthony H. and Abraham R. Wagner. *The Lessons of Modern War, Volume I: The Arab-Israeli Conflicts, 1973-1989*, paperback reprint edition. San Francisco: Westview Press, 1991.

_____. *The Lessons of Modern War, Volume III: The Afghan and Falklands Conflicts*, paperback reprint edition. San Francisco: Westview Press, 1991.

_____. *The Lessons of Modern War, Volume IV: The Gulf War*. San Francisco: Westview Press, 1996.

Crabtree, James D. *On Air Defense*. The Military Profession Series, ed. Bruce Gudmundsson. Westport, CT: Praeger Publishers, 1994.

Crane, Conrad C. *American Airpower Strategy in Korea, 1950-1953*. Modern War Series, General Editor Theodore A. Wilson. Lawrence KS: University Press of Kansas, 2000.

Creveld, Martin van with Steven I. Canby and Kenneth S. Brower. *Air Power and Maneuver Warfare*. Maxwell AFB, AL: Air University Press, 1994.

Crosby, Francis. *A Handbook of Fighter Aircraft*. London: Hermes House, 2003.

Davies, Steve and Doug Dildy. *F-15 Eagle Engaged: The World's Most Successful Jet Fighter*. Oxford, UK: Osprey Publishing, 2007.

_____. *Red Eagles: America's Secret MiGs*. Oxford, UK: Osprey Publishing, 2008.

Davis, Richard D. *On Target: Organizing and Executing the Strategic Air Campaign Against Iraq*. Washington, DC: Air Force History and Museums Program, 2002.

Dorr, Robert F. and Chris Bishop, eds. *Vietnam Air Warfare: The Story of the Aircraft, the Battles, and the Pilots Who Fought*. Edison, NJ: Chartwell Books, Inc., 1996.

Drew, Dennis M. and Donald M. Snow, Ph.D. *The Eagle's Talons: The American Experience at War*. Maxwell AFB, AL: Air University Press, 1988.

Duffield, John S. *Power Rules: The Evolution of NATO's Conventional Force Posture*. Stanford, CA: Stanford University Press, 1995.

Dupuy, Trevor N. *Elusive Victory: The Arab-Israeli Wars, 1947-1974*, 3rd Edition. Dubuque, IA: Kendall / Hunt Publishing, 1992.

Ethell, Jeffrey and Alfred Price. *Air War South Atlantic*. New York: Macmillan, 1983.

Futrell, Robert Frank. *Ideas, Concepts, Doctrine: Basic Thinking in the United States Air Force, Volume II, 1961-1984*. Maxwell Air Force Base, AL: Air University Press, December 1989.

Gaddis, John Lewis. *The United States and the End of the Cold War: Implications, Reconsiderations, Provocations*. New York: Oxford University Press, 1992.

_____. *The Cold War: A New History*. New York: Penguin Books, 2005.

Gething, Michael J. *Modern Fighting Aircraft*, Vol. 1, *F-15 Eagle*. New York: Arco Publishing, Inc., 1983.

Glantz, David M. *Soviet Military Operational Art: In Pursuit of Deep Battle*. Portland, OR: Frank Cass, 1991.

_____. Glantz, David M. *The Military Strategy of the Soviet Union: A History*. Portland, OR: Frank Cass, 1992.

Green, William and Gordon Swanborough. *The Complete Book of Fighters: An Illustrated Encyclopedia of Every Fighter Aircraft Built and Flown*, Barnes and Noble Edition. New York: Salamander Books, 1994; Barnes and Noble Books, 1998.

Guardia, Mike. *Skybreak: The 58th Fighter Squadron in Desert Storm*. Maple Grove, MN: Magnum Books, 2021.

Halberstadt, Hans. *The Wild Weasels: History of U.S. Air Force SAM Killers, 1965 to Today*. Motorbooks International Mil-Tech Series. Osceola, WI: Motorbooks International Publishers & Wholesalers, 1992.

Hammond, Grant T. *Mind of War: John Boyd and American Security*. Washington, DC: Smithsonian Institution, 2001.

Hastings, Max and Simon Jenkins. *The Battle for the Falklands*, Pan Books Edition. London: Pan Books, 1997.

Herspring, Dale R. *The Pentagon and the Presidency: Civil Military Relations from FDR to George W. Bush*. Lawrence, KS: University Press of Kansas, 2005.

Hess, Gary R. *Presidential Decisions for War: Korea, Vietnam, and the Persian Gulf*. Baltimore, MD: John Hopkins University Press, 2001.

Holley, I.B., Jr., MAJ Gen., USAF, ret. *Technology and Military Doctrine: Essays on a Challenging Relationship*. Maxwell AFB, AL: Air University Press, 2004.

Insight Team of the London *Sunday Times*. *The Yom Kippur War*. Garden City, NY: Doubleday & Company, 1974.

Isby, David C. *Weapons and Tactics of the Soviet Union*. Fully Revised Edition. London: Jane's Publishing Company, Ltd., 1988.

Jane's Information Group. *Jane's Battlefield Air Defence, 1988-1989*. Edited by Tony Cullen and Christopher F. Foss. Alexandria, VA: Jane's Information Group, Inc., 1988.

_____. *Jane's Land-Based Air Defense, Thirteenth Edition, 2000-2001*. Edited by Tony Cullen and Christopher F. Foss. Alexandria, VA: Jane's Information Group, Inc., 2000.

Jones, Johnny, Ltc., USAF. *Development of Air Force Basic Doctrine, 1947-1992*. Maxwell AFB, AL: Air University Press, 1997.

Lambeth, Benjamin S. *The Transformation of American Air Power*. Cornell Studies in Security Affairs, eds. Robert J. Art, Robert Jervis, and Stephen M. Walt. Ithaca, NY: Cornell University Press, 2000.

_____. *Russia's Air Power at the Crossroads*. Santa Monica, CA: RAND, 1996.

_____. *Moscow's Lessons from the 1982 Lebanon Air War*. Santa Monica, CA: RAND, 1984.

Luckett, Perry D. and Charles L. Byler. *Tempered Steel: The Three Wars of Triple Air Force Cross Winner Jim Kassler*, paperback edition. Dulles, VA: Potomac Books, 2005; 2006.

Luttwak, Edward and Stuart Koehl. *The Dictionary of Modern War*. New York: HarperCollins, 1991.

Mason, R.A. and John W.R. Taylor. *Aircraft, Strategy, and Operations of the Soviet Air Force*. London: Jane's Publishing Company, Ltd., 1986.

Mason, Tony, Air Vice Marshal, RAF. *Air Power: A Centennial Appraisal*. London: Brassey's, 1994.

Martin, David C. and John Walcott. *Best Laid Plans: The Inside Story of America's War Against Terrorism*. New York: Touchstone Books, 1988.

Messenger, Charles. *Armies of World War 3*. Greenwich, CT: Bison Books, 1984.

Michel, Marshall L. *Clashes: Air Combat Over North Vietnam, 1965-972*. Annapolis,MD: Naval Institute Press, 1996.

_____. *The Eleven Days of Christmas: America's Last Vietnam Battle*. San Francisco, CA: Encounter Books, 2002.

Moody, Walton S. *Building a Strategic Force*. Washington, DC: Air Force History and Museums Program, 1995.

Mrozek, Donald J. *The U.S. Air Force After Vietnam: Postwar Challenges and Potential for Responses.* Maxwell AFB, AL: Air University Press, 1988.

Murray, Williamson with Wayne W. Thompson. *Air War in the Persian Gulf.* Baltimore, MD: The Nautical and Aviation Publishing Company of America, 1995.

Newdick, Thomas. *Postwar Air Weapons, 1945–Present.* London: Amber Books, Ltd., 2011.

Nordeen, Lon. *Fighters Over Israel: The Story of the Israeli Air Force from the War of Independence to the Bekaa Valley.* London: Greenhill Books, 1990.

_____. *Air Combat in the Missile Age*, 2nd Edition. Washington, DC: Smithsonian Institution Press, 2010.

Olsen, John Andreas. *John Warden and the Renaissance of American Airpower.* Dulles, VA: Potomac Books, 2007.

Peebles, Curtis. *Dark Eagles: A History of Top Secret U.S. Air Force Programs.* Novato, CA: Presidio Press, 1995.

Price, Alfred. *Air Battle Central Europe*, Warner Books Edition. New York: Free Press, 1986; Warner Books, 1990.

Rendall, Ivan. *Rolling Thunder: Jet Combat from World War II to the Gulf War.* New York: Dell Publishing, 1997.

Reynolds, Richard T. *Heart of the Storm: The Genesis of the Air Campaign Against Iraq.* Maxwell Air Force Base, AL: Air University Press, 1995.

Shaw, Robert L.. *Fighter Combat: Tactics and Maneuvering.* Annapolis, MD: United States Naval Institute Press, 1985.

Smallwood, William L. *Strike Eagle: Flying the F-15E in the Gulf War.* Washington, D.C.: Brassey's, 1994.

Richardson, Doug. *Modern Fighting Aircraft*, Vol. 2, *F-16 Fighting Falcon.* New York: Arco Publishing, Inc., 1983.

Richardson, Doug and Michael Spick. *Modern Fighting Aircraft*, Vol. 4, *F-4 Phantom.* New York: Arco Publishing, Inc., 1984.

Slife, James C., LTC, USAF. *Creech Blue: General Bill Creech and the Reformation of the Tactical Air Forces, 1978-1984.* Maxwell Air Force Base, AL: Air University Press in collaboration with the College of Aerospace Doctrine Research and Education (CADRE), 2004.

Smith, John T. *The Linebacker Raids.* London: Cassell & Co., 2000.

Smallwood, William L. *Strike Eagle: Flying the F-15E in the Gulf War*, Kindle Edition. New York: Brassey's, Inc., 1997.

Spick, Mike. *Fighter Pilot Tactics: The Techniques of Daylight Air Combat*. New York: Stein and Day, 1983.

_____. *All-Weather Warriors: The Search for the Ultimate Fighter Aircraft*. London: Arms and Armour Press, 1994.

_____, ed. *The Great Book of Modern Warplanes*, reprint edition. London: Salamander Books, 2003.

Stanik, Joseph T. *El Dorado Canyon: Reagan's Undeclared War With Qaddafi*. Annapolis, MD: Naval Institute Press, 2003.

Thornborough, Anthony M. *Modern Fighter Aircraft Technology and Tactics: Into Combat With Today's Fighter Pilots*. Somerset, UK: Patrick Stephens Limited, 1995.

Thornborough, Anthony M. and Peter E. Davies. *F-111: Success in Action*. New York: Sterling Publishing Co., Inc., 1989.

Thornborough, Anthony M. and Frank B. Mormillo. *Iron Hand: Smashing the Enemy's Air Defences*. With Tony Cassanova & Kevin Jackson. Somerset, England: Patrick Stephens Limited, 2002; Reprint Sparkford, England: Sutton Publishing, 2002.

Thornton, Richard C. *The Carter Years: Toward A New Global Order*. Washington, DC: Washington Institute for Values in Public Policy, 1991; St. Paul, MN: Paragon House, 2007.

Trest, Warren. *Air Force Roles and Missions: A History*. Washington, DC: Air Force History and Museums Program, 1998.

Watts, Barry D. *Six Decades of Guided Munitions and Battle Networks: Progress and Prospects*. Washington, DC: Center for Strategic and Budgetary Assessments, 2007.

Werrell, Kenneth P. *Archie, Flak, AAA and SAM*. Maxwell Air Force Base, AL: Air University Press, 1988.

Worden, Mike, Col., USAF. *Rise of the Fighter Generals: The Problem of Air Force Leaders, 1945-1982*. Maxwell AFB, AL: Air University Press, 1998.

Trauschweizer, Ingo. *The Cold War U.S. Army: Building Deterrence for Limited War*. Lawrence, Kansas: University of Kansas Press, 2008.

Zaloga, Stephen J.. *Red SAM: The SA-2 Guideline Anti-Aircraft Missile*. New Vanguard Series #134. Oxford, England: Osprey Publishing, 2007.

Articles

Boyne, Walter J. "Momyer." *Air Force Magazine* 96, No. 8 (August 2013): 65-68.

Brereton, Greenhous. "The Israeli Experience." In *Case Studies in the Achievement of Air Superiority*, ed. Benjamin Franklin Cooling, 563-608. Washington, DC: Center for Air Force History,

1994.

Endicott, Judy G. "Raid on Libya: Operation El Dorado Canyon." In *Short of War: Major USAF Contingency Operations*, ed. A. Timothy Warnock, 145–157. Washington, DC: Center for Air Force History, 2000.

Nicklas-Carter, M. "NATO's Central Front." In *Armoured Warfare*, eds. J.P. Harris and F.H. Toase, 205–229. New York: St. Martin's Press, 1990.

Deptula, David A. "Parallel Warfare: What Is It? Where Did It Come From?" In *The Eagle in the Desert: Looking Back on U.S. Involvement in the Persian Gulf War*, ed. William Head and Earl H. Tilford, 127–156. Westport, CT: Praeger Publishers, 1996.

Fino, Steven A. "Breaking the Trance: The Perils of Technological Exuberance in the U.S. Air Force Entering Vietnam." *Journal of Military History*, Vol 77 (April 2013): 625–655.

Fiszer, Michael. "A Soviet Look at El Dorado Canyon." *Journal of Electronic Defense*, Vol 27 (October 2004): 51–56.

Greenwood, John T. and Von Hardesty. "Soviet Air Forces in World War II." In *The Soviet Air Forces*, ed. Paul J. Murphy, 29–69. Jefferson, NC: McFarland & Company, Inc., 1984.

Hanhimaki, Jussi M. "Détente in Europe, 1962–1975." In *The Cambridge History of the Cold War*,

Volume II: Crises and Détente, 5th Edition, eds. Melvyn P. Leffler and Odd Arne Westad, 198–218. Cambridge, UK: Cambridge University Press, 2014.

Haulman, Daniel L. "USAF Manned Combat Air Losses, 1990–2002." Air Force Historical Research Agency Paper, 9 December 2002.

Hine, Sir Patrick. "Air Operations in the Gulf War." In *The War in the Air, 1914–1994*, American Edition, ed. Alan Stephens, 339–360. Maxwell AFB, AL: Air University Press (in cooperation with the RAAF Aerospace Center), January 2001.

Holley, I.B., Jr. "Some Concluding Insights." In *Case Studies in the Achievement of Air Superiority*, ed. Benjamin Franklin Cooling, 609–626. Washington, DC: Center for Air Force History, 1994.

Horner, Charles. A. "New Era Warfare." In *The War in the Air, 1914–1994*, American Edition, ed. Alan Stephens, 361–375. Maxwell AFB, AL: Air University Press (in cooperation with the RAAF Aerospace Center), 2001.

Hurley, Matthew M. "The Bekaa Valley Air Battle, June 1982: Lessons Mislearned?" *Airpower Journal* Vol. 4 (Winter 1989): 60–70.

Kuehl, Daniel T. "Thunder and the Storm: Strategic Air Operations in the Gulf War." In *The Eagle in the Desert: Looking Back on U.S. Involvement in the Persian Gulf War*, ed. William Head and Earl H. Tilford, 111–126. Westport, CT: Praeger

Publishers, 1996.

Mandeles, Mark D. "Command and Control in the Gulf War: A Military Revolution in Airpower?" In *The Eagle in the Desert: Looking Back on U.S. Involvement in the Persian Gulf War*, ed. William Head and Earl H. Tilford, 157–172. Westport, CT: Praeger Publishers, 1996.

Mason, R.A. "Airpower as a National Instrument: The Arab–Israeli Wars." In *The War in the Air, 1914–1994*, American Edition, ed. Alan Stephens, 191–220. Maxwell AFB, AL: Air University Press (in cooperation with the RAAF Aerospace Center), 2001.

Mastny, Vojtech. "Imagining War in Europe: Soviet Military Planning." In *War Plans and Alliances in the Cold War*, eds. Vojtech Mastny, Sven G. Hollsmark and Andress Wenger, 15–45. New York: Routledge, 2006.

Mowbray, James A. "Air Force Doctrine Problems, 1926–Present." *Airpower Journal*, Winter 1995.

Pennington, Rana. "Pilot Initiative in the Soviet Air Force." In *The Soviet Air Forces*, ed. Paul J. Murphy, 149–156. Jefferson, NC: McFarland & Company, Inc., 1984.

Schneider, William. "Soviet Frontal Aviation: Evolving Capabilities and Trends." In *The Soviet Air Forces*, ed. Paul J. Murphy, 133–148. Jefferson, NC: McFarland & Company, Inc., 1984.

Stambaugh, Jeffrey E. "JFACC: Key to Organizing

Your Air Assets for Victory." *Parameters*, Volume XXI (Summer 1994): 98–110.

Watts, Barry D. "Doctrine, Technology, and War." Maxwell AFB, AL: Air and Space Doctrinal Symposium, 30 April–1 May, 1996.

Ziemke, Caroline. "A New Convenant?: The Apostles of Douhet and the Persian Gulf War." In *The Eagle in the Desert: Looking Back on U.S. Involvement in the Persian Gulf War*, ed. William Head and Earl H. Tilford, 290–310. Westport, CT: Praeger Publishers, 1996.

Dissertations and Theses

Dougherty, Stanley J., MAJ, USAF. "Defense Suppression: Building Some Operational Concepts." School of Advanced Airpower Studies (SAAS) Thesis Maxwell AFB, Academic Year 1991–1992.

Eldredge, Maurice C. MAJ, USAF. "A Brief History of ADTAC: The First Five Years," Air Command and Staff College (ACSC) Thesis, April 1985.

Kupersmith, Douglas A., MAJ, USAF. "The Failure of Third World Air Power: Iraq and the War with Iran." SAAS Thesis, Academic Year 1991–1992.

Mead, Nathan A., MAJ, USAF. "A Man For All Reason: General Larry D. Welch, 12th Chief of Staff, U.S. Air Force." SAAS Thesis, June 2012.

Michel, Marshall L. "The Revolt of the Majors: How

the Air Force Changed After Vietnam." Ph.D. Dissertation, Auburn University, 2006.

Mcallister, Branford J., MAJ, USAF. "Air to Air Continuation Training in the Tactical Air Command." ACSC Student Report, April 1985.

Schrader, Jeffrey J., MAJ, USAF. "A History of the Wild Weasels in Southeast Asia." ACSC Student Report, April 1985.

ENDNOTES

1   Chris Hobson, *Vietnam Air Losses: United States Air Force, Navy and Marine Corps Fixed-Wing Aircraft Losses in Southeast Asia 1961-1973* (Hinckley, England: Midland Counties Publications, 2001), 247.

2   Hobson, 240-247.

3   Wayne Thompson, *To Hanoi and Back: The U.S. Air Force and North Vietnam, 1966-1973* (Washington, DC: Smithsonian Institution Press, 2000), 302.

4   Harry S. Truman, *Memoirs of Harry S. Truman, Volume 1, 1945: Year of Decisions*, Konecky & Konecky Leaders of Our Time Series Reprint, no editor given (New York: Time, Inc. 1955; Konecky & Konecky, undated reproduction), 524 and *Memoirs of Harry S. Truman, Volume 2, 1946-52: Years of Trial and Hope*, Da Capo Paperback Unabridged Edition (Garden City, NY: Doubleday, 1956; Da Capo, undated reproduction), 35-39.

5   Dwight D. Eisenhower, *The Eisenhower Diaries*, Robert H. Ferrell, ed. (New York: W.W. Norton & Company, 1981), 136-153 *passim*; James Forrestal, Frank Pace, and Clark M. Clifford, Memorandum for the President of the United States, "Subject: Revision of the National Security Act," classified CONFIDENTIAL (declassified April 12, 1974), dated February 10, 1949,

PSF, Truman Presidential Library; Walton S. Moody, *Building a Strategic Force* (Washington, DC: Air Force History and Museums Program, 1995), 255-335; and Truman, *ibid.* For a more detailed discussion of the United States Navy's concerns, please see Jeffrey G. Barlow's *Revolt of the Admirals* (Washington, DC: Government Reprints Press, 2001).

6   Boyne, *Wild Blue*, 35-52. This discussion is somewhat a simplification, as the Air Force briefly subordinated TAC to the Continental Air Command (ConAC) in the months preceding the Korean War. However, this arrangement was shortly lived and was primarily administrative in nature.

7   Boyne, *ibid.*; Moody, *ibid.*; Trest, 111-138.

8   Some recent general histories include Conrad C. Crane, *American Airpower Strategy in Korea, 1950-1953* (Lawrence, KS: University Press of Kansas, 2000) and Kenneth P. Werrell, *Sabres over MiG Alley: The F-86 and the Battle for Air Superiority in Korea* (Annapolis MD: Naval Institute Press, 2005).

9   For sake of comparison, the P-51 *Mustang* was considered one of the best fighters in the world, with a top speed of 450 miles per hour at sea level. In comparison, by 1950 the USAF had already begun to employ the F-80 *Shooting Star* (543 mph) and by 1952 would also have the F-84 *Thunderjet* (587 mph) and *Thunderstreak* (613 mph) ground attack fighters. All speeds from

Enzo Angelucci with Peter Bowers, *The American Fighter: The Definitive Guide to American Fighter Aircraft From 1917 to the Present,* First American ed. (New York: Orion Books, 1987), 274–275, 334–335, and 402–405.

10   Conrad C. Crane *American Airpower Strategy in Korea, 1950–1953,* Modern War Studies, ed. Theodore A. Wilson (Lawrence, KS: University Press of Kansas, 2000), 136 and Kenneth P. Werrell, *Archie, Flak, AAA and SAM* (Maxwell Air Force Base: Air University Press, 1988), 74–81. It could be argued that better coordination between U.N. artillery and Air Force sorties contributed as much as jets' inherent speed to lower losses in the last two years. It became common practice for artillery to fire suppressive barrages when a CAS flight reported it had arrived on station, with the fighters attacking shortly after the shells had finished impacting.

11   Crane, 82–92; Werrell, *Sabres,* 75–93; National Museum of the United States Air Force website fact sheets for the B-29 (http://www.nationalmuseum.af.mil/factsheets/factsheet.asp?id=2528), B-36 (http://www.nationalmuseum.af.mil/factsheets/factsheet.asp?id=2544) and B-47 (http://www.nationalmuseum.af.mil/factsheets/factsheet.asp?id=2605); and Xiaoming Zhang, *Red Wings Over the Yalu: China, the Soviet Union, and the Air War in Korea* (Texas Air University Press, 2002), 121–138.

12   For examples of these impassioned

discussions, please see Jack Broughton's *Thud Ridge* (Philadelphia: Lippincott, 1969) and *Going Downtown* (New York: Orion Books, 1988); Ed Cobleigh's *War for the Hell of It* (New York: Berkely Caliber, 2005); Craig C. Hannah's *Striving For Air Superiority: The Tactical Air Command in Vietnam* (College Station, Texas: Texas A&M University Press, 2002); and Colonel Mike Worden's *Rise of the Fighter Generals: The Problem of Air Force Leaders, 1945-1982* (Maxwell AFB, AL: Air University Press, 1998).

13   Werrel, *Sabres*, 156-212 and Zhang, 107-109. Considering the demographics of most successful F-86 pilots, the available statistics regarding the increased lethality of fighter pilots after their tenth combat sortie, and the indifferent training received by North Korean and People's Liberation Army Air Force (PLAAF) pilots, it is readily apparent that the Communist forces were fortunate that their losses were not far worse versus the Far East Air Force.

14   John S. Duffield, *Power Rules: The Evolution of NATO's Conventional Force Posture* (Stanford, CA: Stanford University Press, 1995), 75-100; John Lewis Gaddis, *The Cold War: A New History* (New York: Penguin Press, 2005), 63-68 (henceforth Gaddis, *Cold War*); Gaddis's *The United States and the End of the Cold War: Implications, Reconsiderations, Provocations* (New York: Oxford University Press, 1992), 8-9, 58, and 65-86 (henceforth Gaddis, *United States*); Gordon Gray, Resignation Letter as Special Assistant for National Security

Affairs Effective 20 January 1961, dated 13 January 1961, Ann Whitman Files, Box No. 16, Eisenhower Presidential Library, Abilene, KS; Chester J. Pach, Jr. and Elmo Richardson, *The Presidency of Dwight D. Eisenhower*, revised edition (Lawrence, KS: University Press of Kansas, 1991), 23 and 26; and Geoffrey Perrett, *Eisenhower* (New York: Random House, 1999), 424-428. Eisenhower's New Look relied most heavily on getting Europe to the point where it could defend itself by providing economic assistance and access to conventional military equipment. However, the threat of Massive Retaliation was expected to deter any temptation to influence Western Europe's recovery via insurgency or direct military action.

15   This section of the dissertation relies heavily on research conducted for James L. Young, Jr.'s "United States Air Force Defense Suppression Doctrine, 1968-1972" (master's thesis, Kansas State University, 2008). As such, there may be some overlap between this section and passages in that document..

16   Edward Luttwak and Stuart Koehl, *The Dictionary of Modern War* (New York: HarpersCollins, 1991), 170.

17   Department of Defense, Joint Publication 1-02, *Dictionary of Military and Associated Terms April 2001 (As Amended Through 9 June 2004)* (Washington, DC, 2004), 165.

18   For example, Pearl Harbor is mentioned several times in Curtis LeMay's *America is in*

Danger (New York: Funk & Wagnalls, 1968). Likewise other contemporary authors, such as Henry Kissinger, spoke several times of a nuclear Pearl Harbor. It is clear that the Japanese assault and subsequent debacle in the Pacific made a lasting impression on those who lived through it.

19   Steven L. Rearden, "U.S. Strategic Bombing Doctrine Since 1945," *Case Studies in Strategic Bombardment*, R. Cargill Hall, ed., (Washington, DC: Center for Air Force History, 1998), 412–413.

20   Robert R. Bowie and Richard Immerman, *Waging Peace: How Eisenhower Shaped an Enduring Cold War Strategy* (New York: Oxford University Press, 1998), 97–108; Boyne, *Wild Blue*, 99–113; and Budiansky, 361–368.

21   General Twining served as Air Force Chief of Staff from 1953 through 1957. General White served as Vice Chief of Staff under Twining than became Chief of Staff from 1957 through 1961. General LeMay, perhaps the most famous and influential officer in Air Force history, served as Commander in Chief (CinC) Strategic Air Command (1948 through 1957), Vice Chief of Staff of the Air Force (1957 through 1961), then as Chief of Staff from 1961 through 1968.

22   In many cases, the yields employed by these fighter warheads were larger than those employed by contemporary "strategic" warheads. In addition, many of the infrastructure (command post, depot, airfields, etc.) targets

intended for these weapons were collocated near Eastern European urban centers. In effect, had Massive Retaliation ever been executed, those on both the delivering and receiving ends would have been hard pressed to tell the difference in targets or weapons. .

23   Department of the Air Force, AFM 1-3, *Theater Air Operations*, 1 September 1953 ed. (Washington, DC: Department of the Air Force, 1953), 6 and 20-23; Robert Frank Futrell, *Ideas, Concepts, Doctrine: Basic Thinking in the United States Air Force, Volume 1, 1907-1960* (Maxwell AFB, Alabama: Air University Press, 1971; Washington, DC: Government Reprints Press, 2002), 440-443; Earl H. Tilford Jr., *Setup: What the Air Force Did in Vietnam and Why* (Maxwell AFB, Alabama: Air University Press, June 1991), 30-32; and Budiansky, 372-373.

24   *Ibid.*; Walter S. Moody and Warren A. Trest, "Containing Communism," *Winged Shield, Winged Sword: A History of the United States Air Force, Vol. II: 1950-1997*, Bernard C. Nalty, ed. (Washington, DC: Center for Air Force History, 1997), 129-160; Hannah, 20-30; Trest, 176-177; and Worden, 74-79. For purposes of this work, CAS are airstrikes delivered in support of enemy forces which are within direct fire weapons range and/ or close proximity of friendly forces. Battlefield Area Interdiction BAI are airstrikes delivered against hostile targets that are nominated by a supported ground commander (e.g., a corps or division headquarters) in support of an ongoing

or imminent ground operation.

25   *Ibid.*

26   Steve Fino, "Breaking the Trance: The Perils of Technological Exuberance in the U.S. Air Force Entering Vietnam," *Journal of Military History* (April 2013): 625-655.

27   Fino, *ibid.*

28   Angelucci, 105-106.

29   Ray Bonds, ed., *Modern Fighting Aircraft. Vol. 4, F-4 Phantom* (New York: Arco Publishing, Inc., 1984), 34-37; Walter J. Boyne, *Aces In Command: Fighter Pilots as Combat Leaders* (Washington, DC: Brassey's, 2001), 160-162; and James E. Whitt, Major, USAF, "F-4 Employment of Air To Air Missiles In Southeast Asia: A Special Report," Project CORONA HARVEST, February 1970 (Maxwell AFB: AFS-HRCA), 18-29. BVR is nebulously defined due to changing conditions (e.g., engine smoke, clouds, atmospheric composition, etc.), but is generally accepted to be any engagement over 8-10 nautical miles. Within Visual Range (WVR) is used to define any engagement in which eyesight is used as the primary means of acquisition and tracking.

30   This distinction was not mere sophistry. An interceptor, in general, placed the ability to rapidly transition from standby alert to airborne status at a designated point and altitude above all else. The primary prey of interceptors was expected to be the slow, non-maneuverable

bomber, either individually or in massed groups. Therefore, these airframes were relatively benign in their handling qualities and not designed to be subjected to high-speed maneuvering, much less to operating at low altitude. Fighters, on the other hand, were typically designed with the intent to control a given region of airspace against primarily their own kind. Therefore, unlike interceptors, fighters were typically built with maneuverability in mind, with performance across the entirety of a possible flight envelope necessary to be successful. The United States Air Force, after the F-100, generally ceased to consider maneuverability a necessary attribute for their aircraft. The USN, when designing the F-4, still maintained the F-8 *Crusader* as a dedicated "fighter" to backstop the missile-armed F-4s should ACM, a.k.a. "dogfighting" be necessary.

31   Bonds, 8-10; Boyne, *Phantom*, 36-43; and Hannah, 55-65.

32   Perry D. Luckett and Charles L. Byer, *Tempered Steel: The Three Wars of Triple Air Force Cross Winner Jim Kasler*, paperback edition (Dulles, VA: Potomac Books, 2005, 2006), 19-53 *passim* and Broughton, *Downtown*, 1-10, 34-42, and 70-71.

33   Cleo M. Bishop, Brig. Gen., USAF (ret.), interview by Lt. Colonel J.N. Dick, Jr., USAF, 7-8 July 1976 U.S. Air Force Oral History Program, AFS-HRCA, 209-211; Marshall L. Michel III, *Clashes: Air Combat Over North Vietnam, 1965-1972*

(Annapolis, MD: Naval Institute Press, 1997), 10-20; Robin Olds with Christina Olds and Ed Rasimus, *Fighter Pilot: The Memoirs of Legendary Fighter Ace Robin Olds*, Kindle Edition (New York: St. Martin's Press, 2010), 229-240; Bishop, 209-211; Cobleigh, *War*, 145-146; and Whitt, 27-28 and 36.

34   Bishop interview, 86-147, *passim*; Hannah, 89-95; Olds, *ibid.*; and Worden, 103-155, *passim*.

35   Alexander H.C. Harwick, "F-4 Phantom," *Flying American Combat Aircraft: The Cold War*, Robin Higham, ed., (Mechanicsburg, PA: Stackpole Books, 2005), 301-318.

36   Robert E. Mersserli, "Slipping the Surly Bonds With Zip: The F-104," *Flying American Combat Aircraft: The Cold War*, Robin Higham, ed., (Mechanicsburg, PA: Stackpole Books, 2005), 106-119; Angelucci, 282-287; and Broughton, *Downtown*, 42-51.

37   Broughton, *Downtown*, 49-51 and *Thud Ridge*, 106-107. The F-105s engines were unreliable in the initial stages of flight until improvements were made later in the *Thunderchief*'s production.

38   George J. Marrett, *Contrails Over the Mojave: The Golden Age of Jet Flight Testing at Edwards Air Force Base* (Annapolis, MD: Naval Institute Press, 2008), 137-140; Major Donald L. Gish, USAF, "F-4 Air to Air Training," *Fighter Weapons Review*, Fall 1975, 2; Ed Rasimus, *Palace Cobra: A Fighter Pilot In the Vietnam Air War*, Paperback

ed. (St. Martin's Press, April 2006; St. Martin's Paperbacks Edition, September 2007), 34-35; Boyne, *Phantom*, 112-116; and Harwick, "F-4 Phantom," 301-318. Harwick, on page 311, has a far differing opinion than most on how susceptible the F-4 was to departure. However, he is also acknowledged (on 318) as a pilot who "has more time in the F-4 than any other pilot in the world--3,900 hours." This is, to be charitable, akin to someone with multiple rally race championships stating that he or she does not see the problem with your average driver being unable to operate in adverse weather or road conditions.

39   Werrell, *Archie*, 71-81.

40   Conrad C. Crane *American Air power Strategy In Korea, 1950-1953* (Lawrence, KS: University Press of Kansas, 2000), 136 and Werrell, *Archie*, 74-81. It could be argued that better coordination between U.N. artillery and Air Force sorties contributed as much as jets' inherent speed to lower losses in the last two years. It was common practice for artillery to fire suppressive barrages when an Air Force flight reported it had arrived on station.

41   Angelucci with Bowers, 407-409; Bell, 155-157; Hobson, 239 and 269; and Rasimus, *Thunder*, 272-277. USAF jets were simultaneously able to suffer multiple direct hits from 23mm cannons yet succumb to small-caliber damage to fuel and hydraulic systems.

42   Jane's Information Group, *Jane's Land-Based Air Defense, Thirteenth Edition, 2000-2001*, edited by Tony Cullen and Christopher F. Foss (Alexandria, VA: Jane's Information Group, 2000), 285-288; Jeffrey L. Schrader, MAJ, USAF, "A History of the U.S. Air Force Wild Weasels in Southeast Asia," (Student Report, ACSC, April 1985 [declassified December 2006]), 6-7; and Stephen J. Zaloga's, *Red SAM: The SA-2 Guideline Anti-Aircraft Missile* (Oxford, England: Osprey Publishing, 2007), 16-21.

43   Terrain masking is the process of using a large natural feature, e.g. a ridge or mountain range, to block a radar's transmissions. In the case of the *Fan Song*, this could also be accomplished by flying lower than 5-7,500 feet.

44   Pacific Air Forces (PACAF), "Air Tactics Against NVN Air Ground Defenses, December 1966-1 November 1968," Volume I, 1-4; Anthony M. Thornborough and Frank B. Mormillo, *Iron Hand: Smashing the Enemy's Air Defences* with Tony Cassanova & Kevin Jackson (Somerset, England: Patrick Stephens Limited, 2002; Reprint Sparkford, England: Sutton Publishing, 2002), and Michel, *Clashes*, 37-38.

45   Bishop, 209-211; Cobleigh, *War*, 145-146; Michel, *Clashes*, 10-20 and Whitt, 27-28 and 36. Terrain masking is the process of using a feature such as a ridge or mountain to block a radar's transmissions. This maneuver thus prevents the radar from tracking the target aircraft.

46 A.J.C. Lavalle, MAJ, USAF, ed., *The Tale of Two Bridges and The Battle for the Skies Over North Vietnam*, USAF Southeast Asia Monograph Series, Series Editor Major A.J.C. Lavalle, Volume I, Monographs 1 and 2 (Maxwell AFB, AL: Air University Press, 1976; Washington, DC: Office of Air Force History, 1985), 120.

47 Caroline Ziemke, "A New Convenant?: The Apostles of Douhet and the Persian Gulf War," *The Eagle in the Desert: Looking Back on U.S. Involvement in the Persian Gulf War*, ed. William Head and Earl H. Tilford (Westport, CT: Praeger Publishers, 1996), 299.

48 H.R. McMaster, *Dereliction of Duty* (New York: HarperCollins, 1997; HarperPerennial, 1998), 222-234; Wayne Thompson, *To Hanoi and Back: The U.S. Air Force and North Vietnam, 1966-1973* (Washington, DC: Smithsonian Institution Press, 2000), 2-38; and Tilford, 89-95.

49 Hobson, 268-282.

50 Thompson, 2-38, McMaster, 222-234; and Tilford, 89-95.

51 Jacob Van Staaveren, *Gradual Failure: The Air War Over North Vietnam, 1965-1966* (Washington, DC: Air Force History and Museums Program, 2002), 33-67 and 310-315 ;Clodfelter, 39-72; and McMaster, 217-242.

52 Major John C. Pratt, *Air Tactics Against NVN Air Ground Defenses, December 1966-1 November 1968 (U)* (Maxwell AFB, AL: Project CHECO

(Contemporary Historical Examination of Current Operations) Report, Pacific Air Force (PACAF) Tactical Evaluation Directorate, 30 August 1969 (Declassified July 1991)), 10.

53   PACAF, "Linebacker: Overview of the First 120 Days," 2.

54   William Momyer, Gen., USAF (ret.), *Airpower in Three Wars (WWII, Korea, Vietnam)*, 2003 Reprint Edition (Maxwell AFB, AL: Air University Press, 2003), 378.

55   Broughton, *Thud Ridge*, 95.

56   Broughton, *Ibid.*, 95–96.

57   Cobleigh, *War*, 4.

58   For further discussion of this issue, see T.R. Fehrenbach, *This Kind of War: The Classic Korean War History*, Brassey's Edition, (New York: Macmillan (as *This Kind of War: A Study in Unpreparedness*), 1963; Washington: Brassey's, 1994), 216 –242 and 320–346 and Max Hastings, *The Korean War* (New York: Touchstone, 1988), 115–147. As historiography of the Vietnam War illustrates, the specter of Korea constantly haunted President Johnson's thoughts.

59   Drue L. DeBerry, R. Cargill Hall, and Bernard C. Nalty, "Flexible Response: Evolution or Revolution?" *Winged Shield, Winged Sword: A History of the United States Air Force, Volume II, 1950-1997*, Bernard C. Nalty, ed. (Washington, DC: Air Force History and Museums Program, 1997), 163–200 and Tilford, 45–60.

60   Dale R. Herspring, *The Pentagon and the Presidency: Civil-Military Relations from FDR to George W. Bush* (Lawrence, KS: The University Press of Kansas, 2005), 110-115, 120-123, and 148-149 and Trest, 171-196 *passim.*

61   Momyer, *Airpower,* 378.

62   Ricky James Drake, MAJ, USAF, "The Rules of Defeat: The Impact of Aerial Rules of Engagement on USAF Operations in North Vietnam, 1965-1968" (Thesis presented to the faculty of the School of Advanced Airpower Studies, May 1992), 32.

63   James D. Crabtree, *On Air Defense* (Westport, CT: Praeger Publishers, 1994), 134; James Frank Futrell, *et. al.,* eds., *Aces and Aerial Victories: The United States Air Force in Southeast Asia, 1965-1973,* ed. by James N. Eastman, Jr., Walter Hanak, and Lawrence J. Paszek (Maxwell AFB, Alabama: 1976), 4; and Momyer, *Airower,* 133.

64   Walter J. Boyne, *The Influence of Air Power Upon History* (New York: K.S. Giniger Company, 2003), 330-331; Budiansky, 390-394; Clodfelter, 131-133, and Momyer, *Airpower,* 132-165.

65   Ironically, the North Vietnamese methodology was somewhat close to the USAF's perspective on Theater Air Defense. AFM 1-3, on page 25 discussed theater air defense from the USAF's perspective in this manner [emphasis added]:

(c) Theater Air Defense:

(1) The complete neutralization of the enemy's air force is seldom possible; therefore, the establishment of an air defense system for the theater is necessary. Although some of the attacking air forces will still penetrate theater defenses and attack vital targets, **the maintenance of an effective air defense system compels the attacker to rely heavily on tactics of maneuver and deception which divert part of the attacking force to noneffective operations, and which tend to minimize the effects of the attack.**

The NV–IADS easily meets this description of an ideal air defense system. Therefore, arguments that the ferocity of the North Vietnamese defenses was "unforeseen" by Air Force leaders are somewhat hard to believe.

66   Michel, *Clashes*, 44–45 and Thompson, 40–41.

67   Crabtree, 106–107 and 135–136 and Werrell, *Archie*, 101–103.

68   Broughton, *Downtown*, 119 and Pratt, x.

69   Pratt, 2.

70   Correspondence from Robert L. Simon, LTC, USAF, 7th Air Force Director of Combat Tactics, to PACAF, located in Pacific Air Forces (PACAF), *Air Tactics Against NVN Air Ground Defenses, December 1966–1 November 1968, Volume II––Supporting Documents (U)* (Maxwell AFB, AL: Project CHECO (Contemporary Historical Examination of Current Operations) Report, Pacific Air Force (PACAF)

356 | JAMES L. YOUNG JR.

Tactical Evaluation Directorate, 30 August 1969 (Declassified July 1991)); Broughton, *Downtown*, 117–137; Budiansky, 394–395; Crabtree, 134–135; Michel, *Clashes*, 121; and Pratt, x (Figure 1 which follows this page number). All sources agree that a great majority (Michel cites 85 percent) of casualties to AAA were accrued between 3,000 and 6,000 feet. I have chosen 5,000 feet altitude for illustrative purposes.

71   Angelucci with Bowers, 407–409; Bell, 155–157; Hobson, 239 and 269; and Rasimus, *Thunder*, 272–277.

72   Jeffrey L. Schrader, MAJ, USAF, "A History of the U.S. Air Force Wild Weasels in Southeast Asia," Student report, ACSC, Maxwell AFB, April 1985 (declassified December 2006)), 7; Budiansky, 393–394; and Hobbs, 26.

73 Interview of Major Hal Dortch, USAF, found in Pacific Air Forces (PACAF), *Air Tactics Against NVN Air Ground Defenses, December 1966–1 November 1968, Volume II--Supporting Documents (U)*; Bell, 101; Broughton, *Downtown*, 158–159, and Handley, 124.

74   Energy, in this case, refers to an aircraft's ability to move throughout space. Aircraft with low energy may be capable of maintaining straight and level flight, but they will be capable of little else for fear of stalling.

75   Bell, *ibid*. and Jenkins, 90–91.

76   Bell, 101–103; Momyer, *Airower*, 100–113;

and Rasimus, *Thunder*, 92–99. The Route Package System arose due to interservice rivalry in the initial stages of Rolling Thunder. Rather than attempting to unify all strikes against North Vietnam under a single commander, Admiral Shaw, CINC of the Pacific region (CINCPAC), had chosen to divide North Vietnam into seven "Route Packages," or target areas. A monument to interservice rivalry at its worst, the Route Package system meant that joint USAF/USN strikes usually required coordination at the CINCPAC level. Considering that CINCPAC was located in Honolulu and would then have had to ensure these strikes were approved by the JCS in Washington, joint attacks were extremely rare.

77   Wild Weasels will be discussed later in this study.

78   Jenkins, 93. One of the many needs for up-to-date intelligence was due to the ECM pods' requirements to be set to a given frequency on the ground. In other words, if an aircrew needed to jam a *Fire Can* radar versus a *Fan Song*, the early ECM pods had to be set to the *Fire Can*'s frequency at the expense of nearby aircraft not being able to jam (or in some early pods' cases, *detect*) a *Fan Song*. Carrying two different types of ECM pods for each radar on the same aircraft had the perverse effect of cancelling *both* pods' protection.

79   Hannah, 77–78.

80   Pratt, 21.

81   Jenkins, 93-96; Michel, *Clashes*, 71-72.

82   Michel, *Clashes*, 73-74.

83   *Ibid.*, 44; Spick, *Fighter*, 150-151; and Thompson, 44-47. If the American aircraft jettisoned its ordnance and caused collateral damage, this could often be exploited for propaganda purposes.

84   See Bell; Drake; Momyer, *Air Power*; Broughton (both *Downtown* and *Thud Ridge*); and Rasimus throughout for examples of these arguments.

85   AFM 1-3, 18. Ironically, the North Vietnamese methodology was somewhat close to the USAF's perspective on how a theater-level air defense operation should be conducted. AFM 1-3, on page 25 discussed theater air defense from the USAF's perspective in this manner [emphasis added]:

(c) *Theater Air Defense:*

(1) The complete neutralization of the enemy's air force is seldom possible; therefore, the establishment of an air defense system for the theater is necessary. Although some of the attacking air forces will still penetrate theater defenses and attack vital targets, **the maintenance of an effective air defense system compels the attacker to rely heavily on tactics of maneuver and deception which divert part of the attacking force to noneffective operations, and which tend to minimize the effects of the attack.**

86   *Ibid..* For example, each of the F-105 wings began to modify their approach to targets based on losses. This, in turn, meant that their escorting F-4s had to plan different techniques based on low, medium, or high-level ingress.

87   Michael Cooper, "Navy / Air Force Joint Iron Hand," in *First In, Last Out: Stories by the Wild Weasels (First Person Stories By Wild Weasel Pilots, EWOs and Their Associates)*, Colonel Edward T. Rock, USAF (ret.), ed. (Bloomington, IN: Authorhouse Press, 2005), 23-25.

88   Young, 51-57.

89   In contrast, during the tests at Eglin AFB, most of the missiles had been maintained, loaded, and serviced post-flight by contractors from their respective manufacturers. They were usually also stored in climate controlled buildings in between flights. This was decidedly not the case in Southeast Asia.

90   Young, 58-61.

91   Ed Rasimus, *Palace Cobra: A Fighter Pilot In the Vietnam Air War*, Paperback ed. (St. Martin's Press, April 2006; St. Martin's Paperbacks Edition, September 2007), 23-42; John Darrell Sherwood, *Fast Movers: Jet Pilots and the Vietnam Experience* (New York: The Free Press, 1999), 59-61; and Tilford, 215-217.

92   Hobbs, 271.

93   C.R. Anderegg, Col., USAF (ret.), *Sierra Hotel: Flying Air Force Fighters in the Decade After*

360 | JAMES L. YOUNG JR.

Vietnam (Washington, DC: Air Force History and Museums Program, 2001), 39-40; Clancy, 95-110; Anderegg, 39-40; Clodfelter, 134; and Sparks, 20-22.

94   Anderegg, *ibid.* The majority of these pilots were departing flight billets due to their advanced age. A pilot who had been inducted into the Army Air Corps at 18 in 1945 was, by 1968, a 42-year-old senior officer with over 20 years of service. The performance of several Rolling Thunder squadron and wing commanders notwithstanding, the Air Force felt that this was far too old for continued, regular flying duties.

95   Futrell, *Vol. II*, 318-323.

96   *Ibid.*, 235 and 470-471.

97   Anderegg, 22-26 and 63-65; Clodfelter, 131; Hobbs, 14-170 and 270-271; Michel, *Clashes*, 149; and Rasimus, *Palace Cobra*, 23-42. Hobbs' work especially indicates the lethality of small arms and AAA throughout Southeast Asia, as the overwhelming majority of USAF losses were due to these systems. Although the 7th Air Force would conduct a wholly different war during the Linebacker Operations, the fact that TAC continued to train pilots in methods which were proven to lead to increased losses indicates a lack of Air Force focus.

98   Robert E. Belli, USAF, Interview by Major Lyn R. Officer, USAF, and Mr. Hugh N. Ahmann, 29 January, 1973, transcript of interview by same, U.S. Air Force Oral History Program #645,

declassified 31 December 1981 (Maxwell AFB, 25 January 2006), Air Force Historical Research Center, Maxwell AFB, 108.

99   Schrader, 50-53 and Thornborough and Mormillo, 93-98. Schrader indicates that part of the reason for this decision was a desire to maintain F-4D strength in Europe. Thompson and Mormillo detail than the F-4C *Wild Weasel* was initially deployed to Korea in 1969, but due to the continued electronic problems was not considered wholly operational by the Air Force.

100 Schrader, 50-53; Thompson, 266-267; and Thornborough and Mormillo, 125.

101 Dortch interview; Bishop 206; and Schrader, 46-47.

102 Michel, *Clashes*, 181-185.

103 *Ibid.* and Rasimus, *Palace Cobra*, 23-42.

104 Anderegg, 20-21.

105 Michel, *Clashes*, 181-185; Worden, 188-189.

106 Worden, *ibid.* Worden also served as a fighter pilot during the Vietnam War and later became a Major General in the Air Force.

107 AFM 1-1, 28 September 71 edition, 3-2.

108 *Ibid.*, 2-1. Numbering is as presented in original text.

109 *Ibid.*, 2-4. Numbering is as presented in the original text.

110   Futrell, *Vol. II*, 490-498 and Trest, 213-214.

111   Chapter 4 and Chapter 5, respectively. The six years includes three years of Rolling Thunder and the entire Korean War.

112   R.A. Mason, "Airpower as a National Instrument: The Arab Israeli Wars," in *The War in the Air, 1914-1994*, American edition, Alan Stephens, ed. (Maxwell AFB, Alabama: Air University Press [in cooperation with RAAF Aerospace Center], January 2001) 191-220 with particular attention to 200-201; Belli, 108-109; Futrell, *Vol. II*, 472-475 and 490-492.

113   Richard Nixon, *The Memoirs of Richard Nixon* (New York: Grosset & Dunlap, 1978), 394-397 and 400-418.

114   Stephen P. Randolph, *Powerful and Brutal Weapons: Nixon, Kissinger, and the Easter Offensive* (Cambridge, Massachusetts: Harvard University Press, 2007), 7 and Nixon, 289. Nixon stated in his memoirs that President Eisenhower expressed doubts not once but twice about Laird's duplicity. As President Nixon ostensibly agreed with Eisenhower, it is hard to understand why he decided to still nominate Laird as Secretary of Defense

115   Nixon, 380-385 and 388.

116   *Ibid.*, 400, 407, 433, 450, 509.

117   Boyne, *Wild Blue*, 256.

118   Tilford, 166 and 215; and Trest, 207-208.

119 Tilford, 215.

120 Worden, 192-196.

121 Futrell, *Ideas, Vol. II*, 478.

122 Boyne, *Wild Blue*, 256 and Worden, 192-193.

123 Boyne and Worden, both *ibid*.

124 Bell, 216-218; Broughton, *Downtown*, 98-99 and Thompson, 59-61.

125 *Ibid*. and Clodfelter, 123. For example, according to Clodfelter, Ryan directed the bombing of a North Vietnamese village despite protestations that there was little evidence that a suspected SAM facility was actually present. Another example, cited by Bell and Broughton, was Ryan's actions during the *Turkestan* incident.

126 Thompson, 193-210.

127 Boyne, *Aces*, 190 and Sherwood, 34-35.

128 Worden, 194-195.

129 Blesse, 120-126.; Boyne, *Aces*, 178-181; and Broughton, *Downtown*, 99-100.

130 The existence of these meetings is indicated in the notes from the various CHECO reports cited in this paper. However, unlike these reports, the majority of these documents have yet to be unclassified.

131 William W. Momyer, Gen., USAF (ret.), interview by Dr. Edgar F. Puryear, Jr., 9 September 1981, Part I interview transcript, U.S. Air Force

Oral History Program, AFS–HRCA, 10.

132   Momyer, CORONA HARVEST enclosures, 3.

133   *Ibid.*, 4.

134   Bishop, 206–207.

135 Michael Maclear, *Vietnam: The Ten Thousand Day War, 1945-1975* (New York: St. Martin's Press, 1981), 304-305; John Pimlott, *Vietnam: The Decisive Battles* (London: Marshall Editions, 1997; Edison, NJ: 2003), 160-171; John Schlight, "Vietnamization and Withdrawal, 1968-1975," *Winged Shield, Winged Sword: A History of the United States Air Force, Volume II, 1950-1997*, Bernard C. Nalty, ed. (Washington, DC: Air Force History and Museums Program, 1997), 295-336; Lieutenant Colonel James H. Willbanks, USA ret., *Thiet Giap!: The Battle of An Loc, April 1972* (Fort Leavenworth, KS: Combat Studies Institute, 1993), 3; and Randolph, 22-31.

136 Richard Nixon, *The Memoirs of Richard Nixon* (New York: Grosset & Dunlap, 1978), 394-395 and 588.

137 Tilford, 234.

138 Michel, *Clashes*, 210; Thompson, 229; and Tilford 233-234. Linebacker II was so dubbed due to its being a sequel to the first operation. "Linebacker 'began' long before it was initiated," and most sources only consider there to be a division between Operation Freedom Train and Linebacker I due to the ferocity of operations on May 10th, 1972. Since there was no operational

pause or, for that matter, change in tactics between Freedom Train and Linebacker I nor did the 7th Air Force cease striking Vietnam from October–December, 1972, this paper will consider Freedom Train, Linebacker I, and Linebacker II as "Linebacker operations." For a contemporary discussion of this lack of divide, see PACAF Office of History, *Linebacker: Overview of the First 120 Days (U)*, by Melvin F. Porter.

139 Clodfelter, 154–157; Randolph 80–101 and 114, Tilford, 228–234

140 Clodfelter, 154; Michel, *Clashes*, 211; Porter, *Linebacker: Overview*, 8–11; Smith, 77; and Tilford, 228.

141 Clodfelter, 166–167; Porter, *Linebacker Overview* 53–55; Tilford, 233–237; and Worden 197–198.

142 Colonel G.H. Turley, USMCR ret., *The Easter Offensive: Vietnam, 1972* (Novato, CA: Presidio, 1985; New York: Warner Books Edition, 1989), 30–37; Randolph, 30–39; and Tilford, *ibid*.

143 Bernard Nalty, *Air War Over South Vietnam, 1968-1975* (Washington, DC: Air Force History and Museums Program, 2000), 333–402.

144 Clodfelter, 155–158; Randolph, 160–181; and Thompson, 220.

145 Maclear, 249–254; Randolph, 23–26; and Turley, 28–29.

146 Clodfelter, 152–158; Randolph 160–181 and

331–338; and Thompson, 250–253.

147 Thompson, 301–302.

148 PACAF CHECO/CORONA HARVEST Division, *The F-111 In Southeast Asia, September 1972 – January 1973,* by A. A. Picinich, Col., USAF, et. al., Project CHECO Report, U.S. Air Force (Maxwell AFB, 21 February 1974 (declassified 16 January 2000). TFX stood for "Tactical Fighter Experimental," the Secretary McNamara-directed program intended to force the USAF / USN to adopt a common airframe to meet a series of interceptor and attack requirements.

149 PACAF Directorate of Operations Analysis, *Guided Bomb Operations in SEA: The Weather Dimension, 1 FEB —31 DEC 1972,* by Patrick J. Breitling, Col., USAF, Project CHECO Report, U.S. Air Force (Maxwell AFB, 1 OCT 73 (Declassified 31 December 1980); PACAF Office of History, *Linebacker: Overview of the First 120 Days (U),* by Melvin F. Porter, Project CHECO Report, U.S. Air Force (Maxwell AFB, 27 September 1973 (declassified 31 December 1983)), *passim*; and *Ibid.,* 229–236.

150 Michel, *Clashes,* 203–207.

151 *Guided Bomb Operations,* 1–7 and *Linebacker: Overview,* 20–21 and 58–59.

152 *Guided Bomb Operations,* 7–10.

153 As its name implies, "fire and forget" weapons are those that will perform the necessary maneuvers to impact their target without further

input from any external sources. In the case of the EOGBs, certain models possessed the ability for an F-4 weapons officer to provide steering input throughout the bomb's launch rather than simply being locked onto its target before release.

154 Out Country Air Operations PACAF Office of History, *Linebacker Operations: September-December 172 (U)*, by Calvin R. Johnson, MAJ, USAF, Project CHECO (Contemporary Historical Examination of Current Operations) Report, U.S. Air Force (Maxwell AFB, 31 December 1978 (declassified 8 July 1991)), 37-40; United States Air Force Operations (Strategic and General Operations Section), J-3, briefing entitled "The Employment and Effectiveness of Missile and Guided Weapons in SEAsia," located at AFS-HRCA, 50-55 and AG-VU (slides) 1-7; *Guided Bomb Operations*, 10-39; and *Linebacker Overview*, 59.

155 John T. Smith, *The Linebacker Raids* (London: Cassell & Co., 1988; 2000), 75 and Michel, *ibid*. The shortage was due to the *Pave Knife* still being technically in development rather than accepted for production.

156 *Linebacker: Overview*, 44-60 and Momyer, *Airpower*, 144-145.

157 Thompson, 230-236.

158 Benjamin S. Lambeth, *The Transformation of American Air Power* (Ithaca, NY: Cornell University Press, 2000), 27 and William W. Momyer, Gen.,

USAF (ret.) in memorandum to General Ellis, "SUBJECT: CORONA HARVEST (Out Country Air Operations, Southeast Asia, 1 January, 1965 – 31 March, 1968)," with enclosures (Maxwell AFB, Alabama: AFS-HRCA, General Momyer Correspondence, Declassified December 31, 1982), 6-7 and 14-15. Memorandum is undated, but is stamped for archival entry 23 JUL 1974. Henceforth "Momyer, Ellis Memo."

159 Smith, 142-165.

160 Thompson, 250-253. Interestingly enough, many of the leadership and infrastructure targets were vetoed by Secretary Laird without President Nixon's knowledge. However, given the difficulty the 7th Air Force had in striking even those targets assigned, Laird's decisions did not have much impact on Linebacker operations

161 Maclear, 249-254; Randolph, 23-26; and Smith, *ibid.*

162 William Park, *Defending the West: A History of NATO* (Boulder, CO: Westview Press, 1986), 100-101; Duffield, 194-202; and Nixon, 372-373 and 394-395. The ROKAF information is based on the author's own discussion with USAF personnel while stationed in Korea.

163 Russell F. Weigley, *The American Way of War*, The Wars of the United States, ed. Louis Morton, (New York: Macmillan Publishing Co., Inc., 1973), 467-477; C.R. Anderegg, 126-127; Futrell, *Vol. II*, 475-485; and Lambeth, *Transformation*, 54-55.

164 Anderegg, 39–67 and Clancy, 125–136.

165 Michael L. Michel III, *The 11 Days of Christmas: America's Last Vietnam Battle* (San Francisco: Encounter Books, 2002), 223 and 235; Randolph, 220; Rasimus, *Palace Cobra*, 294–296; and Thompson, 243–244.

166 Der Baron (pseud.), "Anything Else Is Rubbish," *Fighter Weapons Review*, Summer 1972, 32–34 and Donald L. Gish, MAJ, USAF, "F–4 Air to Air Training," *Fighter Weapons Review*, Fall 1975, 1–5.

167 Momyer, Ellis memo and enclosures *passim*, and Michel, *Christmas*, 222–231.

168 Boyne, *Wild Blue*, 253–260 and Budiansky, 395–402.

169 Nixon, 726–735.

170 Nixon, 733–734.

171 Budiansky, 394–395 and Michel, *Christmas*, 1–4.

172 Crabtree, 106–109 and Goure, 181–186.

173 Edward Luttwak and Stuart Koehl, *The Dictionary of Modern War* (New York: Harpers–Collins, 1991), 570–571 and *Linebacker Operations*, 62–64.

174 Randolph, 118–128 and Thompson, 224–227.

175 *Linebacker Operations*, 31–34 and Michel, *Christmas*, 44–47.

176 Head, 74-78 and McCarthy and Allison, 39-85.

177 Head, *ibid.*

178 Karl J. Eschmann, *Linebacker: The Untold Story of the Air Raids Over North Vietnam* (New York: Ivy Books, 1989), 205-211; Michel, *Christmas*, 54-70; and Worden, 199-201.

179 The experience level of the North Vietnamese SAM operators had definite impact on their successful adjustment to operating against the B-52s. For further discussion, see Belli, 118-125; Michel, *Christmas*, 139-143; Dougherty, 11-14; Momyer, Ellis memorandum; and Schrader, 58.

180 Clodfelter, 167-169 and *Linebacker Overview*, 62.

181 John J. Zentner, LTC, USAF, "The Art of Wing Leadership and Aircrew Morale in Combat," The Cadre Papers, Cadre Paper No. 11, (Maxwell AFB, Alabama: Air University Press, June 2001); Johnson, 60-70; Michel, *Christmas*, 185-186 and 239-242; and Schrader, 55-59.

182 McCarthy and Allison, 86 and Johnson, 31-34.

183 Head, 80 and Nixon, 737.

184 Michel, *Christmas*, 232-234. The Battle of Dien Ben Phu was a decisive victory for the Viet Minh against the French Army. It is usually considered the defeat which broke France's will and desire to retain Indochina.

185 Maclear, 310-312 and Tilford, 271-272.

186 Spick, *All-Weather*, 133-136.

187 Goure, 161-165 and Spick, *ibid.*

188 Walter J. Boyne, *The Influence of Air Power Upon History* (Gretna, LA: Pelican Publishing Company, Inc., 2003), 337-341; Luttwak and Koehl, 93-94; and Tilford, 55-62. One possible counterargument to these thoughts would be that B-52s would have been equipped with stand-off weaponry in a general conflict. This theory ignores the fact that PVO *Strany* interceptors and SAMs would have been equipped with nuclear warheads as well.

189 Dave Brog (WW #420), "The Black SAM," *First In, Last Out: Stories by the Wild Weasels (First Person Stories By Wild Weasel Pilots, EWOs and Their Associates)*, Colonel Edward T. Rock, USAF (ret.)ed., (Bloomington, IN: Authorhouse Press, 2005), 509-511; Jim Winzell (WW #1098), "Linebacker-II: The Eleven Days Of Christmas," *First In, Last Out: Stories by the Wild Weasels (First Person Stories By Wild Weasel Pilots, EWOs and Their Associates)*, Colonel Edward T. Rock, USAF (ret.)ed., (Bloomington, IN: Authorhouse Press, 2005), 361-372; *F-111 CHECO*, 63-65; *Linebacker Operations*, 41-70; and Worden, 199-204.

190 Robert F. Dorr and Chris Bishop, ed., *Vietnam Air Warfare: The Story of the Aircraft, the Battles, and the Pilots Who Fought* (Edison, NJ: Chartwell Books, Inc., 1996), 214 and Hobson, 268-271.

191   Der Baron (pseud.), "Anything Else is Rubbish," *Fighter Weapons Review*, Summer 1972, 32–34; Ed Cobleigh, "Top Gun Navy Style," *Fighter Weapons Review*, Spring 1973, 5–7; Donald L. Gish, "F–4 Air to Air Training," *Fighter Weapons Review*, Fall 1975, 1–5; Alexander Harwick, "Thoughts on Flight Leadership," *Fighter Weapons Review*, Summer 1973, 6–8; _____., "USAFE Tactical Employment School," *Fighter Weapons Review*, Summer 1973, 25 and 34; and Vincent P. Roy, "Double Attack Revisited," *Fighter Weapons Review*, Spring 1971, 26–32; Anderegg, 4–27 and 59–61; Michel, *Clashes*, 277–291; and Sherwood, 182–184.

192   *Ibid.* Please see Robert Wilcox's *Scream of Eagles* (New York: John Wiley and Sons, Inc., 1990) for a more detailed discussion of the "loose deuce" versus "fluid four" evolution in the USN during Vietnam

193   Anderegg, 63–67; 71–82, and 119–142 and Thornborough and Mormillo, 92–98.

194   AFM 1–1 (SEP 71), 28

195   Momyer, *Airpower*, 179 and Ellis memo, 1–3.

196   Momyer, Ellis memo, *passim.*

197   *Ibid.* In effect, Momyer created the exercises by stripping TAC funds and equipment from other authorized events and emergency wartime training accounts.

198   Momyer and Ellis memo, 3 and Mike Press,

"Meet the Aggressors," *Fighter Weapons Review*, Fall 1973, 30-33.

199 Steve Davies, *Red Eagles: America's Secret MiGs* (Oxford, UK: Osprey Publishing, 2008), 16-34; Robert J. Hoag, "Symposium 1972," *Fighter Weapons Review*, Winter 1972, 9-11; Cobleigh, *ibid.*; and Press, *ibid.*

200 Branford J. Mcallister, MAJ, USAF, "Air to Air Continuation Training in the Tactical Air Command," ACSC Thesis, April 1985, 19-21; Author phone conversation with Stan Goldstein, former president of the Wild Weasel Association, 27 September 2016 (henceforth Goldstein 27 September 2016); Robert D. Russ, COL, USAF, "Air to Air Training Under the DOC System," *Air University Review*, January-February 1977, http://www.au.af.mil/au/afri/aspj/airchron-icles/aureview_toc/AUReview1977/AUReview-1977Jan-Feb.htm; and Anderegg, 71-88.

201 As noted in previous citations, the memorandum is undated. However, given some of the references involved, the fact that Momyer signs the memorandum as head of TAC, and the general tone of its contents, it can be inferred that it was written at some point after mid-1973.

202 Momyer, Ellis memo enclosures, 17.

203 Ibid., 17-21.

204 Ibid., 11-12 and 16-21.

205 Momyer memo, 3-4 and ibid., 12-14.

206 Momyer memo, Ellis enclosures, 14-17.

207 Momyer memo, Ellis enclosures, 15.

208 Momyer memo, 3-5 and Ibid., 14-22 *passim*.

209 Momyer memo, 3.

210 Momyer memo and Ellis enclosures, *passim*. Momyer acknowledges at several points in the memorandum that he is approaching personnel problems while addressing other issues. This writing style reflects the interconnectedness of the contemporary air combat arena, an issue that a man trained on fighters in the 1940s was clearly wrestling with.

211 Momyer, Ellis memo, 11.

212 Ibid., 11-12.

213 Ibid., 6.

214 Ibid.

215 Ibid.

216 Ibid., 6-8.

217 Ibid., 1-2.

218 Walter J. Boyne, "Momyer," *Air Force Magazine* 96, no. 8 (August 2013): 65-68.

219 Buddy Bowman, "To Fly and Fight," *Fighter Weapons Newsletter*, December 1970, 10-11; Steve Davies and Doug Dildy, *F-15 Eagle Engaged: The World's Most Successful Jet Fighter* (Oxford, UK:

Osprey Publishing, 2007), 17–51; and Angelucci, 317–320.

220 Ibid.; Anderegg, 149–164; and Handley, 100–114.

221 Goldstein 27 September 2016. In 1973, Mr. Goldstein was serving as the deputy to the USAF Air Staff's Electronic Warfare Office in the Pentagon and thus was heavily involved in attempts to expand the number of attendees for the Wild Weasel school as well as increase the funding for Wild Weasel training.

222 Goldstein 27 September 2016 and Thornborough and Mormillo, 146–147.

223 Author phone interview of Stan Goldstein September 2016 (henceforth Goldstein Interview #1) and Thornborough and Mormillo, 92–98.

224 Robert Coram, *Boyd: The Fighter Pilot Who Changed the Art of War*, Paperback Edition (New York: Little, Brown and Company, 2002; Back Bay Books, 2004), 243–256 and Goldstein Interview #1.

225 *Ibid.*; Budiansky, 398–402; and Davies and Dildy, 66–71 and 87–92.

226 Boyne, *Wild Blue*, 255–260 and Momyer memo, *passim*.

227 Robert M. Collins, *More: The Politics of Economic Growth in Postwar America* (New York: Oxford University Press, 2000), 42–51; Duffield, 112–151; and Gaddis, *Cold War*, 64–68.

228 Duffield, 186–187

229 Jussi M. Hanhimaki, "Détente in Europe, 1962–1975," *The Cambridge History of the Cold War, Volume II: Crises and Détente*, Melvyn P. Leffler and Odd Arne Westad, eds., 5th Edition (Cambridge, UK: Cambridge University Press, 2014), 198–218 and Collins, 84–128, *passim*.

230 Collins, *ibid.* and Duffield, *ibid.*

231 Department of the Army Center of Military History, *Department of the Army Historical Summary, Fiscal Year 1972* (Washington, DC: Army Center of Military History, 1972), 8–10 and 122–125 and Duffield, 189–192. The *Department of the Army Historical Summary* is available online at http://www.history.army.mil/books/dahsum/1972/ch08.htm#b3 .

232 JP 1–02, 96.

233 Luttwak and Koehl, 166.

234 Ingo Trauschweizer, *The Cold War U.S. Army: Building Deterrence for Limited War* (Lawrence, KS: 2008), 190–194 and Duffield, 194–208.

235 David M. Glantz, *The Military Strategy of the Soviet Union: A History* (Portland, OR: Frank Cass, 1992), 188–200, *passim*; Hanhimaki, *ibid.*; and Duffield, *ibid.*; Once the Soviet Union had achieved strategic parity, such a stance was unsurprising. The majority of Soviet reinforcements in a NATO / Warsaw Pact military conflict would move through population centers in the western USSR, Poland, or East Germany. It was

generally assumed in Soviet doctrine that once NATO employed nuclear weapons tactically, it would shortly do so *operationally* in order to stop these forces. Given the geography, a warhead was ostensibly being employed against a tank division on a railhead moving through an Eastern bloc city would in effect still be targeting a major population center under the Soviet nuclear umbrella.

236 Trauschweizer, 37–47 and 162–165.

237 Using only standing forces in from the East Germany–Polish border to the North Sea, the Warsaw Pact enjoyed an advantage of ~2.5:1 in tanks, ~2.8:1 in total armored vehicles, over 3:1 in dismounted infantry, and over 3:1 in artillery pieces throughout the period covered in this paper. If forces in Poland and the western Soviet Union were added, this advantage became over 3:1 in all categories. According to traditional staff planning, an attacker requires a 2–2.5:1 advantage in force ratios to be successful against a non–fortified defense, 3:1 if an opponent has had time to prepare fortifications.

238 Kevin N. Lewis, "Historical U.S. Force Structure Trends: A Primer," RAND Corporation Paper P–7582, July 1989, 17–33 and 42–45; Brian McAllister Linn, *The Echo of Battle: The Army's Way of War* (Cambridge, MA: Harvard University Press, 2007), 151–192, *passim*; and John L. Romjue, *From Active Defense to AirLand Battle: The Development of Army Doctrine, 1973–1982* (Fort Monroe, VA: U.S. Army TRADOC Historical Office, 1984), 3–11.

239 M. Nicklas-Carter, "NATO's Central Front," *Armoured Warfare*, J.P. Harris and F.H. Toase, eds. (New York: St. Martin's Press, 1990), 205-229; Andreas Wenger, "The Politics of Military Planning: Evolution of NATO's Strategy," *War Plans and Alliances in the Cold War*, Vojtech Mastny, Sven G. Hollsmark and Andress Wenger, eds. (New York: Routledge, 2006), 165-198; and Trauschweizer, 70-80

240 Charles Messenger, *Armies of World War 3* (Greenwich, CT: Bison Books, 1984), 19-45 and M. Nicklas Carter, *ibid.*

241 Martin van Creveld with Steven L. Canby and Kenneth S. Brower, *Air Power and Maneuver Warfare* (Maxwell AFB, AL: Air University Press, 1994), 198-200; Lewis, *ibid.*; M. Nicklas-Carter, *ibid.*; Trauschweizer, *ibid.*

242 Vojtech Mastny, "Imagining War in Europe: Soviet Military Planning," *War Plans and Alliances in the Cold War*, Vojtech Mastny, Sven G. Hollsmark and Andress Wenger, eds. (New York: Routledge, 2006), 15-45 and Gaddis, *Cold War*, 108-109 and 134-135.

243 David M. Glantz, *Soviet Military Operational Art: In Pursuit of Deep Battle* (Portland, OR: Frank Cass, 1991), 211-217; David C. Isby, *Weapons and Tactics of the Soviet Army*, Fully Revised Edition (London, UK: Jane's Publishing Company, 1981, 1988), 24-26 and 54-58; and Harriet Fast and William F. Scott, *The Armed Forces of the USSR* (Boulder, CO: Westview Press, 1979), 41-59

passim and 375-383

244 Glantz, *Military Strategy*, 200-213 and *ibid.*

245 R.A. Mason and John W.R. Taylor, *Aircraft, Strategy, and Operations of the Soviet Air Force* (London: Jane's Publishing Company, Ltd., 1986), 26-57; Thomas Newdick, *Postwar Air Weapons, 1945-Present* (London: Amber Books, Ltd., 2011), *passim*; and Anthony Robinson, *Soviet Air Power* (London: Bison Books, Ltd., 1985), 68-81 and 90-99. Newdick discusses various weapons throughout his work, which is arranged by type of ordnance. The most common weapons in NATO's arsenal through 1975 were 500, 750, and 1000-lb. bombs, with various guidance kits becoming available from 1973 on. The majority of the Warsaw Pact's command posts, like their NATO counterparts, were hardened against all but direct hits from 2,000-lb. bombs. While the shock from smaller weapons would have likely harmed delicate electronics and stunned personnel, these were both relatively easy to replace.

246 *Ibid.*

247 *Ibid.* and Isby, 306-313

248 Gaillard R. Peck, *America's Secret MiG Squadron: The Red Eagles of Project CONSTANT PEG* (Long Island City, NY: Osprey, 2012), 99-101 and Mason and Taylor, *ibid.* and 204-206.

249 John T. Greenwood and Von Hardesty, "Soviet Air Forces in World War II," *The Soviet*

Air Forces, Paul J. Murphy, ed. (Jefferson, NC: McFarland & Company, Inc., 1984), 29–69 and Steven J. Zaloga, *Soviet Air Defence Missiles: Design, Development and Tactics* (Alexandria, VA: Jane's Information Group, 1989), 166–190. By comparison, the Western Allies established air superiority prior to Operation Overlord in June 1944. Despite the *Luftwaffe*'s efforts, the Western Allies did not face significant *Luftwaffe* interference with their operational maneuver from that point on.

250 Zaloga, *ibid.* and Isby, 306–313.

251 Zaloga, *ibid.*, 232–250.

252 Zaloga, *ibid.*, 273–284.

253 Zaloga, *ibid.*, 191–205 (SA–4) and 206–232 (SA–6).

254 Zaloga, *ibid.*, 256–272 and 327–351.

255 Isby, 306–313 and Zaloga, *ibid.*, 77–108.

256 Rana Pennington, "Pilot Initiative in the Soviet Air Force," *The Soviet Air Forces*, Paul J. Murphy, ed. (Jefferson, NC: McFarland & Company, Inc., 1984), 149–156 and William Schneider, Jr., "Soviet Frontal Aviation: Evolving Capabilities and Trends," *The Soviet Air Forces*, Paul J. Murphy, ed. (Jefferson, NC: McFarland & Company, Inc., 1984), 133–148.

257 Budiansky, 401–402 and Isby, *ibid.*

258 *Ibid.*

259 Trevor N. Dupuy, *Elusive Victory: The Arab-Israeli Wars, 1947-1974*, 3d. ed. (Dubuque, IA: Kendall/Hunt Publishing, 1992), 221-340; Brereton Greenhouse, "The Israeli Experience," *Case Studies in the Achievement of Air Superiority*, Benjamin Franklin Cooling, ed., (Washington, DC: Center for Air Force History, 1994), 412-413; and Creveld, 160-170.

260 Eliezer "Cheetah" Cohen, *Israel's Best Defense: The First Full Story of the Israeli Air Force* (New York: Orion Books, 1993), 314-320; Anthony H. Cordesman and Abraham R. Wagner, *The Lessons of Modern War, Volume I: The Arab Israeli Conflicts*, Paperback Edition (San Francisco, Calif: Westview Press, 1991), 18-23; and Dupuy, 344-348.

261 Cohen, 254-320 and Dupuy, 343-383

262 Kenneth M. Pollack, *Arabs at War: Military Effectiveness, 1948-1991* (Lincoln, NE: University of Nebraska Press, 2002); 96-97; Cohen, 254-320; and Dupuy, 343-383. Pollack notes that the IAF had little difficulty in dealing with the SAM Belt until the arrival of the more advanced SA-3, SA-6, and ZSU-23-4.

263 Merav Halperin and Aharon Lapidot, *G-Suit: Combat Reports from Israel's Air War* (London: Sphere Books, 1990), 55-94; Iftach Spector, *Loud and Clear: The Memoir of an Israeli Fighter Pilot* (Minneapolis, MN: Zenith Press, 2009), 286-290; Cohen, 314-319; and Dupuy, *ibid.*

264 Cohen, *ibid.*; Crabtree, 151-153, and Pollack,

96-97 and 484-485

265 Cohen, 337-354; Halperin and Lapidot, 95-100; and Spector, 302-309.

266 Len Nordeen, *Fighters over Israel* (London: Greenhill Books, 1991), 123-140 and *Ibid*.

267 *Ibid.*

268 *Ibid.*

269 Victor Israelyan, *Inside the Kremlin During the Yom Kippur War* (University Park, PA: The Pennsylvania State University, 1995), 55-61; Budiansky, 401-402; Crabtree, 153-158; Futrell, *Vol. II*, 540-543; and Cordesman and Wagner, *Volume I*, 73-104, *passim*.

270 Insight Team of the London *Sunday Times, The Yom Kippur War* (Garden City, NY: Doubleday & Company, 1974) 199-205; Dupuy, 465-467; and Nordeen, 135-148.

271 Crabtree, 152-158; Cordesman and Wagner, *Volume I*, 73-98; and Werrell, *Archie*, 138-146

272 Lon O. Nordeen, Jr. *Air Combat in the Missile Age* (Washington, DC: Smithsonian Institution Press, 1985), 162-165 and *ibid*.

273 General Robert J. Dixon, Oral History Interview, Air Force Historical Research Agency, 18 July 1984, K239.0512-1591 C.I, 246-250; Robert H. Reed, "On Deterrence: A Broadened Perspective," *Air University Review*, May-June 1975, http://www.au.af.mil/au/afri/aspj/

airchronicles/aureview/1975/may-jun/reed.
html; Budiansky, 400-403; and Test, 227-249.

274 Anderegg, 181-184 and Dixon, *ibid.*

275 John Robert Greene, *The Limits of Power:
The Nixon and Ford Administrations* (Bloomington,
IN: Indiana University Press, 1992), 204-220;
John Lewis Gaddis, *Strategies of Containment:
A Critical Appraisal of American National Security
Policy During the Cold War*, Revised and Expanded
Edition (New York: Oxford University Press,
Inc., 2005), 279-307, *passim*; George C. Herring,
*From Colony to Superpower: U.S. Foreign Relations
Since 1776* (New York: Oxford University Press,
2008), 770-775 and 810-824; Dale Herspring,
*The Pentagon and the Presidency: Civil Military
Relations from FDR to George W. Bush* (Lawrence,
KS: University Press of KS, 2005), 212-236; and
Collins, 152-157.

276 Coalition for a Democratic Majority, "For
An Adequate Defense," John Marsh Files, Gerald
R. Ford Library, Box 8; Gaddis, *ibid.*; and Duffield,
196-221.

277 Greene, 214-22 and Herspring, *ibid.*

278 Gaddis, *Strategies*, 343-349.

279 Brian J. Auten, *Carter's Conversion: The
Hardening of American Defense Policy* (Columbia,
MO: University of Missouri Press, 2008) 44-47
and 101-111; Jimmy Carter, *Keeping Faith: Memoirs
of a President*, paperback edition (New York:
Bantam Books, 1983), 76-83 and 235-236;

Duffield, 205–221; Futrell, *Vol. II*, 498–512; Herring, 830, 833–834, and 860; and Herspring, 246–248.

280 *Ibid.*; Congressional Budget Office (CBO), "Strengthening NATO: Pomcus and Other Approaches," February 1979; Auten, 149–173. It is telling that the majority of the Air Force's advanced weapons systems purchased in large numbers by President Reagan and employed in Desert Storm were first acquired by the Carter Administration. Furthermore, it was under Carter that the Department of Defense received funding for developing the means to rapidly deploy, support, and employ large scale military formations outside of NATO. Within NATO, persuading allies to either develop their own modern systems or purchase the United States' served to ease the nation's overall military burden even as budgets were reduced due to the effects of inflation.

281 Marcelle S. Knaack, *Encyclopedia of U.S. Air Force Aircraft and Missiles Systems, Volume II: Post-World War II Bombers, 1945-1973* (Washington, DC: Office of Air Force History, 1988), 578–592; Anthony M. Thornborough and Peter E. Davies, *F-111: Success in Action* (New York: Sterling Publishing Co., Inc., 1989), 57–72; and Trest, 214–217; TAC Staff Memorandum, "Secretary of the Air Force Objectives—1976," dated 28 April 1976 (Maxwell AFB, Alabama: AFS–HRCA, General Dixon Correspondence), vii–ix.

282 Richard G. Davis, *The 31 Initiatives: A Study*

in Air Force-Army Cooperation (Washington, DC: Office of Air Force History, 1987), 25.

283 Staff Message from General Donn A. Starry, USA, to Lieutenant General Edward C. Meyer, Deputy Chief of Staff for Operations and Plans, USA, entitled "TACAIR Support in Europe," dated 15 November 1977, in *Press On!: Selected Works of General Donn A. Starry*, Lewis Sorley, ed. (Fort Leavenworth, KS: Combat Studies Institute Press, 2009), 2-3; Major Paul H. Herbert, *Deciding What Has to Be Done: General William E. Dupuy and the 1976 Edition of FM 100-5, Operations*, Leavenworth Paper #16 (Fort Leavenworth, KS: Combat Studies Institute, 1988), 70-79, *passim*. For purposes of this paper, direct fire is that employed using a line-of-sight (LOS) weapons system such as a tank main gun, missile launcher, or small arms. Indirect fires are those employed using artillery, multiple rocket launchers, mortars, or other weapons that do not require LOS.

284 Dixon, 125-127 and 187-191.

285 Letter from General Donn A. Starry, USA, to Lieutenant General Edward C. Meyer, Deputy Chief of Staff for Operations and Plans, USA, entitled "Army-Air Force AirLand Battle Issues," dated 28 December 1978, in *Press On!: Selected Works of General Donn A. Starry*, Lewis Sorley, ed. (Fort Leavenworth, KS: Combat Studies Institute Press, 2009), 4-5; Davis, *31 Initiatives*, 25-32, and *Ibid*. Air interdiction is the employment of air strikes to constrict an enemy's movement along lines of communication. It differs from BAI

in that it targets ground forces whose ultimate mission is unknown or who may not yet be involved in an operation against friendly forces. According to Fontenot, USAF F-111 squadrons intended to interdict LOCs from the Polish border to mid-East Germany. As part of its defense policy, the Carter administration began putting pressure on NATO allies for their governments to start purchasing aircraft that could perform these missions as well as set aside the funding to conduct the requisite training. This would lead to several policy decisions that will be covered as appropriate in the main text.

286 *Ibid.*

287 Dixon, 271-274.

288 *Ibid.*

289 Dixon, 273-274.

290 *Ibid.*, 274.

291 *Ibid.*, 275-276.

292 Herbert, 67-73

293 AFM 1-1, 15 January 1975 edition, 1-3 and 3-4 to 3-5.

294 AFM 1-1, 28 September 71 edition, 2-2.

295 AFM 1-1, 15 January 1975 edition, 3-3.

296 AFM 1-1, 28 September 71 edition, *ibid.*, and AFM 1-1, 15 January 1975 edition, *ibid.*

297 Herbert, *ibid.* and Romjue, 24-27 and

33–34.

298 Herbert, 73, 86–87, and 99–104; Romjue, 39; and Trauschweizer, 193–214.

299 AFM 1-1, 15 January 1975 edition, 3–6.

300 *Ibid.*

301 Joseph H. Stodder, "Aspects of Air Force Strategy Today," *Air University Review*, November–December 1975, http://www.au.af.mil/au/afri/aspj/airchronicles/aureview/1975/nov-dec/stodder.html; Dixon, 299–302; and Reed, "On Deterrence: A Broadened Perspective," *ibid.*

302 AFM 1-1, 15 January 1975 edition, 3–2.

303 *Ibid.*

304 AFM 2-14 / FM 200-42 *Airspace Management in an Area of Operations*, 1 November 1976, 2–2.

305 Dixon, 251 and 258–260. In addition to Dixon and Kidd's "handshake" operations, the USN Chief of Naval Operations and USAF Chief of Staff signed several memorandums of agreements regarding pilot exchanges and the use of USAF aircraft for anti-shipping operations. Surprisingly, the latter included use of SAC B-52s for mine laying, anti-surface warfare (ASuW), and sea surveillance operations. For more information, see Peter M. Swartz with Karin Duggan, "U.S. Navy – Air Force Relationships, 1970-2010," a CNA Strategic Studies Division Presentation (June 2011).

306 Ray Bonds, ed., *The Modern U.S. War Machine: An Encyclopedia of American Military Equipment and Strategy* (New York: Military Press, 1988), 100-111; Douglas N. Campbell, *The Warthog and the Close Air Support Debate* (Annapolis, MD: Naval Institute Press, 2003), 71-81; Futrell, *Vol. II*, 498-512; and Handley, 100-114.

307 General Robert J. Dixon memorandum to Tactical Air Command entitled "Commander's Information Letter," dated 3 AUG 1976.

308 Futrell, *ibid*.

309 Norman Friedman, *Fighters Over the Fleet: Naval Air Defense from Biplanes to the Cold War* (Annapolis, MD: Naval Institute Press, 2016), 356-370 and 382-391 and Lewis A. Frank, "The Decision to Respond: What Forces Do We Need In A Crisis," *Air University Review*, March-April 1975, http://www.au.af.mil/au/afri/aspj/airchron-icles/aureview/1975/mar-apr/frank.html.

310 Friedman, *ibid*. and Swartz, *ibid*.

311 Friedman, *ibid*., 346-348, 356-370, and 382-391.

312 *Ibid*.

313 Angelucci, 251-254 and *ibid*.

314 Angelucci, *ibid*.

315 *Ibid*.

316 Angelucci, *ibid*.; Freeman, *ibid*.; and Spick, *Fighter Combat*, 90-93. Ironically, the F-14

would be delivered to Iran mere months before the fall of the Shah. It would then be used by the Islamic Republic of Iran Air Force (IRIAF) during the Iran-Iraq War. During this conflict, due to the powerful AWG-9, it would serve as an airborne early warning (AEW) platform as well as an interceptor. Additionally, models were provided to the Soviet Union and played a major role in the development of the MiG-31 *Foxhound* interceptor.

317 Davies, *Eagle*, 7-43 and Dixon, 244-252. The *Foxbat*'s performance would be greatly overrated due to NATO intelligence agencies ignorance of the materials used in that fighter's construction and its flight envelope limitations. These fears would not be dispelled until a MiG-25 pilot defected to Japan in September 1976. See Spick, *Fighter Combat*, 70-73 for more information on the *Foxbat*.

318 Anderegg, 149-164 and Angelucci, 317-320.

319 George W. Hawks, Jr., "Flying the F-15 Eagle," *Flying American Combat Aircraft: The Cold War*, Robin Higham, ed., (Mechanicsburg, PA: Stackpole Books, 2005), 1-19. Mr. Hawks was an experienced F-4E pilot with over 299 missions in Southeast Asia. Much of his selection on the F-15 and the comparisons between the *Eagle* and *Phantom* are written from the perspective of comparing the two fighters.

320 Bill Gunston and Mike Spick, *Modern Air Combat* (New York: Crescent Books, 1983),

38-47; Patrick Higby, "Promise and Reality: Beyond Visual Range (BVR) Air-to-Air Combat," (Air War College Thesis, March 2005); William A. Flanagan, "The Fighter Force: How Many Seats?" *Air University Review*, May-June 1981, http://www.au.af.mil/au/afri/aspj/airchronicles/aureview/1981/may-jun/flanagan.htm; Spick, *Fighter Combat*, 19-20. This belief was based both on operational experience and the expected nature of a European conflict. With regard to the former, USAF fighters had shot down almost as many USN fighters (two) as North Vietnamese MiGs (2-3) with BVR engagements in Vietnam. There had been several other near misses with both USN and USAF *Phantoms* as the initiating culprits. These incidents had provided much of the impetus for the requirement for all U.S. fighters to visually identify possible targets before engaging with AIM-7s. While the introduction of Combat Tree had led to the loosening of these restrictions, this had resulted in only 1-2 of the possible BVR air-to-air kills. The Israelis had added possibly one more BVR kill during Yom Kippur. According to the Air Staff and NATO's projections, any Central European conventional conflict was expected to involve a high number of contacts, with even friendly aircraft hailing from multiple nationalities. These aircraft would, in turn, be operating in an environment potentially saturated with a high degree of electronic "noise" due to airborne and ground-based jammers of various frequencies. Given all these factors, the *Eagle*'s detractors were quick to point out that even if the *Eagle*'s moderately powerful radar was able to find and track targets, 2 ATAF/USAFE were unlikely to allow the F-15 to engage BVR given the high possibility of fratricide.

321 Comptroller General of the United States, "Operating and Support Costs of New Weapons Systems Compared With Their Predecessors," 17 October 1977 and "Summaries of Conclusions and Recommendations on Department of Defense Operations," 13 January 1977, 30-31; Doug Richardson, *Modern Fighting Aircraft*, Volume 2, *F-16 Fighting Falcon* (New York: Arco Publishing, Inc., 1983), 4-17; and Flanagan, *ibid*. The *Eagle* required less maintenance hours than the *Phantom* but, like the entire airframe, its subsystem components were at least double those of its predecessor. This difference in cost would eventually be solved by McDonnell Douglas as the Air Force ordered larger production runs.

322 Doug Richardson, *An Illustrated Survey of the West's Modern Fighters* (London: Salamander Books, Ltd., 1984), 72-75; Richardson, *F-16*, *ibid*.; and Padfield, 207-221.

323 U.S. Government Accounting Office (GAO), *Status of the F-16 Aircraft Program*, GAO PSAD-77-41 (Washington, DC: April 1977) (henceforth *GAO F-16 Report*), 1-5 and Richardson, *ibid*.

324 Grant T. Hammond, *The Mind of War: John Boyd and American Security* (Washington, DC: Smithsonian Institution, 2001), 8-10 and 83-100.

325 Bill Gunston, *USAF: The Modern U.S. Air Force*

(New York: Arco Publishing, Inc., 1982), 58–65; Angelucci, *ibid.*; and Stan Goldstein Interview #2. This view would become ironic given the eventual production of the F-16CJ SEAD aircraft in the mid-1990s.

326 Tuck McAtee and Loren Timm, "Pease Tower, Zoom Flight is Number 1," *Fighter Weapons Review* (Summer 1980), 2–13.

327 Mike Spick, *An Illustrated Guide to Fighter Combat* (New York: Arco Publishing, Inc., 1987), 102–105 and *ibid.*

328 Dan Hampton, *Viper Pilot: A Memoir of Air Combat*, Kindle Edition (New York: Harper Collins, 2012), 43.

329 Goldstein Interview #2; Hammond, *ibid.*; and Richardson, *F-16*, 36–37.

330 Richardson, *F-16*, 40–42 and Spick, *Modern Fighter Combat*, 13–21. The exact analogy is the author's, but variants of it have been uttered to him F-15, British *Tornado*, and F-14 *Tomcat* pilots to Republic of Korea and USAF F-16 officers in his presence.

331 Peck, *MiG Squadron*, 100–101.

332 Author written interview of Mr. Edward "Victor" Ballanco, 9 May 2017.

333 Society of Wild Weasels, "A Word from Willie," February 2017 Newsletter and Blanco, *ibid.* Newsletter regularly includes personal history vignettes from society members. Majority

of information was provided by Mr. Howard Plunkett, WW #2445, a former member of the Spangdahlem F-4G tactical fighter wings.

334 Thornborough and Mormillo, 163-174; Ballanco, *ibid.*; and February 2017 Newsletter.

335 *Ibid.*

336 *Ibid.*

337 *Ibid.*

338 Bonds, *War Machine*, 173; Dixon, 244 and 313-318; and Gunston, *USAF*, 34-39

339 *Ibid.*

340 *Ibid.* The author would like to thank LTC Antonio "Pumba" Alvarado, USAF, and former AWACS squadron commander for discussing the system at length during Command and General Staff College, August to November 2010 and reconfirming this line of argument in June 2017.

341 Brian Laslie, *The Air Force Way of War: U.S. Tactics and Training After Vietnam*, Kindle Edition (Lexington, KY: University Press of Kentucky, 2015), Location 813.

342 Laslie, *ibid.*, Location 754-1139, *passim.*

343 Tom Clancy with Chuck Horner, Gen., USAF (ret.), *Every Man A Tiger*, Berkley Paperback Edition (New York: G.P. Putnam's Sons, May 1999; Berkley Caliber, May 2000), 118-155 *passim.*

344 For a full discussion, please see Marshal L.

Michel III, "The Revolt of the Majors: How the Air Force Changed After Vietnam" (Phd. Diss., Auburn University, 2006).

345 Michel, "Iron Majors," 189–238, *passim*.

346 Michel, "Iron Majors," 183.

347 Clancy with Horner, *ibid*. and Michel, *ibid*.

348 Russ, *passim*.

349 *Ibid*.; Anderegg, 51–62 and 72–83; Handley, 100–114; S.J. Deitchman, "The Implications of Modern Technological Developments for Tactical Air Tactics and Doctrine," *Air University Review*, November 1977, http://www.au.af.mil/au/afri/aspj/airchronicles/aureview/1977/nov-dec/deitchman.html; and Captain John Jumper, "Training Towards Combat Capability," "Us Guys At Nellis," "Instincts of the Fighter Pilot," "Training for the Threat," and "Air-to-Air Training to Win," *Fighter Weapons Review*, Winter 1976, 2–7 and 16. This process also served to "train up" those pilots who had been transferred to fighters in support of USAF's "one tour" policy.

350 *Ibid*.

351 *Ibid*. and Handley, 100–114 and 177–190. The *Fighting Falcon*, due to its lighter construction, location of the fighter's air intake, and fly-by-wire controls, was able to maintain a higher angle of attack than the *Eagle*. This disrupted the airflow to the F100 engine and, when combined with aggressive throttle inputs, caused loss of power.

At higher altitudes, the engine could sometimes be restarted. Below 1,000 feet, this necessitated almost immediate ejection lest the pilot be lost with the aircraft. See *GAO F-16 Report*, 1-10.

352 Anderegg, 56-60; Dixon, 50-51 and 244-252; Michel, "Iron Majors," 186-188.

353 Michel, "Iron Majors," 189-194.

354 Momyer, *Air Power*, 125-179, *passim*.

355 Dixon, 298-300 and Sherwood, *ibid.*

356 Der Baron (pseud.), "Anything Else is Rubbish," *Fighter Weapons Review*, Spring 1975, 10-14 and the entirety of the Winter 1976 issue of the *Fighter Weapons Review* are the best examples of this trend.

357 Anderegg, 72-87; Roy, "Double Attack" and "Double Attack Revisited," *passim*.

358 *Ibid.*; McAllister, 23-28; and Michel, "Iron Majors," 190-196.

359 Russell A. Everts, "BFM and the *Eagle* Jet," *Fighter Weapons Review* (Fall 1978), 15-17; Gunston, *USAF*, 62-64; Tuck McAtee and Loren Timm, "Pease Tower, Zoom Flight is Number 1," *Fighter Weapons Review* (Summer 1980), 2-13; Davies, *Eagle*, 87-91; and Spick, *Fighter Combat*, 96-99 and 102-105

360 Anderegg, 89-94 and Dixon, 247-259.

361 James G. Clark, "The Visionary Moody Suter," *Air Force Magazine* 99 (July 2016), 76-79;

Ronald L. Rusing, "Prepare the Fighter Force—
Red Flag/Composite Force" (CGSC Thesis, June
1980), 8-16; and Anderegg, 89-95.

362 Letter from General William DePuy, USA to
General Dixon dated 1 March 1976 and located in
General Dixon Correspondence, AFHRA.

363 Anderegg, *ibid.*; Davies, *Red Eagles*, 50-65;
Michel, "Iron Majors," 218-221; and Peck,
MiG Squadron, 54-98 *passim*. Michel's passage
highlights that General Jones and General Dixon
got in a public shouting match over the high
accident rate at Red Flag II and III. The latter
pointed out that this initial bill was a result of the
Air Force not having performed realistic training
for decades. This thinking was vindicated as
the accident rates began dropping once the DOC
system's training took hold.

364 "23rd Tactical Fighter Wing Unclassified
Unit History," Volume 3 (Maxwell AFB: AFHRA,
Microfiche Roll 32839, 14 April 1978), 760.

365 Dixon, 248-251 and Rusing, 14-15. The RCAF
became so impressed with the Red Flag concept
that it established its own facility, Maple Flag,
in 1978. As with Red Flag, Maple Flag enjoyed
regular participation by NATO members after its
construction.

366 AFM 1-1, 14 February 1979 edition, ii.

367 *Ibid.*, 1-3.

368 *Ibid.*, 1-7.

369 *Ibid.*, 2-1.

370 *Ibid.*

371 *Ibid.*, 1-7 to 1-8.

372 *Ibid.*, 2-11through 2-13.

373 *Ibid.*, 2-14.

374 *Ibid.*

375 Maurice C. Eldredge, MAJ, USAF, "A Brief History of ADTAC: The First Five Years," ACSC Thesis, April 1985.

376 Dixon, 307-310; Nordeen, *Fighters*, 152 and 163-168; and Richardson, *F-16*, 52-53. The first group of F-16s was originally designated for the Imperial Iranian Air Force. After the Iranian Revolution, these aircraft were immediately allocated to Israel.

377 Creech, 212-214

378 Laslie, location 1338-1350.

379 Specifically, the AGM-86's testing and acquisition would later greatly expedite the development of the "C" version for conventional use, while attempts to develop an anti-radar variant of the SRAM would aid later upgrades to the Air Force's version of the AGM-88 *HARM* anti-radiation missile.

380 Kenneth J. Coffey, "Defending Europe Against Conventional Attack," *Air University Review* 31, No. 2 (January-February 1980):

47-59; CBO, "Strengthening NATO," xx-xxiii; and Duffield, 204-208.

381 Sir John Hackett and others, *The Third World War, August 1985* (New York: Macmillan, 1979), 359.

382 *Ibid.*, 223.

383 *Ibid.*, 226-232.

384 Shelford Bidwell, ed., *World War 3* (Englewood Cliffs, NJ: Prentice Hall, Inc., 1978), 139-153, *passim*.

385 *Ibid.*, 87-89, 95-104, and 154-167.

386 CBO, "Strengthening NATO," 7.

387 *Ibid.*, 14.

388 Donald J. Alberts, Maj., USAF, "A Call From the Wilderness," *Air University Review*, http://www.au.af.mil/au/afri/aspj/airchronicles/aureview/1976/nov-dec/alberts.html and Nigel B. Baldwin, Wing Commander, RAF, "European Weather and Round-the-Clock Air Operations," *Air University Review*, May-June 1981, http://www.au.af.mil/au/afri/aspj/airchronicles/aureview/1981/may-jun/baldwin.html.

389 Jack F. Matlock, Jr., *Reagan and Gorbachev: How the Cold War Was Ended*, Kindle Edition (New York: Random House, Inc., 2004), Location 168-497 and Casper Weinberger, *In the Arena: A Memoir of the 20th Century* (Washington, DC: Regnery Publishing, 2001), 327-329

390 Weinberger, 291–329.

391 Joyce P. Kaufman, *A Concise History of U.S. Foreign Policy*, 2nd Edition (New York: Rowman & Littlefield Publishers, Inc.: 2010), 116–118 and Weinberger, *Arena*, 275–279.

392 Richard C. Thorton, *The Reagan Revolution II: Rebuilding the Western Alliance*, 2nd Ed. (Oxford, UK: Trafford Publishing, 2005), 9–10; Duffield, 221–228; and Herring, 862–871. The most well-known of these exercises was Operation Reforger, which actually exercised NATO's intended plans to airlift personnel from North America to fall in on equipment stationed in Europe.

393 Weinberger, *Arena*, 278.

394 Herspring, 275–278 and Weinberger, *Arena*, *ibid.*

395 Weinberger, *Fighting for Peace*, 45–79.

396 Creech, 190–191.

397 *Ibid.*

398 AFM 1-1, 14 February 1979 edition, 2-28.

399 Mel Copeland, "Air to Air: Comm Out," *Fighter Weapons Review* (Winter 1982), 13; Creech, 192; and Thornborough and Mormillo, 174–175.

400 *Ibid.*

401 Creech, 192–196.

402 *Ibid.* and Bonds, *War Machine*, 183.

403 Robert L. Shaw, *Fighter Combat: Tactics and Maneuvering* (Annapolis, MD: United States Naval Institute Press, 1985), 322–323, Creech, 192–196, and Thornborough and Mormillo, *Ibid.*

404 Creech, *ibid.* and Laslie, location 1457–1463.

405 Creech, 197 and McAllister, 25–26.

406 Bonds, *War Machine*, 222; Gunston, *USAF*, 154–157; and Newdick, 146–149.

407 James C. Slife, *Creech Blue: General Bill Creech and the Reformation of the Tactical Air Forces, 1978–1984* (Maxwell AFB, AL: Air University Press, 2004), 62–65. LANTIRN was an acronym for Low Altitude Navigation and Targeting Infrared for Night, as the pod combined a navigational system along with the FLIR camera.

408 Curtis Peebles, *Dark Eagles: A History of Top Secret U.S. Air Force Programs* (Novato, CA: Presidio Press, 1995), 158–179, *passim*.

409 *Ibid.*

410 *Ibid.*

411 Davies and Dildy, 66–71; Davies, *Red Eagles*, 134–137, 163–168, 231–232, and 249–251; Shaw, 45–52 and 291–295; and Spick, *Fighter Tactics*, 161–170.

412 Bonds, *War Machine*, 230 and Luttwak and Koehl, 550–551.

413 *Ibid.* and Luttwak and Koehl, 536–537.

414 Mike W. Shoenfeld, "New Guy on the Street-the AIM-9L," *Fighter Weapons Review* (Spring 1980), 2-6. As the "all aspect" description implies, the AIM-9L could be fired at a target aircraft's front or either beam as well as the rear.

415 Joseph E. Merrick, "Combat Capability," *Fighter Weapons Review* (Spring 1981), 16-22 and Luttwak and Koehl, 529-531.

416 V. Dubrov, "A Soviet View," Rana J. Pennington, ed., *Fighter Weapons Review* (Spring 1981), 23-27; Davies and Dildy, 66-71; Davies, *Red Eagles*, 134-137, 163-168, 231-232, and 249-251; Shaw, 45-52 and 291-295; and Spick, *Fighter Tactics*, 161-170

417 Mike Press, "Aggressor Reflections," *Fighter Weapons Review* (Spring 1981), 2-6; Davies, *Red Eagles*,193-220 *passim* and 276-291 *passim*; and Peck, 121-168, *passim*.

418 Larry D. New, "Reentering the Fight," *Fighter Weapons Review* (Winter 1981), 22-24; Paul Stucky, "Blocking and Tackling," *Fighter Weapons Review* (Winter 1981), 24-28; Laslie, 1051-1100; and *Ibid.* At the time these tactics were being developed, it was vigorously debated whether Warsaw Pact pilots conducted the necessary academic work to be familiar with American missile envelopes. Aggressor pilots, being quite knowledgeable of the *Sparrow*'s limitations as well as how Red Flag "scored" radar engagements, often ignored radar missiles "launched" from poor angles. This, in turn,

encouraged what *Eagle* pilots considered a false bravado that made slashing attacks seem less effective than the F-15 community expected them to be in combat conditions. Subsequent events in the Bekaa Valley and during Operation Desert Storm would be cited as evidence that Red Flag's algorithms for determining missile "kills" during training were too strict with regard to the AIM-7F and AIM-7M.

419 Craig Brown, *Debrief: A Complete History of U.S. Aerial Engagements, 1981 to the Present* (Atglen, PA: Schiffer Military History, 2007), 13-18. The Libyan aircraft were Sukhoi Su-22s, an aircraft roughly analogous to USAF/USN A-7 *Corsair II*s in aerial combat capability.

420 Max and Simon Jenkins, *The Battle for the Falklands*, Pan Books Edition (London: Pan Books, 1997), 61-136 and Sandy Woodward with Patrick Robinson, *One Hundred Days: The Memoirs of the Falklands Battle Group Commander* (Annapolis, MD: Bluejacket Books, 1997), 68-75.

421 Anthony H. Cordesman and Abraham R. Wagner, *The Lessons of Modern War, Volume III: The Afghan and Falklands Conflicts*, Paperback Edition (San Francisco, Calif: Westview Press, 1991), 260-266 and 302-311 and Jeffrey Ethell and Alfred Price, *Air War South Atlantic* (New York: Macmillan, 1983), 231-233. The RAF *Harriers* not only lacked an air-to-air radar, but were flown by pilots that had only rudimentary ACM training.

422 *Ibid.*

423 Ethell and Price, 60-70 and Woodward, 138-145. The *Sea Harrier* pilots, knowing their aircraft's limitations and aware that the Argentinians would have to attack at low level, steadfastly refused to climb to meet the AAF's fighters. Despite possessing faster aircraft with a higher ceiling, the Argentineans were forced to descend to around 10-15,000 feet where the *Sea Harrier* had an advantage in maneuverability. The ensuing dogfight seemed to present a completely hapless situation to the AAF. From the FAA's view, the combat's outcome had been close enough that a sustained series of attacks may have ultimately started to result in *Sea Harrier* losses. Failing that, combat air patrols constantly having to be on the lookout for attacking *Mirages* and *Daggers* was a consistent fear for Rear Admiral Woodward and his staff throughout the conflict.

424 Sources vary, but the Argentinians launched 3-4 missiles while the British launched 21-24. In the FAA's case, there were several occasions where the same target was engaged by two different *Sea Harriers* with both missiles observed to hit. This has led to some difference in percentages depending on source.

425 Ethell and Price, 214-217; Hastings, 356-364; and Weinberger, *Fighting For Peace*, 215-217.

426 Ethell and Prince, 214-221 and Cordesman

and Wagner, *Volume III*, 294-303.

427 Nordeen, *Fighters*, 163-168 and Coheen, 436-460. In the case of the Osirak raid, the Iraqi air defense network had been consciously oriented towards the east. Fully aware of the F-4 *Phantom*'s capabilities and believing neither Saudi Arabia nor Jordan would allow the IAF to fly over their airspace to penetrate into Iraq. This was, obviously, a mistaken impression. The Syrian Air Force's interceptors repeatedly challenged the Israeli Air Force over Lebanon or the Mediterranean in areas outside of their ground-based defenses.

428 Weinberger, *Fighting For Peace*, 140-144 and Cohen, 460-465.

429 Pollack, 526-551. The Syrian armed forces were one of the largest recipients of Russian military aid in the aftermath of the Yom Kippur War. The air force, navy, and army had all been equipped with new platforms, to include more advanced SAMs and anti-tank missiles.

430 Amos Amir, *Fire in the Sky: Flying in Defence of Israel* (Barnsley, South Yorkshire, UK: Pen & Sword Aviation, 2009), 273-280 and Nordeen, *Fighters*, 170-175.

431 Matthew Hurley, "The Bekaa Valley Air Battle, June 1982: Lessons Mislearned?" *Airpower Journal* Vol. 4 (Winter 1989): 60-70 and Cohen, 462-475.

432 *Ibid.* and Nordeen, *ibid.* Much of the intel-

ligence about the *Flogger* came from the USAF's tests of the aircraft. This was provided in exchange for the IAF's delivery of a Syrian defector's MiG-23. The MiG-21 was a known entity both from captured examples and previous experience against the *Fishbed*. In the case of both fighters, their radar-warning gear was mounted in such a manner that the MiG's own fuselage created dead spots. For instance, an Israeli *Eagle* or *Falcon* approaching from directly abeam or from certain angles above and below the *Flogger*'s plane of flight could lock onto the MiG without the Syrian pilot being aware of imminent danger.

433 Amir, *ibid.*; Cohen, *ibid.*; and Nordeen, *ibid.*.

434 *Ibid.* Israeli sources claim that only one aircraft (an F-4) was lost to Syrian MiGs. However, four aircraft losses were listed as "unknown." Although radar intercepts indicate no MiGs were present in one case, it is possible that any or all of the remaining three may have been destroyed by Syrian MiGs.

435 *Ibid.*

436 Bejamin S. Lambeth, *Moscow's Lessons from the 1982 Lebanon Air War* (Santa Monica, CA: RAND, September 1984), 13–17 and Pollack, 532–534 and 542–543.

437 Eden, Paul, ed., *The Encyclopedia of Modern Military Aircraft* (London: Amber Books, 2004), 312–314 and 452–461; Benjamin S. Lambeth, *Russia's Air Power at the Crossroads* (Santa Monica,

CA: RAND, 1996), 123-161and *Moscow's Lessons*, 32-33; Alexander Zuyev with Malolm McConnell, *Fulcrum: A Top Gun Pilot's Escape from the Soviet Empire* (New York: Warner Books, 1992), 21-32, 112-115, and 123-157, *passim*; and Jane's Information Group, *Jane's Land-Based Air Defense*, 140-151.

438 Dick Anderegg, "Meeting the Threat: Sophistication Vs. Simplicity," *Fighter Weapons Review* (Fall 1982), 2-6.

439 Ballanco interview and Society of Wild Weasels February 2017 Newsletter.

440 Davis, 3-4.

441 "Air Force: AirLand Battle," Interview of General Donn A Starry, USA, conducted by Dr. Harold Winton, 13 May 1995, in *Press On!: Selected Works of General Donn A. Starry*, Volume II, Lewis Sorley, ed. (Fort Leavenworth, KS: Combat Studies Institute Press, 2009), 1274-1292; Romjue, 57-76; and Trauschweizer, 222-227. Starry stresses in this interview how critical General Creech's influence was with regard to the Air Force fully participating in AirLand Battle and doctrinal development.

442 Andrew J. Bacevich, *The New American Militarism: How Americans Are Seduced by War* (New York: Oxford University Press, 2005), 44-47 and *ibid*.

443 U.S. Army, FM 1-100 *Doctrinal Principles for Army Aviation in Combat Operations* (February

1989) and *ibid.*

444 Davis, 74-86 and 91-155, *passim.*

445 Trest, 229-240.

446 Ronald Reagan, *The Reagan Diaries* (New York: HarperCollins, 2007), 103-194, *passim*; Herspring, 278-285; and Weinberger, *Fighting for Peace*, 135-174.

447 David C. Martin and John Walcott, *Best Laid Plans: The Inside Story of America's War Against Terrorism* (New York: Touchstone Books, 1988), 158-160 and 202 and Weinberger, *Fighting for Peace*, 433-445.

448 Martin and Walcott, *ibid.* and Weinberger, *Fighting For Peace*, 188-189.

449 Shuttle missions are those that do not entail permanent basing rights. The Air Force regularly planned operations that would involve a minimalist support element (e.g., portable refueling bladders, sufficient munitions for self-defense only, and rudimentary repair) that would fit into one or two C-5 *Galaxy* transports. These personnel and equipment would be landed in a host nation, remain only long enough for a potential strike package to land, refuel, and rearm. Once this operation was complete, the transports would then accompany the strike package back to a friendly base, thus allowing the airfield providing nation to claim plausible deniability of support.

450 Robert E. Venkus, *Raid on Quaddafi* (New

York: St. Martin's Paperbacks, 1993), 33-47 and Martin and Walcott, 258-277.

451 *Ibid.*; Michael Fiszer, "A Soviet Look at El Dorado Canyon," *Journal of Electronic Defense*, Vol 27 (October 2004): 51-56; and Pollack, 417-419.

452 Martin and Walcott, 285-288.

453 Reagan, *Diaries*, 403-406 and Weinberger, 191-192.

454 Judy G. Endicott, "Raid on Libya: Operation El Dorado Canyon," *Short of War: Major USAF Contingency Operations*, A. Timothy Warnock, ed., (Washington, DC: Center for Air Force History, 2000), 145-157; Barry D. Watts, "Six Decades of Guided Munitions and Battle Networks: Progress and Prospects," Center for Strategic and Budgetary Assessments Paper, March 2007, 243-246; Martin and Walcott, 272-274; Peebles, 170-171; and Thornborough and Davies, 169-176. The White House's unwillingness to risk B-52s motivated the Air Force to accelerate development of a conventional variant of the AGM-86. Having initially planned on introducing the new cruise missile into service in 1990 or later, this impetus to production led to the AGM-86C being made available in December 1986.

455 Thornborough and Davies, *ibid.*

456 Stanik, 148-166.

457 *Ibid.*

458 *Ibid.*

459 *Ibid.*; Endicott, *ibid.*; and Thornborough and Morillo, 185-187. At the time, U.S. officials believed that this squadron was also partially manned by Warsaw Pact or North Korean pilots. This has never been confirmed.

460 Weinberger, *Fighting for Peace*, 195-201.

461 Stanik, 199-205 and Venkus, 144-150.

462 *Ibid* and Pollack, *ibid.*

463 Boyne, *Wild Blue*, 295-296; Martin and Walcott, 318-321; Stanik, 222-240; and Venkus, *ibid.*

464 John Andreas Olsen, *John Warden and the Renaissance of American Airpower* (Dulles, VA: Potomac Books, 2007), 130-131 and Laslie, 2088-2095.

465 Goldwater-Nichols Department of Defense Act of 1986, Public Law 99-433, 1986; Herspring, 291-296; and Trest, 235-240.

466 *Ibid.*

467 Goldwater-Nichols Act, "§164. Commanders of Combatant Commands: Assignment; Powers" and duties.

468 *Ibid* and Jeffrey E. Stambaugh, "JFACC: Key to Organizing Your Air Assets for Victory," *Parameters*, Volume XXI, Summer 1994, 98-110.

469 Stambaugh, *Ibid.*

470 *Ibid.*

471 Ballanco interview.

472 Joint Chiefs of Staff, JP 3-01.2 *Joint Doctrine for Theater Counterair Operations* (1 APR 1986), VI-1. Although its publication date is prior to Operation El Dorado Canyon, it is highly unlikely that this document influenced the planning process given the DoD's publication and distribution technology at the time. No mention of it is made in any of the primary sources that address Operation El Dorado Canyon.

473 Department of the Air Force, AFM 2-8 *Electronic Combat (EC) Operations* (30 June 1987), 9-10.

474 *Ibid*, 34-35.

475 Nathan A. Mead, "A Man For All Reason: General Larry D. Welch, 12th Chief of Staff, U.S. Air Force," SAAS Thesis, June 2012.

476 Department of the Air Force, *Mission Employment Tactics and Fighter Fundamentals F-4G* (Langley, VA: Headquarters Tactical Air Command, 15 March 1989); T. Bear Larson (WW #952), "The F-4G/APR-38/HARM Evolves as a Weapons System," *First In, Last Out: Stories by the Wild Weasels (First Person Stories By Wild Weasel Pilots, EWOs, and Their Associates)*, ed. Edward T. Rock, Col., USAF (ret.) (Bloomington, IN: Authorhouse Press, 2005), 566-573; and Thornborough and Mormillo, 188-192.

477 *Ibid*.

478 *Ibid*.

479 Ballanco interview and Hampton, 47-60 and 129-132.

480 Ballanco interview; Department of the Air Force, *F-4G*; Larson, *ibid.*; and Hampton, *ibid.*

481 *Ibid.*; Olsen, 65-74 and 101-108; and Thornborough and Mormillo, *ibid.*

482 *Ibid.* and Bradley C. Hosmer, "American Air Power and Grand Tactics," *Airpower Journal*, Vol. 1, No. 1 (Summer 1987): 9-14.

483 GAO, *NATO-Warsaw Pact Conventional Force Balance: Papers for U.S. and Soviet Perspectives Workshops*, GAO NSIAD-89-23B (Washington, DC: December 1988); Bonds, *War Machine*, 18-22; Duffield, 226-232; and Mason, *Air Power*, 94-133. Although hardly an exhaustive list, examples of analysts' changed viewpoints can be found in William Baxter's *Soviet AirLand Battle Tactics* (Novato, CA: Presidio Press, 1986); Alfred Price's *Air Battle Central Europe*, Warner Book Edition (New York: Warner Books, 1990); Steven J. Zaloga's *Red Thrust* (Novato, CA: Presidio Press, 1989); and Bond's *War Machine*.

484 Crabtree, 110-113 and Zaloga, *Soviet Air Defence*, 21-25 and 184-190.

485 Mike Spick, ed., *The Great Book of Modern Warplanes* (London: Salamander Books, 2003), 488-491 (*Fulcrum*) and 512-517 (*Flanker*) and Zuyev, *ibid.*

486 Lambeth, *Crossroads*, 181-190 and Zuyev, 135-159, *passim* and 184-215, *passim*.

487 Stephen Kotkin, *Armageddon Averted: The Soviet Collapse, 1970-2000* (Oxford, UK: Oxford University Press, 2001), 67-90 and Gaddis, *Cold War*, 238-252.

488 Archie Brown, *The Gorbachev Factor*, Oxford Paperback Edition (Oxford, UK: Oxford University Press, 1997), 212-25; Herspring, 297-303; and *ibid*.

489 Gary R. Hess, *Presidential Decisions for War: Korea, Vietnam, and the Persian Gulf* (Baltimore, MD: John Hopkins University Press, 2001), 153-165.

490 *Ibid.*, 164-170.

491 Williamson Murray with Wayne W. Thompson, *Air War in the Persian Gulf* (Baltimore, MD: The Nautical and Aviation Publishing Company of America, 1995), 7-41; Diane T. Putney, *Airpower Advantage: Planning the Gulf War Air Campaign, 1989-1991* (Washington, DC: Air Force History and Museums Program, 2004), 50-97; Herspring, 317-319; and Hess, 165-174.

492 John A. Warden, *The Air Campaign*, Revised Edition (New York: Excel Press, 2000), ix-xix; Richard T. Reynolds, Col., USAF, *In the Heart of the Storm: The Genesis of the Air Campaign Against Iraq* (Maxwell AFB: Air University Press, 1995), 71-130, *passim*; Olsen, 145-151; and *ibid*.

493 Budiansky, 414-417 and Olsen, 175-179.

494 *Ibid*.

495 Pollack, 232-241.

496 Cordesman and Wagner, *The Lessons of Modern War, Volume IV: The Gulf War* (San Francisco, Calif: Westview Press, 1996), 118-122 and 125-135.

497 Putney, 103-107.

498 Pollack, *ibid.* and Putney, *ibid.*

499 Murray, 68-70 and *ibid.*

500 Department of Defense, "Conduct of The Persian Gulf War," Final Report to Congress Pursuant to Title V of the Persian Gulf Conflict Supplemental Authorization and Personnel Benefits Act of 1991 (Public Law 102-25), April 1992, D-11 to D-20 and Murray, 68-70.

501 Richard G. Davis, *On Target: Planning and Executing the Strategic Air Campaign Against Iraq* (Washington, DC: Air Force History and Museums Program, 2002), 101-127 and Hess, 167-179.

502 *Ibid.* and Putney, *ibid.*

503 Davis, *ibid.* and Hess, *ibid.*

504 Putney, *ibid.* and 204-207.

505 Edward M. "Victor" Ballanco (WW #1774), "Wild Weasel Planning for Desert Storm," *First In, Last Out: Stories by the Wild Weasels (First Person Stories By Wild Weasel Pilots, EWOs, and Their Associates)*, ed. Edward T. Rock, Col., USAF (ret.) (Bloomington, IN: Authorhouse Press, 2005), 574-582; Ballanco interview; Davis, 127-145 and

Putney, 201–207.

506 Mike Guardia, *Skybreak: The 58th Fighter Squadron in Desert Storm* (Maple Grove, MN: Magnum Books, 2021), 85–98 and 143–145; Rick Tollini, *Call-Sign Kluso: An American Fighter Pilot in Mr. Reagan's Air Force* (Havertown, PA: Casemate Publishers, 2021), 104–108 and 113–115; and *ibid.*

507 Ballanco, *ibid.*, Davis, 127–145, and Putney, 201–207.

508 Author written interview of Mr. Warren Fontenot, 27 March 2017; Ballanco interview; Budiansky, 416–423; and Davis, 174–179.

509 *Ibid.* and Brown, *Debrief*, 23–50.

510 Cordesman and Wagner, *Volume IV*, 389–411and Guardia, 84–88.

511 Brown, *Debrief*, 51–73; Guardia, 168–178; and Tollini, 119–125.

512 Cordesman and Wagner, *Volume IV*, 425–429 and Murray, 102–109.

513 Brown, *Debrief*, 51–101, *passim*; Cordesman and Wagner, *Volume IV*, 404–407, Davis, *On Target*, 247–261; and Murray, 186–189. Most ignominiously, one of the final aircraft shot down in this period was an Ilyushin transport believed to have been shuttling Iraqi officers attempting to coordinate the postwar return of the IQAF's airframes to Iraq.

514 *Ibid.*

515 Brick Eisel and Jim Schreiner, *Magnum! The Wild Weasels in Desert Storm*, 96–180, *passim*; Dan Hampton, Capt., USAF, "Combat Defense Suppression: The F-4G / F-16C Wild Weasel At War," *Fighter Weapons Review* (Summer 1991), 4-8; and Thornborough and Mormillo, 200–254, *passim*.

516 *Ibid.*

517 *Ibid.* and Cordesman and Wagner, *Volume IV*, 406–419.

518 Hampton, *Viper*, 155–157; Laslie, location 3102–3406; and Thornborough and Mormillo, 255–276.

519 Figure courtesy of CIA.gov, accessed 30 October 2016.